INDIAN SUMMER

WILL RANDALL

An *Abacus* Paperback Original

First published in Great Britain in 2004 by Abacus

A CIP catalogue record for this book
is available from the British Library.

ISBN 0 349 11678 4

Typeset by Palimpsest Book Production Ltd,
Polmont, Stirlingshire
Printed and bound in Great Britain by
Clays Ltd, St Ives plc

Abacus
An imprint of
Time Warner Books UK
Brettenham House
Lancaster Place
London WC2E 7EN

www.TimeWarnerBooks.co.uk

Acknowledgements

Wherever I found myself on the Indian subcontinent, I was greeted with breathtaking kindness and friendliness by people from all walks of life. There were, however, a number of individuals who eased my passage through India, and I would like to take this opportunity to thank them.

Lindsay Baker introduced me to the inspirational Shaheen Mistri, and I wish her and all the teachers, volunteers and fundraisers at Akanksha (www.akanksha.org) much success in the tremendous work they do for the children of the slums of Mumbai and Poona. Anu Aga made me most welcome and her thoughtful generosity was very much appreciated. My friend, Ganesh V. More, his colleagues and his family gave me a gourmet's guide to fine Indian cuisine, and helped me to understand the importance, in the greater scheme of things, of cricket.

Claire Price was great company and through her I met the indomitable Uma da Cunha who opened the doors to the world of Indian cinema which provided me with endless fun and a whole raft of new friends.

Elsewhere, Sarah Grimes provided me with great encouragement and was wonderful, warm and affectionate company in Perth, Western Australia.

Jean Perier in Trivy, Burgundy, continues to offer sage opinions and a steady flow of pastis.

Back home in England, my friends Robin and Sue Grant-Sturgis have provided me with so much splendid hospitality in Devon. I am thankful that some things never change.

As usual, my family has provided me with unfailing support, advice and help as well as a bed or sofa 'just for the night'. This book is for them with much love.

Without the continued support of my agent Kate Hordern and the confidence of Richard Beswick at Abacus, I would not be typing these words at all. I am very grateful to them both.

Tatyana Demidova is a talented and sensitive illustrator.

Above all, however, I must thank everyone at the Saraswati Anath Ashram for their open-hearted welcome, for their friendship and for so many indelible memories. It is a sincere hope of mine that the children of the ashram may grow up to realise some of the dreams that they told me so much about.

WR
Kasane, Botswana,
October 2003

Author's Note

In *Indian Summer* I have adopted the spelling Poona rather than the more modern Pune. This is simply to clarify pronunciation.

At the time of my stay in India, £1 was worth approximately sixty-five rupees.

This is a book for anyone who thinks it might be worth adding their drop to the ocean.

Contents

INDIAN SUMMER

Prologue

Lord Rama rose giddily from where the searing thunderbolt had struck him down and, drawing the deepest of heroic breaths, prepared yet again to do battle. Around him lay the countless bodies of slain monkey warriors almost motionless in death on the forest floor. Above him, though, still towered the giant figure of Ravana, demon-king of Lanka, his eyes flashing fire from his ten heads, his countless arms flailing, each ready to unleash infinite lethal weapons. Tridents tipped with heart-stopping poison, clouds of insects, howling winds and ferocious animals, lions, serpents and crocodiles were all to be hurled down to destroy the impudent Rama.

'I am no mere mortal,' bellowed Ravana, shaking back and forth with fury, his voice seeming to emanate from the very centre of his being. 'Do you really dare to test my superhuman strength?' he demanded as he took great strides across the earth towards the target of his wrath.

Rama replied gamely by lopping off one of Ravana's heads with a thumping blow of his sword but another slowly appeared to sprout in its place. Suddenly, the brave Lord Rama was struck with dread fear. For it was clear to him now that not one of his weapons was strong enough to defeat the mighty demon.

All was lost.

Slowly he sank to his knees awaiting the final awful moment.

Then he remembered!

Surely now was the moment to avail himself of the deadliest of all the weapons of the universe – the secret to which had been conferred upon him by the great Lord Brahma himself! Should he invoke this power now and use it to destroy Ravana forever then his kidnapped wife, his beloved Princess Sita, would be returned from her captivity in the enchanted Ashoka Grove; Good would conquer Evil; the skies would clear, the sun shine and peace and harmony would return to the Earth once again.

As Rama bravely pulled his shoulders back, and slowly, clearly, firmly began to repeat the chant, Lord Hanuman, King of the Monkeys, who until now had been standing motionless, awe-struck by the ferocity of the mighty combat, began to fidget. He didn't much like his papier-mâché mask, which was itchy and lopsided giving him a blank, simple-minded look like the crazy man who lived at the end of his lane. He pushed it up and rubbed his eyes with the soft balls of his fists. What was more, he thought that his tail, made from half a bicycle tyre and some glued-on straw, looked really stupid. He scratched and jiggled in the most unregal fashion. Anyway, he was tired. He yawned, pulled at the elastic that stretched tightly round the back of his head and yawned again. It was fair enough, I thought. Dulabesh was only nine.

'Hold on, look, how about just five minutes more and then everyone is stopping, *tike*?' I stretched my back and neck and refolded my legs into a fair impression of *sukhasana*. At last I realised that however long I practised sitting cross-legged on the floor I was always going to end up with a backside that felt, when I rubbed it, like it belonged to someone else.

'*Acha*,' somebody muttered in reply and the rest of the children silently wobbled their heads from side to side in assent, smiling gently. As ever, their willingness to be positive and helpful refreshed and enthused me.

'Now, Sahas, just from the bit "Oh, Lord Brahma . . ." OK?'

Sahas, in the role of Lord Rama, drew himself to his full height of five foot six, took a deep breath and started again.

Just at that moment, distractingly for our superhero, an anonymous member of the slain Monkey Army broke audible and lengthy wind.

In the Ashoka Grove a number of the trees were forced to pull down one branch or, in some cases, both to cover their noses. A couple of Ravana's devil apprentices started to giggle and Princess Sita sat up with a start on the pile of woven floor mats deep in the forest. She looked startled, confused at being woken so rudely. She too yawned widely, smiling dreamily at no one in particular. A red ribbon that had held one of her looped plaits in place had come undone and her hair hung lopsidedly on her left shoulder. She sleepily tried to rearrange it.

Unmesh 'the Head', or rather 'the Heads', who was playing the top half of the giant Ravana, pulled off his disguise, rearranged his glasses and looked at me shyly. He held out his hand, his fingers closed but for the little one which he now wiggled slowly at me – the strangely illustrative signal that he was bursting to go to the loo. I nodded and wobbled my head and Prakash 'the Legs' (and 'the Voice' because little Unmesh was much too squeaky) leaned forward letting the small boy slide off his shoulders and down his back. Dumping his costume of solid gold, his bicycle pump and a pile of uninflated 'Devil's Heads' balloons in a heap, Unmesh dashed outside into the evening light.

Just then the tin-shaded light bulbs that hung down in lines from the corrugated roof flickered orange, throwing a dark-room glow across the makeshift stage before finally fizzing out. The moonlight shadows of the normally brisk ceiling fans slowed into a clicking slideshow of the children's paintings on the walls of the classroom. There was no expression of surprise – we were nearly always interrupted by a power cut at about this time in the evening. It would only last an hour or so but now seemed as good a moment as any to stop.

'OK, enough for today, *haan*?' I asked, the Indian word for 'yes' pronounced as a French policeman might on making an enquiry. Standing awkwardly, I picked up a tinfoil and cardboard thunderbolt. Everyone agreed and the trees lowered their branches with a sigh of relief and a good deal of shaking of their arms. Silently but willingly, the children scooped up the various props and bits of home-made costume placing them on their labelled shelves in the creaking wall cupboard at the far end of the room. Occasionally someone climbed up a rough, almost rungless ladder, pushed up by small hands from below, to reach the highest points. Then those that owned them shuffled their feet slowly into their *chupples* and the rest stepped barefoot out on to the porch of the schoolroom, peering up at the shape of the white concrete and smoked-glass office block next door, outlined silently in the magnesium light of the moon. I pulled the brass bolt on the classroom door and clicked the heavy padlock closed.

'So, everyone ready for tomorrow? Bus is coming to the schoolroom at four thirty?' Sleepy agreement. Everyone seemed happy and confident. Well, nearly everyone.

Oh, well. I was sure it would all be fine.

'Come on then, *chelo* – let's go.'

A small, brown hand wrapped around each of my fingers and thumbs, the littlest members of the cast and I launched ourselves out into the wheezing, grunting, roaring chaos of traffic, while the older children dodged the buses, rickshaws, two-wheelers, cars and bicycles with confident ease. I took a deep breath and spluttered as a highly decorated orange and blue truck groaned past blasting us with black exhaust fumes. We took a chance and with small, quick and, in my case, stooping steps we crossed the road into the slum.

My hands were released.

'Thank you, *Bhaiya*, goodnight. Goodnight, *Bhaiya*,' came a chorus of voices as the children turned, skipped and disappeared in separate directions into the alleyways of the coughing, heaving, smoking, muttering muddle of rickety buildings that was their home.

Shooing away a greedy goat that was taking a less-than-literary interest in my script, I went in search of Sanjay and his rickshaw.

Tomorrow was the big day.

1

The School and the Spark Plugs

L ondon in late October is a pretty dreary sort of place.
  In fact, to my mind, London is a pretty dreary sort of
place all the year round but at least in summer, particularly
when the sun makes its brief appearances, the irregular green
expanses of park and the few remaining views of a once
majestic skyline between the architectural offences of the last
century provide a faintly surreal sense of release from the
cloying, confining atmosphere of city life. As long as you can
ignore the ruin wreaked on once admirable façades, there is
still a momentary opportunity to dream, to make plans, to
spread cramped wings and to believe that childhood aspirations are still attainable.

But in late October the hard, wet grey of the pavements
and the general gloom of the days only imbue the scurrying,
downcast citizens with a feeling of melancholic unfriendliness.
Turning up their collars against the needling rain and their
fellow human beings, they head back homewards in search of
the solace of sour alcohol and the vicarious but dull emotions
aroused by the lives of people who only exist behind their
television screens.

Reluctantly, *finance oblige*, I had returned to all this from an
extended period abroad. Life in a small village in the South
Pacific, where I had been sent to administer a small private
charitable fund, had left a gentle but indelible mark on my
soul. Beautiful scenery, the untouched, unspoilt geography,

and the kindly, good-natured people of the Solomon Islands had all conspired to lull me into pastoral reverie. There had been problems, discomforts, even the occasional danger, but I could look back now and be confident, particularly with the softening effects of time and distance, that it had been a near-idyllic way of life. One indeed that I might well have pursued forever had a primeval part of me not begun to call out for family and friends. There was also a part of me that believed, perhaps because I had been told it so often, that I could not really do without the comforts of home.

Before my departure, I had been content with life as a rural secondary school teacher and had enjoyed all the benefits of a varied and busy career in the English countryside. There I had lived a life where competition was healthy – but not as beneficial as simply taking part. People had been friendly for the sake of friendship and still seemed to believe that social intercourse in a shop, in the street or even on the bus was not something to be sniggered at as being old-fashioned eccentricity. Under these circumstances, in this corner of the world, I had enjoyed my teaching life. On the whole, the routines and regulations by which I and my pupils had had to abide had been sensible in their application. Indeed, they had served to provide a comforting shape to the passage of the years.

By luck, I had established an easy rapport with my pupils, who, in the main, were content (despite the occasional and often understandable adolescent niggle) to patiently play the game that had been created for them by us, the adults. Plenty of happy memories had been amassed and, some time in the future, it will be with pleasure that I shall reassess all those old motives and outcomes, those friendships, loves and occasional but thankfully rare enmities.

Perhaps the storyline of my life had developed a little slowly and tamely thus far, but now, I had decided, things were going to hot up sensationally. With the benefit of time away from England, with the focusing effects of distance, I could now make decisions about a new career. Teaching had been fun, undoubtedly, but equally I knew that I was never really going to be considered successful. Well, was I? I mean, everybody else knew it too. I was the man who looked after their children while they did something more important – publicly 'highly respected' but, out of earshot, a 'bit of a loser'.

If indeed the curmudgeonly George Bernard Shaw believed his own suggestion that 'He who can, does. He who cannot, teaches', it was perhaps only in response to his treatment at the hands of his own wretched teachers. Sadly for the rest of us, the public (not, of course, without exception) seemed to have adopted this sentiment as their own. His suggestion that any educator in the country is a useless no-hoper seems to have taken a firm hold on the British consciousness. It is this same trite phrase that is almost invariably trotted out by bar-room bores in the same breath as '. . . and anyway they get the bloody holidays'. Eluding them in the mists of fag smoke and alcohol fumes is that 'he that can' and is at present 'doing' medicine or law or business or art or music – even politics – would be pitifully inept, unstructured and ungrounded had it not been for the constructive guiding influences of his or her teachers. After all, even bloomin' old 'Enery 'Iggins must have learnt his skills from a professor before him.

In the more reflective moments of my runabout youth, rarer than I care to remember, I was often painfully aware that the public denigration combined with idealistic, cotton-woolly, political decisions that were made on a seemingly daily basis meant that Education, a surprisingly sensitive and thoughtful creature who just wanted to get on and do the job, was now face down on a graffitied desk, hands over ears, trying to block out the belittling jeers.

Perhaps when I was a younger, more energetic teacher I should have been more radical, more militant, defended my corner more vocally, but now, like a footballer nearing the end of his career, I could only sit in the stands and watch as we got thrashed once again.

Anyway, I had decided that I would not now return to that career. Now was the time for me to become a man of some importance and, with this aim, it was to our capital city that

I headed. Perhaps I had not swung the stick and spotty handkerchief of optimism over my shoulder with the same confidence as young Dick Whittington, but I knew – because all the papers said so – that London was where everything 'happened'.

'Diversification' was a suitably technical term, I thought, for what I planned to do: to make the most of my experience, and live an enriching life in all senses of the word. My bank manager, the rather inappropriately named Mr Jolly, assisted me in my endeavours. Sadly as that dank winter wore on he became increasingly unable to live up to his name. There were a variety of walks of life that I thought I might be well suited to: the law, for example. I gripped my lapels, and paced about the mildew-scented flat lent to me by an absent friend. As I ran a hand over my head, I realised the increasing attraction of a career that provided a wig.

Life in the City had its attractions too: I would, because you could, make a huge amount of money, becoming fantastically rich, as a number of my peers had seemed to do in a matter of months. I would have cars and boats and a wife, even wives, and dogs and possibly horses too, although I didn't like them much. I would live in Berkshire or Sussex or, even better, Hampshire, perhaps have somewhere abroad that I might, with a bit of luck, have to retire to for tax reasons. Buckling on a stockbroking belt sounded very appealing, very reassuring. I wondered if you needed to be good at maths.

Of course, I remained realistic, kept my feet firmly on ground that I knew was not paved with gold. No, I did not have any intention of ending up as Lord Mayor of London – although, now I came to think of it, he was allowed to wear a wig too.

Unhappily I was never to discover my true potential; suitable posts seemed rarely to be advertised, applications seldom responded to and offers of interviews arrived as often as invitations to Millennium celebrations. The few meetings I attended felt like staff training exercises in public humiliation.

More positively, though, it appeared that I was hardly ever over-qualified.

Eventually, Mr Jolly and I decided, after another consultation about the state of my current account, that the world of finance was perhaps not where my future was most certain. Finally, after all the bills of an expensive Christmas had been added up and could no longer be ignored, the only credit to be found was a few new pairs of socks. It was time for desperate measures: it became clear now that any sort of a job would do – even teaching.

Public libraries are a reasonable alternative to public bars if you find yourself, as I did now, with too much time and too little money with which to do anything useful. Arriving late one February morning at the Fulham Road library, I discovered that I had been beaten to the newspaper section by the rough-sleeping regulars. Consequently I found myself with next to no reading alternatives. The *Caterer's Weekly*, my first choice, I quickly discarded, deflated by the cover story: 'The Rise and Rise of Frozen Dough'. It was with some real physical and mental effort that I forced myself to reach up for the pristine copy of *The Times Educational Supplement*. Half-horrified, half-resigned, I flicked through the several dozen pages of small ads. In the past I had done this with genuine interest, to find out how I might head onwards and upwards; now I turned the pages with the desperation of someone who had no idea how to go on the dole and even less of an idea how to survive on it.

The recently renamed establishment on a London estate was definitely a school – the battered sign at the gate said so (you could just make it out under some black, priapic graffiti) but it was not at all how I, or indeed anybody else in the outside world, imagined a school to be. A few years earlier, when it had been known by another name, things had not looked rosy for the school – truancy was high, vandalism commonplace and achievements barely visible. With a heavy heart, particularly when it thought of the additional paperwork, the local council decided to close it down at the end of the summer term. It was perhaps a fitting end to this seat of learning that the school was destroyed by a fire started in a Year 8 domestic science class a few days before the holidays began.

Since my experiences there I have often thought of other suitable institutions with which to compare it but none seems in any way appropriate: prisons are considerably less dangerous, mental asylums more sane, anarchist groups better organised. The youngsters, who fitfully attended, seemed to view life in or out of school as a permanent and strenuous competition to get one over on everybody else. Everyone, particularly adults (perhaps because they were so unused to having any normal contact with them), was perceived as a possible threat – to be kept at arm's length. Undeniably some of these children came from homes that provided little more than protection from the elements. Many of them lived in households that lacked any recognisable familial structure and where emotional warmth had been replaced long before by a flickering TV in the bedroom.

School work and academic achievement were not priorities for most of these youngsters. That said, it would be unfair to say that they were not without certain skills: they could break almost anything that did not belong to them, could swear with a fluency that would have astonished an Irish working men's club and could list the top ten most expensive pairs of trainers and mobile telephones as respectfully as if they were reciting verses of Milton. They also seemed to have an encyclopedic knowledge of their rights.

Once they had gained access to the classroom for the first lesson on that frighteningly cold morning in early March, and had wholly ignored my invitation to come in 'nice and quietly', they set about each other with cheerful, murderous intent.

This particular period had been marked down on the official timetable as a music lesson. Now I am not musical – at all – but the pleasant although curiously numb teacher in charge of staff absences had not let this worry her. Instead, she had smiled and handed me a pile of paper.

'Here you are – this is for Year Eight.'

I looked at the sheets. Relieved, I understood what I saw: the same note repeated from top to bottom in the simplest of rhythms of quavers and crotchets.

'So you get them to go through it. Like this, you see,' she waved her finger up and down in time. 'Dum-dum-dum-dum-di-dum-dum.'

'OK . . .'

'Fine, thanks, err, Will. You're doing a great job – really appreciate your help. Thanks.'

She began to wander off towards a crowd of nervously twitching supply teachers – it seemed to be their first day at school too.

'Yes, fine. OK. So what about after that then?'

'No, just that; that'll be fine.'

'What – for an hour and a half?'

But she was gone.

Dum-dum-dum-dum-di-dum-dum.

In the event I need not have worried.

The children – they were twelve years old – only sat down after the first forty minutes and then only if they were tired or injured; the other half continued to run around in a desperate attempt to prove the Random Theory despite my gentle and then not-so-gentle suggestions that they might like to take their places.

Well, I supposed I might as well give it a go.

'So here we are. Music.' I thought it worth pointing this out.

I started to hand out the sheets. Placing one in front of a boy whose back was turned three-quarters away from me and who was engrossed in conversation with his mate, I tapped it with my hand to attract his attention.

'Here you are; have a look at this. Should be quite good fun this . . . Just write your name on the top of it, please.'

As I looked down, the boy slowly placed his hard-bitten fingers flat down on the piece of paper. Then with an equal lack of haste, without turning towards me, or even complicitly winking at his friend, he scrumpled it up and tossed it back over his shoulder from whence it had come.

Dum-dum-dum-dum-di-dum-dum.

'Just remember, it's not you, it's them!' a whisky-soaked Scottish teacher had breathed thickly into my ear after the last bell of the first day rang and I was limping my way to the barbed-wire-topped school gates. I tried to remember, I really did, but in the thick of battle, in the midst of one of the four hour-and-a-half-long lessons of the day, it was really very difficult to remember anything more than where the door was.

At least the pay was pretty good – by teaching standards – and, in truth, in time, things did get a little better. Often, though, I found myself wondering from where or from whom these youngsters had adopted this antagonistic, unhappy attitude to the world in which they lived. It was therefore with a combination of trepidation and intrigue that I attended my first parents' meeting.

Entering the school hall one March evening I smiled as I remembered the imaginative variety of threats that my charges had issued with straight-faced earnestness during the course of the school day. Whatever happened I must not say the wrong thing.

As it turned out, the exercise was of relatively little use as the parents of the most ill-behaved children, and hence those who most needed to be addressed, failed to appear. However, as a nervously shaky colleague pointed out, this was probably something of a blessing in disguise. The rest of the parents seemed to divide themselves squarely in three: one group were righteously concerned about the progress of their children and were going to give them 'a proper pasting' for any reported misdemeanours when they got them home. Inevitably, feebly, not having the heart to be responsible for the meting out of this punishment, I found myself not only hopelessly diluting the truth but also, in front of more heavyweight parents, simply lying. Their offspring, squirming in their grey plastic seats, were consequently astonished to find themselves portrayed by me as students worthy of the greatest academic recognition. Unbeknownst to them, I planned to have run away a long time before the flaws in this judgement became only too evident.

A second group of parents suggested that they would be giving *me* 'a good pasting' unless their kids 'had fun' and I didn't 'have a go at them when they just wanted to talk to their mates'. Their youngsters were accordingly described by me, with an eloquence born of self-preservation, in terms that suggested that they were so angelic that they were nudging for a place at the Right Hand.

The remainder of the parents seemed only to have a sketchy idea why they were there at all. Greatly irritating for them was the hazy realisation that all the time that they spent in the austere, strip-lit classroom was time that they could otherwise have been spending in the innumerable pubs and clubs that fringed the estate. Fumbling with the buttons on their mobile telephones, they tended to reply only with slow, befuddled 'I see's, 'Oh, yeah, is that right?' and 'Wassall that about then?'

Actually, I had forgotten those families that fitted into no particular category. They were just extraordinarily but quite individualistically odd:

'Sorry, I can't really help Neeta with her French!' Neeta's mother informed me as she flicked at a crisp crumb and hauled the edge of a yellowing cardigan over a copious, black-basqued bosom.

No, I knew. I had every sympathy. I had tried too.

'But I have been good, en'I, sir?' squawked Neeta as she hawked and spat on her glasses and wiped them around amongst the various other liquids that stained her skirt.

'Well, I suppose yess . . .' Flashing at the headmaster had strictly speaking been outside the school rules and had given him a nasty shock, but it was true, she had done no permanent damage that half of term.

'By the way, sir. This is Matthew.' She gestured to a slack-mouthed teenager next to her who sat immobile, gawping at me with heavily ringed eyes; a skateboard was laid flat over his knees, a fistful of spots were splattered across his face. 'He's my fiancé!'

'But Neeta, you're only thirteen.'

'Yeah, but we get up to all sorts of things! You know, naughty . . .' She giggled and wriggled as she slipped her bottle-bottom glasses back on. Rearranging her considerable self, she folded her arms as best she could and gave me an almost opaque wink. Matthew just looked exhausted.

'No, I just speak Flemish.' Somewhat surprised, I turned my attention back to Neeta's mother and her faded husband – old, exhausted, a Matthew forty years on.

'Flemish? Did you say Flemish? God, why?'

'Oh, I go to Belgium a lot,' she replied loftily. 'It's for my husband. For his spark plugs.'

'His spark plugs? What?'

'That's right.' Neeta's mum tossed back her mane of synthetic, static-charged hair and licked the inside of a now empty crisp packet that she had just delicately torn open with vermilion nails. 'You heard me.' Slurp. 'Spark plugs.'

'You deal in spark plugs?' I turned to Neeta's dad.

'Nooo. He doesn't work. Couldn't,' replied his wife. 'It's for his collection.'

Collection?

'He's got one thousand five hundred and forty-two of them now. They've got some very rare spark plugs in Belgium. Very rare.'

Ironically, it was Neeta who, having failed to benefit in any way at all from my presence, gave me a box of chocolates and a card from her and her friends on the day that I finally left the school, before crying noisily and wishing me good luck. Most of my days, sadly, were not filled with such fine sentiment. Indeed, rather the contrary.

Not surprisingly, therefore, it was with some considerable dread that I discovered my name on a list of members of staff accompanying an extraordinarily ill-thought-through trip to one of the better-known London art galleries to see an exhibition of 'Art from the Developing World'. In line with government regulations, we were to be five colleagues to forty children but even had the ratio been reversed I would still have been concerned about public safety. That particular morning in the misty playground, two of my colleagues had failed to report for duty and, as the rest of the staff were hiding in classroom cupboards, there was nobody to replace them. Climbing aboard the heavily fortified coach, however, my guard dropped as to my amazement our somnolent charges seemed to be almost compliant. Regrettably, by the time we had reached the venerable portals of the exhibition hall they were all fully, and some rather more than fully, awake.

With a quiet 'psssh' and an unsticking of rubber seals the coach door slid out and open and I made the mistake of standing up and making my way down the steps. As I did so the hordes behind me swarmed down the aisle between the now slashed and chewing-gummed seats and thrust me out on to the pavement, with cries of 'Sir, sir, bloody hell, get out of the way, sir, yer crushing my packed lunch, sir. If it's squashed you'll have to pay for it.' I just had time to see my two colleagues sauntering off the bus last of all and disappearing into the busy London crowds before the first student was pushed into the ornamental pond at the bottom of a flight of marble steps. Miraculously I somehow herded nearly the whole group towards the entrance and armed them with their tickets. As each one clicked through the turnstile I noticed that the museum attendants slipped quietly away in the direction of felt-clad doors – doors that left no trace once they had been closed behind them. I was on my own.

Within five minutes I had heard the two words 'boring' and 'sad' a dozen times each, but at least they all seemed to be following me around – didn't they? Out of the corner of my eye, as I turned to address them, I noticed a fifteen-year-old boy with a fire-extinguisher-sized marker pen on the point of carefully inscribing 'Kik me ere' on the testicles of a surprised-looking marble discus thrower.

'Please don't do that. I would really appreciate it if you didn't do that, you know. You'll get me in loads of trouble. I

could really do without that, you know.' Official Policy recom-
mended I didn't raise my voice and I was very civil to him.
It didn't seem to work.

'Why are you always having a go at me? You got it in for
me, innit? I'm gonna report you when we get back to school,'
he screamed at the top of his tar-lined lungs, ignorant of the
fact that we had actually never spoken before. Furiously he
waved his black pen up at me as if to suggest that if there was
any further insolence on my part then I would be up for much
the same treatment as the discus thrower. I did my best to
take no further notice of him and turned away to address the
very small percentage of my group who still seemed to be
listening to me.

'So, here we are, and although Miss Robinson isn't here
today to tell you what on earth, err . . . why we're here, I think
we'll find it's pretty interesting.' I could see a few of the mob
eyeing up the burglar alarm system but chose to ignore them
and pressed on. 'Now a lot of these pictures are from countries where people live lives rather differently to the way we
do here. Can anybody tell me how they might be different?'

A small, normally speechless Moslem girl adjusted her black
headscarf and, as if invigorated by these new surroundings –
freed momentarily from the shackles of derision that normally
bound her in the classroom – seemed to be about to say something. At that moment a mobile telephone rang and with a
shriek of rage one tall boy leapt on another shouting: ''Ere,
that's my ring tone. I knew you nicked it, you bastard! Give
us it back or I'll have you!' Like the referee of a wrestling
match, I lay with my ear close to the floor and beat the ground
with the flat of my hand until eventually the kerfuffle came
to its natural end.

'Yes, Fatima, what was it you were going to say about
people from other countries?' I asked, but by now the little
girl's cheeks were flushed with embarrassment and she was
looking down at her twisting hands, her moment of self-
expression gone – probably forever. Apologetically, I too stared
down and, to my surprise, noticed amongst the several

thousand pounds' worth of designer footwear a tough pair of brown hiking boots. Running my eye up some equally sturdy-looking green tights, I was taken aback to find myself staring into the intent face of an elderly and much made-up woman who was standing at the edge of my unruly group. She was smiling at me knowingly, almost as if she expected me to recognise her. At first I thought that she must be some long-lost aunt – believing that I recognised a certain familiar eccentricity in the way she dressed; her hair was tied away by a scarf in the fashion of a Dutch milkmaid and clamped down by a broad-brimmed felt hat. A caftan, flowing to her calves, was bespeckled in small mirrors. Beads and other exotic strings of matter, vegetable and mineral, hung around her neck and wrists, accompanied by, on what appeared to be shoelaces, a pair of half-moon spectacles and some oddly modern sunglasses.

'You have no other members of staff with you? No? Oh! Perhaps I can be of assistance?' she asked, in a slightly northern European accent. 'Before the war I was a teacher too. In Holland. My name is Maria-Helena von Würfelwerfer. You are having some problems, I think?'

Of this there was little doubt.

'I will help you if you would like.' She put on her glasses to better inspect the scene.

'Well, yes, that would be nice, thank you.' Distracted as I was, I noticed nothing peculiar about this offer. The children looked at this strange, compact figure with awe and I was almost as surprised as they when, with strict, no-nonsense efficiency, she had rearranged them to stand in pairs in a long line. For a moment I half expected her to ask them to hold hands.

'That is so much better.' She addressed the group as if they had just arrived at Sunday school. 'Now, please only talk if you are asked a question by your teacher or if you want to know something about what you are going to see.'

'Oi, you can't do that! I know what my rights is. You can't tell us what to do – you're not even a teacher, innit!'

As if that unfortunate position made much difference.

Wrestling briefly with Black Marker Pen, which involved the audible connection of hand with soft flesh that made the rest of us wince, she turned back to me holding the offending felt-tipped article. Taking it gratefully, I tried to fit it into my jacket pocket.

With quiet authority, the old lady divided the children into groups of four and set them a number of tasks: inspecting a painting, making notes on anything they found interesting and then waiting until we came to listen to their findings. In near silence, they shuffled off to their chosen picture, glancing entreatingly back to me. Perhaps it was her age or a fear that she might be mad that meant that they followed her instructions with implicit obedience. Even if she was completely loopy, her methods worked extremely well and that was enough for me.

'It is in many years since I was a schoolteacher. Not since the nineteen fifties when I first came to Britain. Yet, it is strange, a part of me has always missed it. You probably know what I mean?'

'No, not really . . .'

'You will, my dear, you will.' She patted me on the arm, with the soft touch of the elderly. 'Even if sometimes they can be very trying, always, but always, you can make some small progress. Isn't it funny but all they really appreciate is some old-fashioned discipline. Let us not worry about them; they will be quiet for a little while now. Remember, my dear young man, always remember: no fear, no, have no fear!'

No fear seemed to have been a byword for her lifetime. Maria-Helena von Würfelwerfer had been born in Germany but her father, strongly opposed to the Nazi regime, had moved to Antwerp in the 1930s. As a teenager, during the war, she had worked for the Dutch resistance; losing her lover to the Gestapo and escaping from an internment camp, she had come alone to London where she had worked for many years running a number of successful private art galleries. Tiring eventually of her professional life, she had married first one of the more important art buyers in London, then, after his demise during a Scandinavian yacht race, a 'rather *boorring* man – he was only interested in bloody golf'. Despite their shortcomings they had both been wealthy men and now in her retirement the old lady could afford to indulge in her two favourite pastimes – art and travel.

'Now, let us have a look at these interesting works.' She drew me away to one of the smooth wooden benches in front of a large canvas – peasants tilling in a field.

'So what do think of this magnificent picture?'

Amazed, I had been staring at a group of children standing grumpily but, much more impressively, silently, beneath a picture some yards away. Now I quickly turned my attentions to the one in front of the two of us – a depiction of great poverty. Women tilled the earth whilst men in the background were guiding bullocks and ploughs along furrows that ran across a flat landscape. The sun, central in a white-blue sky, beat down on the labourers, incinerating the tufts of vegetation, sapping any remaining moisture from the ochre soil and making the picture an image that seared the eye and wearied the viewer.

'Ach, what a wonderful country it is,' the old lady sighed.

'Yes, yes, a wonderful place, wonderful . . .' I agreed. Delighting in this unexpected respite, I had consequently been paying scant attention to what she was saying.

'So you have been there? How interesting. Which parts do you like most?'

'Oh yes, of course . . . Well, I think my favourite area must be . . .'

I peered forward, desperately trying to work out quite literally where on earth this scene came from.

'No, actually, now I look at it I don't think I have been. No, no, my mistake, no. Must be thinking of somewhere else . . . ha, ha, my mistake.'

'Not been to India? But everybody must go to India! There is so much to learn, so much to see.'

Stealthily behind us the children were beginning to fidget. What had started as a little restlessness was now developing into pushing and shoving. Unbelievably, when the little woman turned slightly in their direction they became immediately still.

'I think it would be just the place for you. You are not happy, I can tell. In India you will find many possibilities to think about things differently. You will meet people that will change the way that you see the world. It will be a life-changing experience for you. Yes, you must go. But I think you are quite poor?'

'No, no, not particularly,' I riposted proudly. Only a few weeks before, I had broken even and Mr Jolly and I were back on first-name terms.

'I see, but I think even so it is really quite easy. You carry, I pay.'

'Sorry, I don't know what you mean . . .'

But as usual it was too late.

She had stood up and was already turning to the children. To my delight, I noticed a number of them stand up straighter.

'Very well, are we ready? Good. Now please sit in a semi-circle on the ground.'

Black Marker Pen glanced at me angrily as he crossed his legs and, on the next instruction, folded his arms. So it was for the next half an hour that he sat and they all listened, enraptured against their will, as the curious lady explained in fascinating and sometimes gruesome detail what was hanging on the walls around them. When the lesson was at an end, she arranged them back into a line.

'Good, now follow me but remember: no chitter – no chatter.'

And with that they snaked off across the highly polished parquet floor. With the old lady in full flow, describing in knowledgeable detail all that there was to see in the other runs, they disappeared around the corner of one of the tall white walls. As they vanished out of sight I wondered if the last of these monsters-turned-angels would break into a skip.

At the end of the tour, and with our group assembled outside in a still orderly row beside the waiting coach, Maria-Helena von Würfelwerfer turned to me with a business-like adjustment of the felt lapels of her Miss Marple tweed jacket. With a deft unsnapping of its clasp she reached into her handbag. From it she pulled a notebook much stained and marked with lipstick and face powder. She flipped it open and with the end of a silver propelling pencil she tapped the page.

'So here you are – put your coordinates. Then I will contact you. I am going for six months starting in April.'

Only snapping the lead twice, I scribbled down my name and address – which I took to be my coordinates – and handed the pad and pencil back to her smiling. She was the most extraordinary woman. Mumbling, I tried to thank her but was silenced by her raised arm. Without speaking again she shook my hand with a soft but definite grasp.

'So now I must go. It has been most pleasant meeting you . . . err . . . Will. I very much hope you will find my proposal interesting. Good luck until we meet again.'

Finally patting one murderous Philistine on the head with what looked strangely like affection, she disappeared like a benign spirit into the crowd; the same crowd from which my two absentee colleagues appeared a few minutes later gripping a number of plastic shopping bags and muttering a few ineffectual excuses under breaths that smelled of a great deal of alcohol.

Sure enough, a couple of weeks later I received a blue envelope which contained a letter written in a looping but concise hand. Its proposal was quite simple. If I were to accompany Maria-Helena von Würfelwerfer on her trip to India – carry her bags, accompany her from the airport to her hotel and take her out to restaurants, keep her entertained, that kind of thing – then she would pay for my ticket.

Initially, of course, I dismissed the whole offer out of hand. This would only prove to be a diversion. Anyway, India had never really appealed to me. Friends had been but most had returned exhausted and ambivalent; for they had found it too hot, too big, too crowded, simply too overwhelming. This huge pressure of population would, I was certain, after so many years of comparative solitude in my life both at home and abroad, be impossible for me to bear. A part of me also felt, particularly after my South Pacific experiences, that there was something faintly pointless about travel for travelling's sake. Nothing that you might see as you passed through a city or country could provide you with anything but the most slight understanding of a different culture, the most stereotypical image of a people. Travel was a distraction, an escape from responsibilities, all part and parcel of the *mañana* complex from which I have suffered all my life.

Above and beyond those reservations, of course, was the thought of having to haul about an enormous rucksack which would only serve as a huge beacon for anyone doing the same thing, and would invite the endless, trying conversations about how long you had been away from home and how much they had been ripped off for a massage in Manila or a hotel in Hanoi.

Part of me must have been intrigued, however – as much by the old lady as by her proposal – for a week or so after I received her letter, I agreed to meet her for tea in a West End hotel that seemed not to have changed since Hercule Poirot had last visited it for a swift *sirop à la menthe*. Over crumpets, she further outlined her plan.

We would fly to Mumbai – the city formerly known as Bombay. Post-independence, many British names had been changed to Indian ones, she explained in a didactic tone that I was soon to recognise only too well. Many people, of course, particularly the older generation, stuck to the colonial names out of familiarity.

'This is of course madness. Every Indian has a responsibility to be modern. Today and every day.' The old lady ended her digression with a thump of the table which made the teacups jump.

'So there we will spend a few days,' she explained after she had rearranged herself.

Then on to a place called Poona by train where she would be met by her 'oldest friend from the war'. They would go and stay in the country, 'in a charming place where we always go'. After her safe arrival I would be free to do whatever I chose: either to set off on my own journey through India or to return home immediately.

'You can do what you want, of course. Just come back to England or stay on in India. You have free choice. But I think you will find that you will stay on. You will be fascinated. More tea? You take sugar? How disgusting!'

I laughed out loud at her brusqueness. She did not seem to take offence and I admired her for her forthright independence. No lazy acceptance of everybody else's rules, no easy decline into old age and senility for her, I thought, as she crossed her leather-clad legs.

'Let me give it some thought, please? A few days?'

'Certainly, but write to me, please. I do not allow a telephone in my house. It is too impertinent when people ring you unannounced and without invitation.'

After another day employed as the referee of a series of illicit boxing matches – fights which involved thirty diminutive pugilists of both sexes, a staggering amount of foul language, several chairs, pencils, tables and compasses – my resolve not to do something stupid was weakened. I was open to offers. A quick trip, then, a well-earned break and then back to England for a new career far, far away. Who knew what the trip would involve but at least it was free.

And also, I thought, as I stomped along the Embankment in a fine drizzle and a foul mood, it would be exciting, an adventure. Battersea Power Station, like a giant upturned table, was reflected in the surface of the cold, unkindly Thames as I leaned over the wall and tried to imagine the India I might find. I thought immediately, unoriginally, of the allure of the East, of the exciting espionage adventures of Kim, the sophistication and elegance of the world frequented by Mrs Moore; even the sweltering jungle and its hidden mysteries suffered by Orwell's colonial characters. Tigers, elephants, a friendly bear, Mowgli, a cast of delightful Disney characters and groups of beautiful women in veils and saris dancing their way across beautiful landscapes. Ridiculous, I know.

Still, it was bound to be more inspiring than stomping my

way along a pavement strewn with burger boxes, past home-bound civil servants shaking their mobile phones in despair that no one had rung them; certainly it would turn out to be more thrilling than being sloshed with dirty rainwater by an unstoppable number 73.

2

Where to, Auntie?

There is something deeply deceptive about the airport arrivals hall at Mumbai. In a bright, well-ordered, open, air-conditioned space, people push trolleys piled high with suitcases that seem to fit perfectly one on top of the other. They glide effortlessly across a clean, smooth floor talking in quiet, measured tones to one another. Other luggage bobbles noiselessly along tarmac-coloured rubber carpets. Immigration control seems in no way out of the ordinary and the officer inspects your passport with the normal official disinterest. You exchange gentle nods of the head and smile discreetly as you push your documents back into your pocket. You make your way towards some double frosted-glass doors.

Little do you know.

The heat alone was enough to make me want to turn and dart back indoors: you move from shirt-sleeves cool to pouring sweat and this just to put one foot in front of the other, let alone having to deal with Maria-Helena von Würfelwerfer's ten pieces of matching luggage plus my rucksack. It was only five o'clock in the morning, still dark, but the warmth was almost unbreathable, the air seemingly so thin that it hardly filled my lungs.

All this was nothing compared to the noise; it is like stepping out of the front door of a well-insulated house into a raging storm, like leaping out of a plane in the middle of a stormy night without a parachute. I felt like a Hollywood star – well, a bit like a Hollywood star – cornered by the press pack which, although it has inadvertently left all its cameras and flashbulbs at home, is making sure not to waste the opportunity by bellowing questions at the top of its voice:

'Baba [the much over-used Indian equivalent of 'Squire'], Baba, Baba, Baba, how much for one taxi? Where you go? Baba! Baba! Five hundred rupee too much? Four hundred? Any nice girl? Body massage? Where you go? Cheap hotel? Souvenir? Chocolate?'

Chocolate?

Ten pairs of hands clamped themselves on to the matching suitcases and threatened to whisk them all off in as many different directions. I rushed from one taxi driver to the next trying unsuccessfully to bring them all together again.

'Come, follow, nice hotel, nice girl, come, come, come.' I was beginning to despair imagining the two of us, alone in this swirl of activity, destitute and baggageless, having progressed no further than the front step of the airport.

'Go back! Go back!' Maria-Helena von Würfelwerfer screeched with what at that moment I believed to be Canute-like self-delusion. 'Ach, you are bad men! Shame on you. What are you thinking? I am an old woman! Shame on you!'

Suddenly the scrummage subsided, the drivers slinking back to their vehicles as the old woman, bringing up the rear, stabbed and cut, feinted and poked with her umbrella.

'Oh, sorry, Auntie. Sorry!' The men looked at their feet embarrassed, touched their right hands to their chests in a sign of apology and spat softly by their wing mirrors. Now in control of the situation, the old lady selected one of the taxis with a jab of her umbrella and half a dozen men ran about regrouping our luggage, which was then stowed in the boot and on the front seat of the box-like vehicle.

'It is so nice here how they respect the elderly.' She grunted as she climbed into the back seat and the driver with a nervous smile slammed the door closed before climbing into his own seat in front of the steering wheel which was surrounded by small pictures of men with long grey beards and beatific smiles stuck to the dashboard.

'We are going to Colaba. Meter please,' the old lady demanded but now in a softer tone. The driver leaned across his seat and reached out of the opposite window to turn a curious aluminium box from up to down. With a quiet 'ching' and a few turns of a toybox key the meter started to tick, the driver pulled down the stick shift and with a clunk and a groan we moved away from the airport terminal.

'Always the meter. Never forget this.' She looked up at me seriously and then settled in her seat. As we cleared the entrance to Sahar International Airport I glanced at my companion and noticed that she had nodded off, her head now resting on the walnut-brown material of the canvas lining of the car door. The rear seat of the taxi seemed to be raised slightly higher than the front ones, which caused me immediate problems. First my head was rubbing against the roof of the car which, due to the increasingly uneven nature of the road, was causing me no little discomfort and, secondly, because of my elevated position I was unable to see anything out of the windows. I slid down in the seat, drawing my knees up under my chin, and looked out of the open window. Early sun had lit a yellow strip along the horizon which was beginning to give some contour to the mass of buildings on either side of the road.

It would be wrong, quite wrong, to attempt to give a romantic description of the approach to Bombay City – indeed it would be impossible. Mile upon mile of decrepit housing is surrounded by concrete rubble, stagnant water, and rare patches of scrubland, which is thickly covered in refuse and varieties of vegetable matter each doing their best to outdo the rest in the levels of filthy stink that they can produce. This, however, I would quickly discover, was the norm outside any Indian city centre. What could not yet be seen at this early hour was the enormous concentration of people living here. The city limits, originally seven islands connected by marshland and swamps, most of which had already been reclaimed to provide more or less satisfactory and hygienic building land, were now swollen, distended by an estimated population of eighteen million people. This figure presumably had been reached before they gave up counting, a hopeless task as thousands of people poured into the city every day. As a result good housing is as sought after as it is in Manhattan and real estate prices equal those of Mayfair. Of course, as the vast majority have next to no income, let alone wealth, nearly half the inhabitants of Mumbai live on a mere 5 per cent of the land, pushed by necessity, herded by financial restraint into more and more cramped conditions. In a number of districts of Greater Mumbai as many as two hundred thousand people live per square kilometre. In pockets of the greatest concentration there is barely two square metres of living space for each man, woman or child and it is only as much as this because the statisticians have considered roads and railway lines as habitable. Young hopefuls still arrive, desperate for a chance to earn a living that might go some way to supporting their families. Few ever escape these squalid, unhealthy conditions again and even fewer survive them into old age.

At this early hour, however, the only waking creatures appeared to be a few herds of goats that shied away from the traffic as they timidly approached the road intent on snipping away the few remaining blades of grass that grew on the verge. The road ahead, although wide, was a slalom of potholes and cracks; many of the side roads seemed to go nowhere and ended instead apologetically in a few barrels full of concrete.

Perhaps more remarkable than the dilapidation of the scene was the scale of it; we drove, not fast but at a reasonable speed as the roads were all but empty, for three-quarters of an hour and the panorama hardly changed. Finally, in quite a sudden and surprising change of view, we entered a part of town that seemed to have benefited from some sort of urban planning. The shacks and hovels, the narrow alleyways and patches of wasteland gave way to large municipal buildings built out of curious grey-green stone in straight architectural lines around burnt brown parks – the *maidans* which were large enough, one imagined, to house a cricket match, perhaps two, but which were at weekends the scene of dozens, if not more, ferociously fought overlapping games.

As we slowed to enter a large roundabout I looked down from the skyline and realised that, as the morning had ticked on, the city was beginning to move, the pavements themselves sprouting people who I had not until that moment noticed. Now they made themselves apparent by sitting up wearily from the flattened cardboard boxes on which they had been sleeping, then slowly standing and stretching towards the brightening sky. At least those who lived in the outlying slums had a shelter to call, however derisorily, 'home' – far less fortunate than they were these countless thousands of homeless who possessed nothing but worthless scraps with which they hoped to earn their living.

From secret places old men produced shoeboxes and polishing kits; women sitting cross-legged, the outside of their two knees flat on the ground, began to organise small piles of handkerchiefs, tea-towels, T-shirts and socks. What appeared at first to be wooden hoardings opened out to reveal cigarettes, sunglasses, lengths of cloth, carvings and bundles of incense wrapped in cellophane. A man drew himself to the edge of the pavement and, squatting, drew from a grimy plastic bag a pair of weighing scales such as might be found in millions of Western bathrooms. Placing them down carefully and adjusting the setting cog at the back, he rocked to and fro, still crouching, and waited for his first customer of the day to come and check his weight for a few coins.

Soon the city would take up its blur of activity, a constant traffic of colour and sound: only the beggars, the hawkers, the dying and the dead were static in a world moving on.

Maria-Helena woke as we turned off the straight main road into a residential leafy side street. The houses, although grimy and in poor repair, were substantial and had clearly once been fine residences. As we pulled out of the end of the road we came out on to a corniche that ran alongside a flat, greasy sea which was beginning to blearily reflect the sun that had just appeared over the rooftops of grubby apartment blocks. To sail out on to the surface of this water was to run the risk of disappearing into the haze, to fall in would mean, for even the strongest swimmer, the certainty of being pulled down into the tepid, treacherous murk only to be released much later to float upwards, finally joining the stiff white bellies of the dead fish that bobbed along the sides of the few unhappy fishing boats.

Ahead of us now was a giant, grey, granite ceremonial arch, an *Arc de Triomphe*, through which, from our approach, the only way to march was out to sea.

'Ahh the Gate of India, good,' murmured Maria-Helena.

This colossus, now grimed and somehow unhappily uncomfortable by the slick of sea, must have looked very different when the King Emperor had made a dashing arrival in 1911 to inspect the diadem of his empire. It was here, too, on the last day of February 1948, that the final symbolic enactment of the handover to Indians of their independence had taken place. As the soldiers of the 1st battalion Light Infantry had marched on to the ship that was to take them back to Blighty, the band had played 'Auld Lang Syne'. This, I felt instinctively, would be, for me too, an acquaintance that would not quickly be forgot.

'Yes, please. The Taj Mahal Hotel.'

The taxi swung in a U turn and came to a squeaking halt outside a huge hotel built in much the same style as the buildings that we had passed earlier – a grand meeting of East and West, the windows of which looked out across the Arabian Sea back towards Britain. Ironically, the great industrialist J. N. Tata had built this most famous of all Indian hotels in 1903 for the very simple reason that, as a native, he had been refused entry to any of the establishments frequented by the colonisers.

As I got out of the cab, two men with turbans and thick black beards and dressed in ceremonial uniforms came charging down the red-carpeted steps. Although I could not immediately see their weapons, it was clear that they wished me no good at all. Hastily, I took a couple of defensive steps backwards into the road causing a horse-drawn carriage to pull to a halt with a jingling of bells and an irritated crack of the driver's whip above my head. Still the men kept on coming but it was only when they began to snatch up the endless bags and baggages, tucking them under their warrior-like arms, that I realised that they were simply the doormen. We made our way inside.

Magnificent, wide, pale corridors of marble were lit by small golden lamps that ran with a pleasing symmetry the length of the seemingly converging walls; the intermittent brass-handled double doors were of solid dark wood, as was the enormous reception counter behind which several men and women smartly dressed in brocade uniforms busied themselves with clicking keys, printed bills and credit cards.

'I have a reservation. My name is von Würfelwerfer.'

'Of course. We have your normal room.' From nowhere, a man with a lopsided hat box on his head appeared and started scooping up the old lady's luggage.

'So where will you be staying?' She turned to me, sympathetic to my supposed lot.

'Well . . . this is a very nice place. Maybe I could have a look at your prices, please?' I was passed a leather-bound folder. 'These prices, they are just for the one night, are they? I see.'

I could afford until about half past ten.

'Well, perhaps I'll just have a look round the area to see if there are any other places. I always prefer the smaller sort of places. More of a family sort of feel, you know.'

'Of course, as you wish,' she replied with no suggestion of irony. 'I am going to rest now. Perhaps you would like to have dinner with me here this evening?'

I accepted and made my way back out into the road as nonchalantly as possible. I turned back down the residential road and although I had to keep a careful eye out for the enormous unprotected holes that lurked to swallow up any unsuspecting pedestrian, I noticed that many of these buildings had been converted into hotels. I stopped at the first one I came to: 'Bentley's Hotel'. A large, once white-fronted building had swirls of old wedding cake still stuck to it. A very smelly dog was slobbering and slavering on the black and white tiles of the entrance hall as I enquired about vacancies.

'Oh no, I am very sorry, this is a most busy week,' the only slightly apologetic concierge informed me. And then, with a certainty that I was soon to recognise as being entirely untrustworthy, he continued, 'You will never find anything this week. Everything is fully booked. Oh dear yes, you will never find something!'

'Oh, I see. Anywhere? In the whole of Mumbai?'

'No possibilities. Oh, sorry.' The man demonstrated the pages of his hotel register with an open hand as if it were symbolic of the whole metropolis. 'Oh yes, this is most certainly the number one busy week in Mumbai.'

'Well, thanks. OK, bye now.'

Unsure exactly what the reason for this sudden business might be, I made my way back towards the door. As I did so the man hit a large metal clinger on his desk and a sparkling, piercing note rang out through the building. Turning back, confused, the edge of my rucksack narrowly avoided destroying a stand of yellowing leaflets that stood like a vase of dead flowers on the reception desk.

Rubbing wet hands on the seat of a dirty pair of shorts, a boy, no more than five foot tall, trotted into the room. For a couple of moments they spoke and the boy wobbled his head from side to side in assent.

'Very good, now this boy is taking you to a very nice hotel. My cousin brother's hotel. Very nice, very clean. Come give me twenty rupees.'

Bewildered, I complied as the boy manhandled the rucksack off my back.

'I thought you said that there was nowhere . . .'

'Yes, yes, no problem. OK. Thank you.' The man suggested with a wave of his arm in the direction of the street that I follow the boy.

As he struggled out of the door like a diminutive Atlas, and I tagged obediently behind, I was unaware that I had just experienced a phenomenon that was to shape and form my Indian experiences. For, in informing me that there was no room at the inn, and organising my guide, Bentley's receptionist had already removed any feeble sense of self-determination that I believed I possessed. Despite my every effort to pursue my own course through India, the hugely strong tides of humanity and all the attendant but often unseen, unvoiced decisions, indecisions, agreements, refusals, pacts and enmities meant that although I was always, finally, to reach my destination, it was not often because I had followed a route of my own choosing. Certainties and uncertainties, the possible and the impossible, the real and the whimsical were to slip across one another like swirling clouds casting random shadows over my Indian landscape, leaving me often confused, sometimes enraged but always, in hindsight at least, greatly invigorated. As time went on I came to expect surprises. Unpredictability became a part of daily routine. But what mystified me almost without exception were people's motivations. Often, as now, they were financial, but more often an act was one of simple kindness. Yet in the majority of situations I was and remained utterly bewildered by why things developed as they did. Perhaps it was just a natural working out of my karma.

If, as the Hindu analogy suggested, I was the archer and my arrows were my past actions, then at least one that I had fired in my earlier life seemed to be following an eccentric and idiosyncratic arc, helped on its way by unseen hands; although sometimes it seemed to possess the properties of a boomerang, swinging back to surprise me by stabbing me in the backside, most of the time it eventually seemed to find its target.

Directly opposite Bentley's, no more than five yards away, stood a ragged building with a first-floor veranda. Attached to the wall was a familiar red shield and as we came closer to it I recognised the squirly words 'Salvation Army Hostel'.

'Is this it? Nowhere else?'

I looked down but the boy had gone, leaving me my slumped backpack for company. Smiling as I thought of Maria-Helena now reclining in cushioned comfort, I picked it up, shrugged and made my way up the steps, fully expecting to be greeted by a uniformed brass band led by a redoubtable lady general. Instead I needed to cough, bump into a few things and slam the front door a couple of times before I woke the deeply slumbering receptionist.

Finally, after a great deal of spluttering, hawking and form filling, I was the guardian of an enormous, unpocketable key and the temporary resident of a room that was large enough to accommodate me, my rucksack and a narrow single bed – although not all comfortably at the same time. The ceiling was so low that the fan, which appeared to be the only piece of equipment that worked in the hostel and which whirred at fighter plane speed regardless of what setting I chose on the Bakelite dial, would surely have decapitated me had I sat up in the middle of the night, waking abruptly from one of those dreams in which something dark and lurking is after you – and you know it is probably your guilty conscience.

Through a narrow archway was a bathroom, partly tiled in curiously unmatching colours, which possessed a number of unidentifiable but clearly intentional holes in the floor and half a dozen mysterious taps protruding from the walls at differing heights – as it turned out, a perfect introduction to Indian plumbing. They all seemed to work and they all seemed to run cold. Not that this seemed to be much of a problem as a hot midday breeze blew through the missing corner of one window and helped to dry the sweat running off me. With a nod towards hygiene and away from any prying eyes that might be directed at me from a tenement block across the way, I splashed myself briefly with water from the highest tap – a hip shower, as it were.

The coffee shop of the Taj Mahal Hotel provides an excellent early evening supper, so Maria-Helena had informed me.

'Unfortunately there are many areas of India where it is impossible to find a reasonable hotel.'

'So where do you stay when you visit them?'

'I don't. I never go there.'

'Oh, right . . .'

There was a long pause.

'So,' I asked perkily, worried that she might be swooping towards some sort of depression about the state of Indian hoteliery. 'How long have you been coming to India? I mean, what brings you here?'

'Oh, I suppose you want to hear more about my life story. So many people ask me to tell them everything. It is true that it is very interesting.'

'No, no, not really.' I was only being polite.

'Very well, I will continue if it will make you happy.'

'Oh . . . good . . .'

In 1944 Maria-Helena, working as an assistant nurse in Holland, had been thrilled, along with so many other Dutch people, at the thought that liberation might well be at hand. A Bridge Too Far at the small town of Arnhem put the brakes on an Allied advance and the flags of freedom were rolled up, put away for a later date. Her hospital, a makeshift structure in a bombed-out village hall, had sadly never been more crowded. A permanent cycle of beds filled and emptied, of arriving stretchers and departing walking wounded, and of course, too often, bodies draped in gory sheets, had kept them all busy that summer.

One of the young nurse's charges turned out, once the bandages had been removed, to be a dashing young Indian man, Ayush, the fourth son of a maharaja from the hills of western Maharashtra. Imbued from early childhood with all the traditions of the British Army by his Anglophile father, he had immediately signed up to join the war in Europe, along with hundreds of thousands of other now largely forgotten volunteers from the colonies. For four years he had avoided any injury and even now the damage to his leg and cheek were only superficial.

'Of course, we fell in love. Why not?'

Well, yes. Why not?

Ayush, who, at the age of twenty-three, had been married for nearly seven years, was the father of four children. The affair was impossible. The war over, he returned to India and for almost two decades there was no further contact between them. His family background, his connections, had meant that he had become a politician and successful businessman in post-independence India. It was only by an extraordinary coincidence that they were to meet again in the 1960s at a cocktail party, which had taken place in one of the art galleries that Maria-Helena now managed in London. For years afterwards they had corresponded and when finally Ayush's wife died, he took a deep breath and invited her to visit him.

Now she stayed with him for six months of every year.

'Every year could be the last year.' She looked up at me, her eyes watering. 'I drrread to hear this news. Such happiness we have shared.'

'Perhaps you could stay with him all the year round,' I suggested gently. Imagining we were flickering to the end of an old black and white movie, I was insistent on a happy outcome.

'What! And how do you think I would be able to deal with all my businesses in Britain? And anyway I could never stand to stay in India during the monsoon. No, no, that is a crazy idea.'

'Yes, yes, right . . . sorry, ha, crazy!'

Blimey.

We sipped our soup, in silence, our conversation clearly now at an end. What was I doing with this dotty old dragon? Oh dear, oh dear, I noticed now, as I glanced up surreptitiously, she had put on her sunglasses. Mind you, I could still be stuck at that awful London school, I thought, as I fiddled around with a cold, artificial-tasting bread bun. If for nothing else I should be thankful to her for having rescued me from that particular doom. Enthusiastic slurps from the other side of the table suggested that she was enjoying her minestrone. She wasn't so bad.

Happy that I was not being made to eat spicy food so soon after my arrival, I skimmed the surface of my bowl with a silver spoon. Gastronomically, India was not a good choice: I didn't really like curry, associating it with rugby players, terrible, embarrassing behaviour in restaurants and show-stopping hangovers. Much more to the point, I was quite certain that as soon as I encountered so much as the wafting odours of the local cuisine I would immediately fall griev-ously ill. Indeed, anybody who had given me advice about India – including a few who had actually been there – seemed to limit their certainties about the country to one fact: that I would get horribly, depressingly and messily sick, my system never coming to terms with the spice, the variable levels of hygiene and the microlife contained in the water from the tap. Grappling with that matching luggage, my rucksack and my insides all at the same time would be more than I was capable of.

'So now I will be going to my room. I think you will be going back to your hotel to rest? Tomorrow I think we will see the city, visit some of the main sights and do some shop-ping. Anyway, you must become used to Indian life so that you will enjoy the rest of your stay. If anyone spends a long stay in India it is important that they become used to the local customs as quickly as possible. Perhaps you will be kind enough to meet me at the front entrance with a taxi at seven o'clock tomorrow morning?'

Not at all sure that I would be spending a long stay in India, I set out in the direction of the hostel. Varying my route for the sake of it, I found myself back on the main road that we had driven in on. It was dark now but the street was still hectic as the stalls that I had seen being erected in the morning were now dismantled and packed away carefully for the night. At the same time people were beginning to stretch themselves out on the pavement. A few of them who still had the energy put up their hand to offer me something that I would not like to buy or just to ask for a few coins, before they flopped down and quickly fell into a deep sleep. I was pleased for them that their sleep was so profound as on countless occasions I saw rats – enormous rats, like large cats – run up from the gutters and over their bodies. Occasionally, they would pause over the fresh faces of children before disappearing lazily down alleyways, prepared for a long night scavenging in the streets of the poor. No great fan of rodents, although braver than I used to be, I shuddered and mentally curtailed my holiday even further.

Turning down the side street towards the hostel, I became aware that I had been joined by a small, fragrant figure that skipped alongside me, on and off the pavement. In the gloom it was difficult to see who it was but when we arrived outside the front door of the Sally Army I found myself looking down at a short, slight woman, her grey hair parted; a red splash of powder, *sindoor*, denoting her married status ran down the middle. Under one arm she held a metal tray on which burned a number of cones of incense around a small statue of a rather ferocious deity. A pile of bright red powder was heaped beside it and, with the accuracy of a marksman, she took a pinch between finger and thumb and smeared a dot, a *tika*, in the middle of my forehead. It was, of course, quite a large target.

Lowering her hand she left it cupped in front of me. Clearly this was a financial transaction, good luck at a price, but it all seemed rather more benevolent than 'Lucky Irish heather, lucky Irish heather, kind sir? Lucky Irish heather. Well give me five quid anyway, or I'll put a curse on you' encounters that I had experienced in London. Fumbling in my trouser pocket I pulled out some coins, made a brief attempt to work out their value, gave up and dropped them clattering on to her tray.

'Thank you, Baba. Having a nice time in India, please.'

Hmm.

She turned to head away but then, curiosity seeming to overcome her, she turned back and came closer to me for a better look.

'Baba . . . let me see you in your eyes. For I am a reader of faces, Baba.' She peered at me most solemnly. 'Yes, you are a good man. A very, kind generous man.'

I bet you say that to all the boys who might have a few rupees to spare, I thought, but smiled anyway and thanked her.

'You are a man for who many things will be happening and you must be making the best of them all. If you see a sparkle in the sand you must reach down and pick it up. It might be a broken glass or it might be diamond. You will never know if you do not pick it up.'

'Well, not really. I don't think that's quite right – you see things don't really happen to me. I'm a teacher.'

Mind you, she had a point. After all I did find myself standing in a street in India talking to a soothsayer. Withdrawing my hand from her crooked, stained fingers, I made to move away but with sudden and surprising agility she stepped into my path.

'Waiting please, Baba. Just two more things.'

'Well OK, but I have actually got to go and meet someone at the err, err, at the, well, got to meet someone.'

'Now, no.'

Oh.

'But soon, it is true, you will meet some people and they will be very important people for you. From them you will gain many things, many riches!'

'No beautiful, mysterious lady then?' Well, that was a pity I thought as I looked down into her thin but now deeply thoughtful face. 'No, sorry, just joking. Many riches, eh? I could do with a bit of that!'

'India will be very nice for you.'

'I'm sure it will. Unfortunately I won't be staying very long this time . . . By the way – what was the other thing you were going to say?'

'You look just like a film movie star, Baba.' And, with that, she slipped down a side street in the direction of the sickly sea before I could even reach into my pocket for any more coins.

Ha, ha, I laughed as I made my way past the slumbering Salvo and put my enormous key in the lock of my room. Amazing. Spontaneous chuckling overcame me more than once that night as the meat-slicer fan whirred menacingly above me.

Movie star! Stan Laurel or Jacques Tati perhaps, but hardly a matinée idol!

The next morning I found a taxi amongst the three hundred or so that lined the street outside the hostel and drove to the front entrance of the Taj. The driver, a cheerful expansive man, was in the middle of a long oration about all the possible services with which he could provide me when Maria-Helena appeared on the scene. Her response to his cheerful but no doubt over-familiar 'Morning, Auntie!' kept him sulkily silent for the rest of the day.

'And first to the Towers of Silence!' she commanded. 'You know of these, of course?'

I shook my head. She rolled her eyes and said nothing further.

As it turned out there were no naked bodies on top of the Zoroastrian funeral towers: the Dakonas, the Towers of Silence that stood hidden from view by the trees on Malabar Hill. Unfortunately the vultures who were normally employed to strip the bones bare, as is the funeral custom of this faith, and which were normally to be seen circling greedily, had become fed up with the ever-rising levels of pollution produced by the millions below and had gone to find themselves a more satisfying career in the countryside. Sadly, wherever they went they were increasingly underemployed as there were only eighty-five thousand remaining Pàrsees, the respecters of this faith. The Towers of Silence, smokestacks topped with blackish upturned cupolas, had been designed to avoid pollution either of the sacred Fire – by cremation – or of the Earth – by burial. Once the bones were stripped bare – on a good day in about twenty minutes depending on the number of vultures and their appetites – the bones were then buried at the bottom in pits of dissolving lime.

It was popular urban myth that occasionally one of the birds, whose beady eyes were bigger than its scrawny tummy, would disgorge some part of the incumbent deceased and drop it on an unsuspecting passer-by. I glanced briefly heavenward.

Thwarted in our pursuit of carrion, we drove back to town in the taxi, which had nervously waited our return. Bumping over a roughly constructed bridge, I looked down on what appeared to be an enormous child's paint box. Seemingly hundreds of rough concrete squares stretched away into the hazy housing, but unlike an artist's palette there did not appear to be any gradation of colour. Indeed each of them seemed to contain its own individual washed-out hue. Surrounding them all were men, an army reputably five thousand-strong who appeared to be engaged in mortal combat with formless creatures of every colour and shape. Whirling these weird beasts around their heads, they would bring them dashing down on the sides of the troughs before throwing them lifeless into large wickerwork baskets. Here then were the *dhobi-wallahs* going about their business of washing the city's clothes; thousands of tons of garments passing through their wrinkled hands every year. It seemed astonishing that each individual item of clothing could reappear from this Dantean jumble and ever be returned to its rightful owner. Laundry seemed to be a never-ending cycle, for wherever I found myself in India I was never far out of earshot of the sound of sloshing and scrubbing. Only later did I realise that this was because people owned so few clothes.

On our return, Maria-Helena resorted to diving into a number of fancy-looking boutiques in the smart district of Colaba behind the Taj Hotel and then prowling the seething narrow lanes of the Kalbadevi and Bhelshwar Bazaars on foot – for no vehicle would ever make it through the impenetrable crowds. She was as thorough as a team of secret police in her efforts to hunt down bargains. Finally, having laid waste to the Mangaldas Market and the Zaveri Bazaar, she pronounced herself content with the purchase of two or three *salwar kameez* – smart matching blouses and trousers or Punjabi suits. Next ornaments were meekly displayed by sleek, stunned merchants whose highly honed bargaining skills were no use against her own tenacious, noisy and occasionally physical techniques.

Her purchases complete, she despatched me into the urban hell that is Bombay's Victoria Railway Terminus or 'Vee Tee' as it was enthusiastically known by every taxi wallah in the city. Our driver, a new man since the return of 'Auntie' to her hotel room, set off up the Colaba Causeway and past the pretty white Anglican Cathedral with great aplomb.

'No problem. Vee Tee, it's no problem. Vee Tee. Oh, yes, sir!'

Crash. Smash.

We stopped abruptly.

In front of us a broken and splintered handcart staggered about briefly before one of the wheels fell off and it collapsed, cascading a great number of small tin drums on to the ground. These proceeded to roll randomly around us, some spinning on themselves, some cartwheeling and bouncing and others racing away in every conceivable straight line. One disappeared under the wheels of a large lorry and exploded with a dull 'whoomp'. As the vehicle growled away, I could see that the can had left an unpleasant browny-yellow stain across the tacky tarmac.

Silent in the taxi, the driver and I stared at their owner who now sat, more shocked than angry or hurt, on our bonnet and stared back at us.

'Bloody fool, *dhaba-wallah*!'

'*Dhobi-wallah*?' What was a washer man doing down here away from the *dhobi-ghat* and what were all these cans?

'Not *dhobi*, *dhaba*! *Dhaba-wallah*! Bloody fool.'

This admonition seemed to be addressed non-specifically as he pushed the door open and waved the man from where he sat.

So a *dhaba-wallah* had nothing to do with the service wash industry, after all. Instead, he was engaged in quite a different provision. For each one of those little tin drums, a *tiffin*, contained one man's lunch, an important cargo. Some five thousand *dhaba-wallahs* collected nearly two hundred thousand of these boxes every day from depots in the suburbs where they had been deposited by the recipients' wives. Then piling them high on handcarts they would deliver them, still warm, to offices throughout the city. Each tin was carefully colour-coded, as many of these men were illiterate. So successful was the system that it was thought that hardly more than a handful had ever gone missing. All that, it seemed, as I noticed the widespread chaos all about me, was about to change. The taxi driver was pointing unhappily at a sizeable dint in his bumper whilst the poor *dhaba-wallah* clearly despaired of rescuing many of his six dozen or so boxes. Voices grew louder. Arms waved a little wider.

There did not seem much point in me hanging around so, whistling quietly, I disappeared nonchalantly into the rapidly collecting crowd. All I wanted to do was collect our railway tickets but I suspected that it would still prove to be an extraordinary palaver.

With its gargoyles and towers, the 'Vee Tee' building was dauntingly imposing. A myriad different entrances all appeared to lead almost immediately to an exit as if, like a *trompe l'oeil*, there wasn't actually any interior to the building at all. Every flight of steps just led to another which then returned you to the place where you had started. Extraordinary numbers of people, vehicles, animals, market stalls and the incredible volume of noise coming from these crowds was enough to put off even the most intrepid railway enthusiast.

The passion and skill of the architect, one Frederick Stevens, were manifested in a panoply of styles, meaning that the whole bristled with Italianate arches, neo-Gothic roofs, Roman windows, Eastern domes and Norman buttresses, swirling Indo-Islamic bits of this and sticking-out Venetian bits of that – the whole supported by pillars imported from Aberdeen. Yet, in spite of its architectural pot pourri, it was magnificent. I looked up to the roof and the four-metre-high statue of Patience and wondered whether she might lend me a little of her virtue as I tried to swim through the contradictory currents of people.

'Much too magnificent for a bustling crowd of railway passengers,' the Vicereine had sniffed when the building was unveiled at Queen Victoria's Jubilee. Whether she was right or wrong, the crowd certainly did bustle.

After following what I was to discover was the one and only direction given in India if I ever asked someone the way – a sweeping gesture of the arm finishing with a finger-pointing in the direction that I was already walking and an impassioned instruction to go 'Straight, straight!' (which strangely always seemed to result in me arriving at my destination without any problem at all) – I found myself in an enormous ticket hall at the far end of which was a long line of arched windows.

What was more impressive than the size of the room was the number of people in it; the only time that I had ever seen so many people packed so closely together was at the Hammersmith Odeon in the 1980s when the crowd surged forward to see if the ten-second superstar could really play his keyboard just by slapping it. When I noticed that the seething mob of people was in fact thirty or forty closely packed queues, I initially despaired because, despite my being British, I have never been keen to stand in line. There appeared to be a little glass window for every type of traveller possible: 'soldiers, sailors, today tickets, reserve tickets, long journey, short journey'. Right at the far end: 'tourist ticket'. I raised my arms and waded through the almost entirely male population of the room in its direction.

To my surprise and also slight embarrassment I found that there were only five or six people standing in front of me: every other queue was made up of fifty or sixty slowly shuffling people; anyway, here I was and, after all, I had not made the rules. I smiled at the man on my right and he smiled back reassuringly. I rose up on to my tiptoes to see, through the small glass archway, the top half of which had been smeared with the sweat of innumerable foreheads, the ticket seller closely inspecting a yellow slip of paper, checking and crossing boxes with the very greatest of care. 'Lunch 11.50–12.00' was painted in red letters on the wall behind him.

Something seemed familiar about this piece of paper. What was it? I wasn't sure. Turning, I discovered standing beamingly in the queue behind me, a tall, thickset young man bedecked with all the accoutrements required by the Western round-the-world traveller: sunglasses to keep hair in place, a T-shirt advertising some incredibly frightening 'outdoor adventure', a huge pair of checked shorts, some rather white, rather hairy legs and a colossal pair of hiking boots topped off with dubious-looking thick grey socks – not forgetting, of course, a rucksack the size of a small family car. He grinned at me with chapped lips and waved his piece of yellow paper under my nose.

It seemed evident from this and from the fact that everybody else in the room was also holding a piece of yellow paper that I would need one too.

'Excuse me, do you speak English?'

'I certainly do!' The young man replied and roared with laughter. 'I *am* English!' More gales of, as far as I could see, unsolicited mirth. 'Just getting the hang of the place myself! Ha! Ha! Ha!'

'Yes, I see. Right . . . So, do you know where I can get one of those forms from?'

'Ho, ho, ha, ha! This man just came up to me and gave me one! It was so funny! Just like that, ha, ha!' He grinned like a drunkard at all the other waiting passengers who looked at him and looked at me and smiled weakly. 'Look, there you go!'

To my surprise he pointed towards my groin. Fully expecting to find one poking out of my flies, I looked furtively down. Looking back up at me was a small boy dressed as I had already seen so many other countless small boys, in a filthy cotton shirt, shorts and bare feet. In a thin hand he held out one of the forms, smiling. When I had taken it, gratefully, his hand remained stretched out. Confused, I took it in mine and shook it.

'You're a little beggar, aren't you?' More gales of laughter. 'Get it? Little beggar? You're a little beggar! I don't give money to little beggars like you! No, no, no money for little beggars,' the irrepressible Englishman behind me blethered on in a cutesy, silly voice. In disbelief, the boy shook his head and gave up any notion of trying to earn anything from us. Fortunately I found some coins, change from the taxi that had brought me here, pushed them into his hand and then busied myself filling in the train ticket booking form. As I did so I tried to shut out the conversation that took place behind me.

'Er ... I think ... you are England yes? ... So how long are you staying in India, Sahib?' It seemed that the boy had decided that he might, at least, practise his English and now addressed himself to my fellow traveller. 'India is my country.'

'Yeeess, I think we know that, don't we?' The same daft voice. 'Anyway, what did you ask me? Oh, right, how long have I been here? Just about a week I think, not long ... but doesn't mean that I haven't worked out what you kids are all up to! Ha! Ha! Ha!'

'So, you are liking it in India? I mean, how you are liking India?'

'Oh, I see, serious question, eh? Well, it's OK, ha, ha, ha, not bad if you get a good hotel with air-con – otherwise it's bloody hot. Expect you're used to it? What else? Course, it's very dirty and unhygienic and that. Not surprising that everybody is sick all the time. I'm a medic of course, well, student, so I know how to be careful about these things. What else? What good things? Well, I suppose it is very cheap. Yeah, that must be the best thing ... I've bought some brilliant stuff. Yeah, really great – so cheap! Ha! Ha! Ha!'

Appalled, I could not turn round.

Somehow I paid for the two tickets to Poona and turned to hurry away. Thankfully the boy had disappeared but I could not help but glance up.

'I'm Christian, by the way, mate. Good to meet you. Where you headed? Eh?'

'Will, I'm Will – look I'm just heading off to ...' I dared not tell him my destination for fear that he might offer to tag along. The combination of Christian and Maria-Helena von

Würfelwerfer was unimaginable. I need not have worried – he took none of it on board. 'Just heading off, you know . . .'

'You off then? Great. Well, see you later then. Cheers! Good luck! Ha! Ha! Ha!'

With relief I disappeared into the crowd but not before I heard him bend down to the window of the counter and say, 'Hello, how are you? All right in there, are you? Looks pretty cosy, nice. I was just after a single ticket to Poona.'

Undoubtedly one of the wonders of India is travel by train. Hundreds and thousands of miles of track transport hundreds of millions of people hundreds of millions of miles every year. Casting the shadows of families seated in open doorways on to the flickering countryside, the cream and brown carriages of the trains make their sometimes slow, often hot, often uncomfortable but always determined way across the subcontinent. The wooden benches and racks, the many layers of paint, the ingrained smell of sweat and spice provide a thick patina, proof of journeys redolent with the sorrow of departure and separation, the impending joy of arrival and reunion. Friendship and kinsmanship, long hours of laughing, playing, meditation and argument, food and drink shared with family and strangers, deep sleep in the laps of mothers or fitful dozing on the shoulders of loved ones or unknown neighbours, all form the shape of journeys experienced and coped with in a way not dissimilar to life itself – suffering discomforts, sharing and making do, getting there in the end. The simple carriages, with their doorless and windowless openings, were baking hot on the midday plains or freezing on a mountain pass at night, allowing the experience of travel, of movement and often displacement to be an intensely real one.

Of course the tickets that I had bought for the old lady and me did not provide a similar experience in any way. 'First-class' resembles the interior of a 1950s aeroplane: plastic high-backed armchairs that recline in clunks, clonking the kneecaps or at least sloshing the *chai* or tea of the person behind. The thick windows keep the rugged country safely outside and the goose-bump refrigerated cold in.

Maria-Helena, once she was settled, tiny in her window seat, took the opportunity to give me a short lecture on our destination. Once a teacher, always a teacher. I should know.

'Poona, you see, was once the stronghold of the great Shivaji, the great Maratha leader of the seventeenth century, then came the Peshwas and then the British. In fact it was the summer capital for the whole of this state, Maharasthra. It is in Poona that you will find the great university, often termed the 'Oxford of the East'. The British always kept an important military garrison here and the Indian Army continues to do so when they are not on the Pakistan border making silly faces at each other over the line. You will also find the commune called Oshhhh . . .'

Her voice tailed off into a feathery sigh. Curled up in a bizarre but extraordinarily soft pink shawl, the old lady had fallen asleep. My eyes, too, were persuaded to close by the gentle rocking and bouncing of the train but they snapped open quickly enough when a metal tank of 'Hot, sweet coffee! Hot, sweet coffee!' was swung into my shin. From the moment that I grumpily declined the small waxed-paper cup that was waved enticingly under my nose, I was besieged by offers of nearly every product known to man. Drinks, sweets, savouries, news sellers, toy sellers, shoeshine boys and book-sellers all passed up and down, swirling their trays of wares above their heads. As if expertly choreographed, the vendors sashayed up and down the aisle, missing their colleagues by nothing as they passed. First-class passengers, it seemed, were hungrier and thirstier than those on the rest of the train for the remaining carriages seemed all but empty of these hawkers. Each time the train slowed to a halt at a small station, as it very often did, I stood up and went to the door to watch the chaotic but earnest bustle on the platforms. At one point four men, roped together at ankle and wrist, a prison officer attached at either end, trooped off to buy a bottle of water. The leading warder who paid for it, drank first. A steady clear stream, as if from a tap, poured without a drip into his mouth, the bottle never touching his lips, before he handed it on down the line.

Some three or four hours later, accompanied by screeching whistles, the train concertinaed to a stop.

'Poona. Poona.'

Maria-Helena swiftly organised a team of porters, dozens of whom had burst into the compartment like marauding pirates before we had even come to a standstill. Dressed in red smocks and with matching turbans, the authenticity of their trade demonstrated by a brass plaque tied to their arm with a thin strip of leather, they lifted the bags on to shoulders and heads and made a great fuss of making sure that we all reached the platform without mishap. We set off over a footbridge that reeked of burnt diesel, the old lady leading the way with great excitement.

'Oh, I hope he is here. He will take me to the hills in his car. Oh and then . . .' Her face twitched with anticipation and she flicked her fingers through her thinning hair and fiddled with the buttons of her jacket that despite the ferocious heat she continued to wear.

'Well, I hope you have a wonderful time. When we've made sure that you are safely delivered then I will probably just jump on the train back to Bombay, that's probably the best thing.' I broke into a bottom-swinging power walk to keep up with her.

'You have been a very good companion, I think so, yes. You must enjoy the rest of your time in India – you will have a wonderful time. And remember you will be quite safe – yes, I am sure.' She began to pant either through exhaustion or anticipation. 'But yes, you have been a good travelling companion. Thank you, William.'

As we came out into the blistering, noisy chaos of the Indian street she suddenly shrieked, 'Look, look, he is here! He hasn't changed a bit, has he? Oh, my darling Ayush. I can't believe it! Darling Ayush, it's me – your little Lennie!'

Lennie?

Neither the baggage handlers, the matching luggage wavering on their heads, or I could quite believe what we saw. For in front of the main entrance to the station stood an antiquated but gleaming Rolls-Royce; a chauffeur in a very much too short white jacket stood by the open door from which was appearing a slim, dapper old man dressed in an immaculate double-breasted suit and two-tone shoes. In slow motion she rushed over to him squealing in a most unbecoming way and the porters and I coughed, cleared our throats and gazed at the sky as they engaged in a lengthy, noisy and moist embrace.

Ayush smiled at me politely and bowed slightly while the bags were loaded into the boot of the Roller under the instructions of the car-proud chauffeur. 'Lennie' skipped into the back of the car. With another quiet smile her host climbed in after her. As the car pulled out into the snarling traffic, a magnificent ship sailing out into the middle of a terrible storm, through the back window I saw Maria-Helena tenderly lay her head on the chest of her elderly lover.

I have never seen the old lady again but I have her to thank for this adventure. Sometimes I like to imagine her in the hills high above the mists, on a balcony, tiny in a bamboo swing, hand in frail hand with her darling Ayush.

3

A Most Noble Profession

Poona is a Million City.

In the language of urban planners, it had become in the 1980s one of the dozen or so cities in India whose population had burst over one million. Ten years later, it had more than doubled.

In the centre of Poona the ruins of a fort, the seventeenth-century stronghold of the great warrior Shivaji, had once stood in a fine defensive position. The Maratha raja's view from the stone-carved ramparts had once been almost unspoilt but for a wooden barracks. Sweeping down the hill towards a gentle, winding river, fertile fields had once produced more than enough rice and vegetables to feed the small garrison, but now the remaining grey walls of the fortifications were surrounded by the warren of the bazaar. Hundreds, thousands of tiny shops, some hardly wider than a man's shoulders, have available for sale seemingly everything the planet has to offer: silk, shoes, spices, bicycles, remedies – herbal and physical – palm-readings, fortune-tellings, pots and pans, sweets, bits of bicycles, rugs, ear-cleanings, fruit, jewellery, ornaments, bits to make bicycle bits, soaps, trinkets and, of course, everything manufacturable in plastic in every shape and size; the skilled and the rudimentary, a jumble of beautiful artistry and terrible tat. Temples, churches and mosques, large and small, of every faith and creed, many garlanded with beautiful flowers and reeking of sandalwood and jasmine, stand on street corners, in shabby parks, in marketplaces, at the bus station, dotted along the edge of the highway, even between the petrol pumps on garage forecourts. Newly constructed concrete office buildings with dark glass, white limousines smiling sleekly in their car parks, cast their long shadows over the shanty houses of the old city where cows roam freely amongst the handcarts and thoughtfully inspect the street-sellers as they swirl *pakora* and samosas around in the hot, fizzing oil of their woks.

Thunderous traffic pours down every thoroughfare, revving, swerving, reversing, braking, racing and, above all, of course, hooting: driving in complete defiance of the sketchy Highway Code. Every type of vehicle belches blue, black and white clouds of exhaust fumes into the world, clouds which hang like autumn fog in the neon of the streets at night and mix with the smells of rose and frankincense drifting up in thin lines of smoke from the joss sticks on the barrows that sell peanuts and spiced snacks.

And somehow crammed into these streets among this seething chaos of vehicles, shops, houses and public buildings are over two million people. Poona was bigger by far than (probably) any British city bar London but, of course, alongside the great cities of Calcutta, Delhi or Mumbai, it was just a small country town. Even so I was dazzled to find myself so suddenly in amongst these thronging crowds: all around me people buying, selling, making, losing, stealing, begging, loving, hating, laughing, crying, eating, spitting, urinating, defecating, procreating and child-bearing, surviving and dying. It took more than a little while to realise that this whole great whirling tableau was real.

In a small, shabby but crowded café on the strangley tautologous but aromatic Curry Road Street, I found myself reviewing the situation over a cup of thick, white Indian tea which was saturatedly sweet and strongly flavoured with cardamom and cinnamon. Gazing into my cup, looking for leaves, I was pondering my future. Despite her overbearing bossiness, the departure of Maria-Helena had left me feeling oddly lonely. Although the crowds hustled and bustled around me, I had the sensation of being somehow adrift. For the first time in my life, I realised, I was rudderless, with no aims, no target. After years of timetabled teaching it felt most disconcerting. Perhaps I should just go home? But to return home immediately seemed to be admitting defeat: I could imagine myself, like a recaptured convict, trooping back into the yard of the school in London to the jeers of the other inmates. But then if I were to stay, what would I do?

Lost in a muddle of confused thoughts, I only lifted my head from my hands when a young, serious-looking man was directed, as is the custom in this overcrowded country, to share my table. He slid a briefcase on to the worn, grimy bench, sat down and stared at me for some time; I looked around for something to read. He ordered something to drink in Hindi and then stared at me some more. As time went on, I was to become used to causing almost traffic-stopping interest wherever I went. Tall, very tall by local standards, white and clean-shaven (in India moustaches, at least, are almost ubiquitous), I seemed to make for a very curious sight. Relatively soon I was to become oblivious to the commotion I caused but now I was self-conscious.

Gulping, I finished my tea. I should ring the airline. Although by no means shy, I did not enjoy the intense attention that I was receiving from my fellow diner. What was more, even admitting that Poona was marginally less hectic and certainly a little cooler than Bombay, I was not at all sure how long I could cope with the endless commotion and noise in the everyday street. Just going out of doors was, as far as I was concerned, a full-blown adventure. My reactions, never sharp and now numbed with age, needed to be on full alert if I were to survive the traffic or avoid disappearing beneath the hooves of one of a number of species of horned animal. In India it seemed that simply being out and about was nothing at all short of dangerous.

As I had strolled the length of Curry Road Street – as much as one can stroll when one is propelled along by an ever-moving crowd – I had noticed high up on some railings outside what appeared to be a disused school a large black notice board with white lettering.

Pollution Levels in Poona
Respirable Level 50
Dangerous Level 60
Extremely Dangerous Level 120

And then at the bottom, written in firm chalk lines:

Today's Pollution Level 233

At this rate I would finally have to give up smoking just to allow any remaining oxygen a chance of getting through.

'So excuse me, Sir,' the young man started nervously, readjusting his glasses and bringing me suddenly back to the table of the coffee shop. He cleared his throat. 'So excuse me, Sir. Where are you coming from?'

'I beg your pardon? Sorry, I didn't quite catch you.' His strong accent made him difficult for me to understand.

'Sorry, Sir.' He stopped, blushing warmly, and then tried again. 'Which place are you coming from? What is your place?'

I tried a small smile to relax him. He toyed with one in return but decided in favour of gravitas.

'I'm from England.'

'Oh, you are a Britisher!'

'Well, yes, I suppose so.' Not since the war comics of my childhood had I heard my compatriots so described. I refrained from raising my hands in surrender.

'And so what is being your profession, Sir?' My new bespectacled friend seemed quite confident now and his English began to flow more easily.

I rummaged through various job descriptions, fictional, even fanciful, but eventually opted for honesty. Trying to claim that I was something I was not had, in the past, got me into difficult and, more than once, dangerous situations. I told him that I was a teacher.

'A teacher!' he seemed terribly impressed. 'That is indeed a most noble profession.'

'Well, yes . . . what . . . really? Oh thanks, yes, well, I suppose it is . . .' I agreed, deeply flattered and more than a little surprised.

Nobody had ever described it as a 'most noble profession' in England. In fact most of the time the announcement of my chosen career had resulted in cries of 'Yes, well, must get another pint . . .' and a turning in of shoulders to talk about business or sport or something else more important. A general feeling that I was somehow mentally, or at the very least socially, deficient normally hung over the remaining proceedings – a sentiment that at least whilst ungainfully employed at my last school I had on occasion shared.

'In India we have an expression: "After your parents comes your teacher". Perhaps you have this expression in your country?'

'Err . . . no . . . no, we don't.'

'My father is having a school,' he went on earnestly, removing his glasses and cleaning them carefully on a neatly folded handkerchief. 'Will you come to see it? Well, it is not a school and he is not really my father but will you come and see it? It is an *ashram* – how are you saying "*ashram*" in English?'

'Yes . . . er . . . ashram, did you say . . . Well, I'm not totally—'

'He is living in some area, please coming,' he continued this sudden torrent of words with a new confidence.

A father who was not a father in a school that was not a school that was to be found in some, as yet unidentified, area – well, I was at least intrigued. But really, I ought to be getting back to the booking office at the station. He seemed nice enough, this fellow, but I didn't really want to get involved. I wasn't going to be around long enough to be of any use to him. Probably better not to take it any further.

'Or tomorrow, then?' he asked, crestfallen. 'We can, we can go on my two-wheeler? Yes?'

Well, tomorrow, perhaps. Depends on the trains.

4

Billbhaiya

'Some area' turned out to my great trepidation to be the 'slum areas' – the parts of town that author V. S. Naipaul describes as 'spontaneous communities', 'the colonies of the dispossessed'. But 'slums' for me had only ever been a historical concept to be found in the same contextual pigeonhole as 'workhouse', 'debtor's prison' or 'pauper'. Suddenly they became a modern reality.

Steadily, a blotchy rash is spreading across the face of Mother India and soon, if no cure is found, she will be unrecognisably disfigured. 'Hutments', as planners prefer to euphemistically describe the slums, exist in all sizeable cities of India but they do not appear, as you might imagine, to be located like rundown European housing estates in particular parts of town. Instead they are to be found in small pockets spread evenly throughout the municipality, often in amazing juxtaposition with the new, the clean and the wealthy. Typically they seemed to have been built where there was any existing clear stretch of solid wall – thus requiring the builder only to find the materials required to construct the other three. According to their age, many of the slums had become more or less permanent. The original materials, cardboard and old corrugated iron, had, in time, been replaced with bricks and mortar, a roof of plastic had given way to galvanised sheets; as a sense of permanency settled over the homes electricity was bled from nearby pylons down shockingly bare pieces of wire. Water, too, although not necessarily safe to drink, was eventually provided by a begrudging municipal council, grateful nevertheless that they were thus saved the burden of having to rehouse these swelling populations. This water, once used, ran away down open drains and official sanitary facilities amounted, as far as I could see, to a couple of roadside lavatory booths per thousand people which were advertised at a hundred yards by their unequalled stink.

Perhaps due to the range of materials that had been used to create these homes, and because of the fertile dust that settled on roofs and between houses, and which provided sustenance for plants and bright flowers that blossomed in the most incongruous places, the slum possessed an almost organic character; it breathed and moved like an enormous slumbering creature that smoked and groaned, that roared and spluttered and glowed in the shadows after dark. It was clear that however sordid, unsatisfactory, unsanitary and unacceptable this accommodation might be – and it was, by any standard set for man or beast – the compost warmth of the heart of the slum seemed still to offer some succour, to be trying to nurture the people who lived within it. Despite my initial shock that so many individuals should be forced to live in such circumstances, it was not long before I sensed an intense vibrancy, an essential vigour in those poor narrow lanes, a powerful vitality emanating from the shambolic shacks.

Undeniably, the slum would prefer to disappear or at least to transmogrify into a different, healthier, more hygienic animal but, as long as it plays a role in India, it is determined that it should protect its inhabitants with all the fervour of a mother. The residents in their turn reciprocated this symbiotic affection with a sense of palpable pride – after all, the slum was for them undeniably home.

It was in the slums of Poona that I first learnt to recognise that very particular odour, that curious mix of damp wood smoke, animal and human sweat, rotting vegetation and general decay which is the complex, saddening smell of poverty. It was here too that I was to encounter some of the most perfect human beings I have ever had the good fortune to meet.

Tanjiwadi was like any other slum in the town: noisy, dirty and so severely overcrowded that there was insufficient covered accommodation to enable everyone to lie down and sleep at the same time. Plastic rubbish floated around the ubiquitous dusty red pinnacles of *mandirs*, one-room temples from which more often than not the representation of one of the myriad Hindu gods peered cheerfully out, patiently waiting for some bright, sweet-smelling *pooja* and a spot of devout veneration. Tanjiwadi was shambolic, having been created piecemeal as people found a corner of land on which to have their families, but in a curious, unregulated way it had taken on its own shape, aping more traditional urban planning. Some few hundred yards from the road had been created a small, half-whitewashed cobbled square – downtown, if you like – where four or five men with baskets of vegetables and pulses, spices and fruit piled attractively on their hand-pulled carts, congregated every morning around the ornamental fountain – a wet patch of green, stinking midden soil surrounding a galvanised water pump in the middle of the open area. Hand scales and their brass balancing weights lay alongside wooden cigar boxes in which the vendors kept their spare change – the cost of one of the original Romeo y Julietas, rolled, no doubt, on the thighs of a Havanese lady, would have been enough to have purchased the contents of each stall several times over.

Built into one wall of the square was a small general store, the floor of which was raised a few feet off the ground above the water level of the monsoon floods that would turn the slum into a poor man's parody of Venice. Here a number of sacks, copper bowls and jars containing the essentials of daily life were laid out: rice, sugar, flour, salt, tea, soap and hair oils (for outer appearance, inextricably linked to a feeling of self-worth was, despite financial hardships, as important as inner well-being); bundles of incense sticks, a household necessity with which to properly venerate the gods, were piled high, suffusing the still air of the shop with strong, competing scents. The tiny emporium measured little more than six feet across its front by four feet deep, and was protected by a rickety awning that Old Saran would prop up in the morning to keep the rain or the sun at bay, dropping and locking it again at night before shuffling away home down the dark lane.

Old Saran, an overweight and somewhat down-at-heel character with a dirty twist of turban and bad teeth, sat serenely on the floor from early morning to late at night surrounded by his wares. At his side bulged a large sack of chocolate eclairs (which perhaps accounted for his dental disaster) and being a kind-hearted sort of fellow he would reach into it occasionally and toss a purple and silver wrapped sweet out of the front window to one of the endlessly passing children. He was canny enough to ignore those that lurked about, hoping to pick up more than their fair share.

In the wall that made the corner with the general store, no more than an opening, a cupboard really, with a peeling, flaky green door over which hung a sign that read 'Mutton and Chicken Centre', was the butcher's shop. Opening times were flexible. It depended, really, on how long it took the proprietor, a silent methodical man from the surrounding *ghats* or hills, to sell the two lambs that he carried on his back into Tanjiwadi each morning – a process that left gruesome dark streaks down the back of his long striped shirt. He hung the beasts on a hook on the back wall and, with a practised stroke, carved and hacked off slices and cuts with a hefty, rusty chopper and an Arabian Nights curved knife as and when they were requested by the quietly murmuring lady shoppers. Slapping the meat down on a thin ledge he would deftly wrap it in a couple of sheets of newspaper. By necessity the whole operation had to be performed with only one hand as the other was permanently engaged in flicking away thousands of drooling flies from the carcasses.

The only sign of the money lender's business was a small window with gold-painted metal bars next door to the butcher's. The wooden shutter behind the bars fitted so tightly that the aperture was hardly visible when the owner was away. Sad and embarrassed were the people who queued almost permanently during opening hours.

From each corner of the little square side streets ran deep into the gurgling belly of the slum, alleyways that were forever a foment of people on the move. Tanjiwadi, of course, made up only one patch of the ragged quilt of slum housing that was spread across the surface of Poona, a comparatively tiny area of housing, a minute community in the giant spread of India.

Children rushed around in consternation when I stepped stiffly off the scooter into a pool of stagnant liquid. They were undecided whether they should stay and stare or whether they should rush off to tell their friends of the strange arrival of a tall, blond white man who had been brought by the solemn, bespectacled Abhishekh to be introduced to his adoptive father Charuvat.

Charuvat, a devout Hindu, was the father of the ashram, a refuge, the home which, with his wife Harshada, he had provided for thirty-four orphan boys and girls. He dreamed one day of housing one hundred children but was determined to expand only as his finances allowed. Charuvat was a government 'sweeper', an Untouchable or Dalit, the lowest of the fantastically complex levels of caste. Though he would never discuss caste, he said. No, despite the fact that he was a Hindu, he would never discuss it – either with me or with the children. For, he pointed out, it was an awareness of caste that would hold back these children, all the children of India, and he hoped more than anything that they might benefit from a new, more egalitarian country. Certainly, caste divides had meant a shortening of horizons for generations of Indians but now, increasingly, as Dalits were given greater national political representation and more opportunities for education, the strict fences that had been in place for so long were slowly coming down. As many of the children did not know a great deal about their family backgrounds and lived on an equal footing with their 'brothers and sisters' in the orphanage, they were free of the psychological restraints of the caste system. As long as they were in his care, then Charuvat hoped to protect them from discrimination based simply on their origins.

Suffice it to say that Charuvat, in this life, was responsible for the most menial of municipal tasks and his slender salary was spent entirely on feeding these waifs and strays. He had found them all in a variety of unhappy situations and had plucked them out of harm's reach just as he too, as a small boy, had been rescued from the misery of life living on a train station platform. An elderly, childless couple had found him asleep under a pile of hessian sacks as they stepped off the sleeper from Bangalore and had taken him home to their one-room tenement apartment with them. They had brought him up as their only son. His adoptive father, a retired engineer, had hoped that he might help Charuvat to follow him into the same profession but sadly he and his wife had died when their adopted child was only fourteen. Charuvat, like so many others, had returned to the streets and considered himself to have been very fortunate to find his present job.

Charuvat was a thickset, amiable man and his kindly nature and generosity of disposition shone from two lustrous, humorous eyes set in a permanently optimistic face. He stroked his thick, black beard thoughtfully as Abhishekh explained in Marathi – the local language of Maharashtra – who I was and what I was doing there. I was glad he could, because I was uncertain whether I would have been able to – in any language. When Abhishekh finished, his adoptive father turned to me bringing his hands together at chest height, fingers pointing upwards and, with a slight bow, he smiled.

'*Namaste*,' he welcomed me softly. 'Please come and see our home.'

The perimeter of the small compound that made up the ashram measured only something like forty foot by thirty but in comparison to the other huddled accommodation that crowded in on it on every side it seemed positively spacious. A new, black metal gate opened out on to the small square. Two single-storey adjoining buildings made up the angle of one corner of the yard. They had been newly finished and the shiny windows reflected the slick waters of a chocolate river that could be seen across the small piece of wasteland. Inside I could see the mosquito screens that would protect the inhabitants from the drones that would surely come up from the riverbanks at nightfall. The opposite corner comprised a washblock and a small storeroom. The rest of the area was paved entirely in ill-matching bricks apart from a small area of what appeared to be a small but struggling kitchen garden. In isolation it was curiously clean and functional particularly in contrast to the chaos of the surrounding area.

'Please before you meet our children then perhaps you can say *namaste* to our family pet.'

Charuvat smiled at me and with a gentle motion of his arms he brought me face to face with a huge and singularly unimpressed billy goat. Without showing the remotest flicker of enthusiasm for this new interesting introduction the animal scrunched his teeth and shifted slowly around the small pen where he was housed. The large brass bell that hung round his neck clonked dully as he turned away and nosed a rotting potato. He smelled terrible and I detected a distinctly mean streak in him.

'Oh great! . . . A goat. Is he, err . . . friendly?'

'Oh my yes. Very friendly. Beckham. He is very friendly.'

'What is he called?'

'Beckham. The children are liking this name. I think he is a Britisher football star?'

'Yes, I know, I know.' I wondered whether this rather unattractive animal would undergo as many different transformations of image as his namesake. For the moment he was sporting a goatee – perhaps before long he would adopt a Mohican.

Smiling, as we moved away towards the buildings, I glanced back at the beast half-expecting to discover it signalling something rude behind my back. Instead it was scratching its chin on the worn wooden fence. In hindsight, I still do not understand why Beckham was such a brute – and he was – ready to bite off any of your appendages as soon as look at you with his rolling malevolent eyes. Servicing the female goats of the locality in exchange for unlimited piles of vegetables sounded like quite a good deal to me.

Housed in the two new but spartan blockhouses, the children slept on the floor, boys in one, girls in another. Charuvat and his wife shared a small room between them. Slipping off our shoes, we went into the cool of one of the children's rooms where Harshada sat cross-legged on the floor surrounded by a dozen or so chattering girls wearing pretty but tattered dresses. When they saw me they leapt hurriedly to their feet.

'*Namaste*,' they chorused, bringing their hands together as their father had done and with the same slight bow. I made a vague, self-conscious attempt to return the salutation which made me look as if I was preparing to dive into a cold swimming pool and they all sat down again, carrying on talking happily as they darned and mended a pile of worn clothes in the middle of the floor. With obvious pride Charuvat pointed to a small glass cabinet on the wall: a number of plaques and metal cups stood in front of a background of photographs of the children being introduced to what appeared to be local dignitaries. Funny, I thought, how the supercilious but ingratiating smile seemed to breach all international boundaries, all cultural barriers, as politicians worldwide went about their dubious trade.

'We have many friends now,' he beamed. 'Now they are helping us to look after the children with some presents.'

'I see . . . good . . .'

They had previously lived in a one-room house, the floor space of which was so tiny that they had had to sleep in shifts because, even when the children had been smaller, there had not been enough room for them all to lie down at the same time. A number of donations from rich benefactors meant that, just recently, they had been able to move into this new accommodation. It was immediately clear that in setting up the ashram Charuvat had set himself a considerable challenge, often relying, as he must, on the charity of others. Later I was to discover that there were any number of privately funded such homes, each one dealing with some underprivileged section of society – the blind, the deaf, the handicapped, hospices that cared for lepers and hostels for the mentally ill. The existence of these charitable institutions was often precarious, relying on gifts and donations from individuals who for any number of reasons, ranging from their own financial difficulties to a loss of interest, might withdraw their support. Only rarely, however, did the children here go hungry, quite something to be proud of in this part of town, because every Monday Harshada would open up the little storeroom and painstakingly calculate how much food could be afforded that week.

Now that the construction work was all but finished, daily life had taken on a regular routine but, as a suddenly grim-faced Charuvat explained, the future of the ashram was less than guaranteed. Astonishingly only 16 per cent of the housing in Poona was pukka – that is to say, designed by an architect and constructed by professional builders on land with a building permit. The ashram at Tanjiwadi, indeed the whole of the slum, had been built on land that was not owned by the inhabitants. Due to the pressures of space people had little choice but to build their homes wherever they could find room. Many of the houses were some twenty or thirty years old, built now in bricks and mortar. It seemed unimaginable that suddenly they could be destroyed thereby rendering their occupants homeless but, as Charuvat sadly conceded, if the owners chose to repossess the land there was little that the community could do.

'We will know if the *goondas* arrive – then we will have a problem.'

Goondas? Weren't they from Venice?

In fact the Indian word had provided English with its 'goons' but it transpired they were no comedy act. Hard men employed by 'respectable' businesses to do their dirty work, *goondas* specialised in a variety of skills which ranged from carefully worded threats to destruction of property, arson, maiming and murder. No job too big, no job too small. Their appearance in the slum would mean only one thing – that eventually the developers wanted to commence the rough-handed process of repossessing their land.

Surely there wasn't any risk of this, though, I asked, trying to imagine the chaos and unhappiness that would be caused by the appearance of these bullyboys, a vanguard for the bulldozers.

'Well, you know my friend, sometimes there are rumours, sometimes people tell us bad stories but we mustn't worry too much about these things. We have to instead to be carrying on with our lives. These children's future is what we must think about.' Stroking his beard, Charuvat stepped back out into the yard.

They hoped, explained Abhishekh, to be able to afford these children the possibility of an education that would allow them eventually to escape the slum and to find themselves employment that would lead them to a life more certain than the hand-to-mouth existence of their neighbours.

'We are teaching them Hindi and Marathi and maths, of course, but I think they need more than this.' I was impressed by the young man's earnestness. 'So what we are trying to do here is to provide every boy and girl with some different subjects. They can learn painting and singing and making clothes and how to build things, repairing and fixing, and sometimes they play sport on the land over there.' Abhishekh pointed to the quarter acre or so of rubbish-strewn wasteland the other side of the ashram's low boundary wall. 'But what they really need is to learn English; English is so useful in India now, for some jobs it is absolutely vital, and if you will wish to be successful then it is most important that you speak it to a good standard . . . You agree?'

It sounded like a sensible idea.

In truth English, in a country which lists Hindi, Urdu, Bengali, Marathi, Gujarati, Oriya, Punjabi, Kashmiri, Karnataka, Malayalam, Sindhi, Tamil, Sanskrit and Telugu as its official languages, was the only one that seemed to be accepted nationwide. Hindi, the most widely spoken language of India, was spoken by barely one-third of the population and not at all by southern Indians who appeared to have a strong aversion to it. Reasonable English meant an increased chance to rise out of the slum or at least a greater possibility that these youngsters might in time find reasonably paid jobs that would give them a better chance to provide for their future families.

'Perhaps you could teach them?' he added guilelessly.

'I would be very interested to help,' I said genuinely, for I was extremely moved by what I had seen, 'but unfortunately I have to get back to England to err . . . just to err . . . get back, you know.'

Abhishekh looked resigned. He shrugged and half-smiled.

'So you are teaching in England?'

I thought of the school I had left behind and grimaced. I looked back at the chattering girls as they sat gently, happily on the floor.

'Yes, yes, teaching.' A particularly nasty smell suddenly blew through the little yard from the direction of the river and I retched inwardly. Not normally someone at a loss for words – goodness knew I must have deluged captive classroom audiences with millions of them over the years – now I could think of nothing to say. Here, as I looked across this desolate landscape, the scale of the problem and the enormity of the need overpowered me. There seemed no point in even attempting to involve myself in a challenge without horizon, without confines. I could really think of no worthy way to respond to this request. Looking as straight as I could at Abhishekh, I shook my head glumly.

'Sorry,' I mumbled guiltily at the young man who was looking up at me hopefully, the hot sun shining off his glasses. 'No I'm . . . I'm sorry . . .'

'Well, never mind. I think you are a very busy man in UK. Never mind. But now definitely you must stay to eat with us,' he said firmly.

'Oh don't worry about that – I'm not really very . . .' That smell again, lining my nose and throat with something green and pungent, made me feel anything but hungry. Beckham, I suspected, was at least in part responsible. Just as I was thinking how I might best make a diplomatic exit a man appeared on a bicycle with an enormous cardboard box on the front carrier. The children surrounded the man quietly, expectantly. He came from a factory the other side of the main road that supplied the children on weekdays with a hot lunch from its works canteen.

'Nice one,' said Abhishekh. 'Vegetable *biryani*.'

He handed me a white paper package, which I took unwillingly, whilst the children jostled each other good-naturedly as they waited their turn in an orderly line. As they received their packages they went and found themselves a small corner of the yard, hunkered down and slowly, almost reverentially, opened up their food.

'So, please, what is your name?' asked a grey-eyed teenager as he squatted down beside me and opened his packet. Due to a sporting injury, I cannot squat as Asian people do. Any attempt causes my knee joints to snap like firecrackers on the way down and requires several assistants on the way up. Instead I sat cross-legged on the ground and poked fitfully at the bag.

'Please,' continued the grave-looking youngster, 'tell me what is your name, *Bhaiya*?'

'Buyer?'

'*Bhaiya* means like brother,' Abhishekh explained as he pushed some rice into his mouth with his fingers.

'Oh, I see. Well,' I turned to the boy, 'my name is Will.'

'Will?' said the boy. 'Will? Only?'

'Yes, Will.' I was fond of my name. 'Well, so what is your name anyway?'

'My name is Pushpendra Prakash. I am fourteen years old and I am living in Poona in the west of Maharashtra in India.' He smiled proudly at me.

'Well, nice to meet you, Pshpprraksh. Actually, Will is short for William.'

The boy still continued to look disappointed.

'Sometimes we say Bill,' I continued, 'or some people even say Willy but I don't really like . . .'

'*Billbhaiya.*' Pushprendra Prakash turned it over in his mouth and found it to his liking. 'Billbhaiya. A pleasure to meet you, Billbhaiya.'

And he shook my hand.

'Come, eat,' insisted Abhishekh.

The reek of something dead blew back through the small yard and I gazed down sadly at the red, orange and yellow grains of rice picked out with bright green peas.

Just at that moment, an irritated dog some yards away put its front paws up against the gate and barked angrily at one of the little girls who was sitting on some steps nearby. It was true that the dog had every reason to be disgruntled as it was bone thin and suffered from some virulent infection that meant that its poor skin was broken and raw under the patchy hair. It also bore, across its haunches, the mark of someone's stick but, even so, it had been unkind to take out its discontent with the world on the little girl. She had started at the noise and, in doing so, had flicked the content of her paper package into the dust at the bottom of the steps. Dismayed, her mouth trembling and her eyes crinkling, she tried to scoop bits of her food back on to the wrapper. I leaned forward and offered her my food. She looked up at me and wiped her nose and its pretty gold stud with her sleeve. Tentatively, she took it and smiled shyly. I smiled back: generosity tinged with a slightly guilty feeling of relief.

After we had finished eating, the children folded up their papers before throwing them back into the empty cardboard box, and while the girls got ready for school, the boys set about tidying the yard, watering the little vegetable garden and sweeping the steps before sitting in rows on the floor of their room and with great seriousness setting about their school work. In near silence I drank a cup of super strong tea with the adults who now included a number of curious neighbours.

I was interested in helping, of course I was, voluntarily, but I did not really see how I could. It all seemed too complicated, confusing. Charity seemed to play a clearly defined role in my society and in my life too. Fundraisers, benefit concerts, a raffle for the church roof, a clinking box for guide dogs on the street corner – to all these I could easily subscribe. Once I had even stood in the stocks at a school fête and grinned at wet-sponge-wielding monsters, happy in the knowledge that the money raised was just icing on a relatively well-baked cake. Even helping to create a charitable project in the Solomon Islands had been manageable, the parameters of the task relatively easy to define. Here, though, the challenge was too amorphous, too huge to be tangible. There was nothing I could do that would make any difference. What use was my small drop in the ocean?

Tea over, Abhishekh offered me a ride back into the middle of the town on his 'two-wheeler', a rusting Indo-Italian scooter. I accepted gratefully. It was a long walk back. My legs eventually returned to a reasonably straight position, I waved goodbye to the children who had come to the gate and thanked Charuvat, wishing him all the best, he was doing a jolly good job, well done, keep it up, great stuff, thanks again, sorry, you know, well, see what I could do, bye now. He smiled and saluted me again with his hands.

Abhishekh was working the kick-start as I stepped out into the alley again, not quite avoiding the stagnant pool of black-green water where a small, squatting boy was washing his bottom with absorbed concentration. I hoiked up my trousers and was readying myself to swing aboard the motorbike when the crowd of children parted and the little girl who had eaten my lunch pushed forward.

Her chestnut eyes raised to mine, she reached up and grabbed my cheeks in two soft, slightly greasy hands, and whispered, 'You very nice man, Billbhaiya.'

And with a shy smile she turned her face into the folds of Harshada's sari.

5

Tracheotomy!

Of course, it was hopeless.
I was hooked.

I resolved on the bouncing trip home to teach at the ashram for as long as my return ticket allowed me to stay in India. Some small savings that I had made at the school in London (I had been too depressed to go out and spend anything) would last me for a while and then I would no doubt have to re-embark on that eternal cycle of debt and reloan. On my return Mr Jolly and I could sort out the situation, as we had done countless times before – if he had not already taken early retirement.

Abhishekh was delighted and turned round regularly to thank me as he steered the machine through the honking, hooting traffic. I smiled as confidently as the situation allowed as we dipped in and out of potholes and slipped on and off the pavement in his excitement.

'Oh, but this is cause for great rejoicing,' he exclaimed ecstatically as he accelerated away through traffic lights that were certainly not in our favour.

'Yes, yes, don't mention it. Just look at that bus there! Whoa, that was a big hole. Ha, ha! And don't mention it, just – err – just concentrate.'

I pointed straight ahead of him hoping that he might concentrate on the traffic rather than smiling effusively at me. He seemed to be blithely ignoring the imaginative road safety signs that zoomed past us at great speed.

'You have no need, no need for speed!' one of them pointed out.

'Keep your nerves on the curves!' suggested another.

I was trying, I really was, but by the time we arrived I was almost as shaky as the wobbly hotel near the station in which I was staying.

'Now we will need to find you some nice place, I am thinking? Which place in town are you wanting to stay? Let me see where is best for you. We must have a nice place for our visitor Britisher.' He seemed most certain about this for he went on: 'I don't think the Tanjiwadi is very good for you?'

Feeling guilty again, I agreed.

'No, well it's not that it isn't nice, it's just that it might be easier, you know, if I had somewhere that was, well, perhaps a little bit more . . . central?'

'Oh, yes, I am agreeing with you, Mr Williams. Central, most certainly central. Yes, yes.' Shy and bashful Abhishekh was definitely no longer. 'So where?'

'Well . . .' Although it was clear that I would now need somewhere more permanent to stay, I did not really want to leave myself without some way of escape just in case I should need to get home in a hurry, there was an emergency, or I had a change of heart. No, really, just in case I didn't like it. 'How about somewhere near the station?'

Abhishekh seemed to think that this was an excellent idea and, on his recommendation, I bought a copy of the *Maharashtra Bugle*, one of the local English-language newspapers, from a seller who, sitting on a low wall, must have had a hundred different titles laid out before him – a paper patchwork that stretched all the way to the pavement.

On an inside page I discovered, sandwiched between an advertisement that proclaimed a cure for 'Asthma, Diabetics, Dust, Allergy, Cough, Cold, Sinus, Piles, Medicine like nectar, treatment with live fish, For vegetarian with banana', and another that announced the departure of Mrs Millie Mandhukar 'to her heavenly abode' placed there by her family 'with moistened eye', a small box advertising 'flat available for immediate renting with furnishings and other stirring features'.

We agreed that this sounded suitable and Abhishekh buffed the front mudguard of his motorcycle with a scrap of old cloth that he pulled from his breast pocket, then checked his appearance in the arched reflection as I waited in a queue to use the telephone on a table outside a tailor's shop. Just as I was wondering how I would be able to hear anything above the din of the racetrack road, a small, black car screeched to a halt without warning beside me. The rear passenger window wound down and a friendly face leaned out.

'Excuse me, Sir! Are you from UK?'

'Yes, I am. Umm . . . ?'

But without another word, the window wound up and the car lurched back into the traffic.

When my turn finally came and the dialling tone purred I watched a snake charmer tie a long-suffering cobra in a knot, while the man behind me in the queue cleaned the ears of the man behind him with a small stick.

Strange new world.

'Hello, hello, hello, hello, hello, hello!' Each of these greetings was louder than the last in what I was to discover was more often than not normal Indian telephone etiquette.

'Err . . . yes, hello. I was just ringing to enquire about the flat. Could you tell me how big the . . .'

'Hello?'

'Hello!'

'Hello, hello, hello?' A tiny pause. 'Goodbye!'

Four or five attempts later, I managed to make it clear why it was that I had rung.

My interlocutor turned out to be the appropriately named Mr Rentaparti. Almost entirely oval in shape, his belt a hula-hoop round his middle, he perspired freely and spent much of his time mopping sweat out of the folds of his numerous chins. This faintly disconcerting personal habit and a propensity to call me Mr Ramble apart, he proved to be both a splendid landlord and an incurable dipsomaniac whose hands shook like leaves unless he had consumed at least half a bottle of Superior Challenge Indian Whisky or was settled to the task of counting and sorting banknotes, which he performed with considerable speed and obvious delight. He was, however, a generous and helpful man and soon I found myself comfortably installed on the second floor of a two-storey block of flats, situated in a locomotive whistle-testing area not far from the train station and, I was assured, only a short bus ride from the ashram. Two floors had not been the limit of the architect's vision but the funds required to complete the dream that was 'Ashoka Villas' had not been forthcoming. Consequently the staircase that ran up from the second floor ended in a concrete ceiling, above which there was nothing but a flat roof and a few twisted iron rods rusting forlornly as they waited patiently for the builders who would never return.

However, this was more than modest accommodation for the city, and, although by the standards of ludicrous London it was cheap, it was also beyond the reach of the vast majority of the population. Now I need to confess at this juncture that whilst I felt uncomfortably guilty, I also felt remarkably comforted by the fact that, although the little block of flats was relatively spartan, it was, at least, nearer to what I was used to. The slums, indeed the vast majority of hugely over-crowded, unsanitary hovels that spread across Poona, were frankly totally alien. My feelings of confusion about this extraordinary diversity of rich and poor and of my position within it were not to leave me. In time, however, they were to become clearer. What most unsettled me, catching me off guard, was that occasionally, dangerously, I would see it all as normal. Due to the sweet nature of the people, the smiles and the daily kindnesses shown to me, I sometimes, somehow, allowed myself to believe that all this deprivation was accept-able, that although they had little they were content. Poor but happy.

What did, however, give me much comfort about life at Ashoka Villas was the knowledge, sure and certain, that I was living in the greatest security. For guarding the gate to the leafy compound was the *chowkidar*, the night watchman, the elderly Drupad. Drupad dressed in a uniform of light khaki, which was topped off with a purple beret. A white and rather overlong fluffy feather waved cheerfully at the front of the beret as he leapt from his chair by the gate to salute me, his elbow out at an acute angle, the fingers of one sturdy hand covering half of one eye. In moments of real devotion, like national holidays, his hand reached almost to his nose. The thick, white woolly combinations that his wife made him wear to keep him warm at night protruded to the wrist from underneath his short-sleeved shirt, and matched his smartly clipped toothbrush moustache and his neatly parted hair. Drupad had, as a younger man, worked in the operating theatre of Bombay General Hospital. Every morning as I left and each evening on my return he would regale me with a list of all the surgical interventions at which, over many years, he had been present, and he informed me too of the veneration that he had had for the number of surgeons under whom he had worked.

'Good morning, Mr Williams, tracheotomy!' he would salute me as I left with my briefcase under my arm. 'Doctor Hemanya, he was fine, fine man. Very nice with his scalpel. Oh, yes . . .'

'Oh yes, good evenings of course and also colostomy!' he would greet me as I returned at dusk.

It was Drupad too who introduced me to a man who was to become a key figure in my life in India – Sanjay, autorickshaw wallah extraordinaire and provider and purveyor of all forms of transport, in fact of all things, had screeched to a halt in his black and yellow motorised rickshaw in response to the thin squeal of Drupad's whistle. (Fed up with dying of exhaustion at the age of thirty, the rickshaw wallahs who had once used their skinny legs to convey their passengers around town now drove about in the extraordinary vehicle that is the autorickshaw – a sort of small, open-sided caravan resting on a petrol-driven tricycle. The driver steered the handlebars from a single front seat; the passengers sat on a double bench behind.)

In many ways Sanjay was, if such a person can be approximated, the quintessential Indian man. Dressed in a traditional white shirt and trousers of homespun *khadi*, he wore a narrow white '*Gandhitopi*' cap on his head. Beneath this poked straight tufts of his strangely dyed hair, glowing orange to match his beard. True to the endless contradictions of his country he was a misogynist lover of women, a capitalist Marxist, a dog-beating reverer of holy cows, an atheistic devotee of dozens of the two or three million Hindu gods, who would swear in the most unholy way, spit and cuss, before offering handfuls of *pooja* to the Almighty at a roadside temple.

Our relationship, in many ways, summarised all the complications, confusions and lack of comprehension inherent in the meeting of East and West, English and Indian. Friends, good friends, we still spent much of our time together trying to understand each other's motivations. I am not sure whether we got very far but soon, at least, we were less surprised by one another.

On our first meeting he was delighted to hear that I had left Mumbai in favour of Poona.

'Very good decision, nice decision. I think in Mumbai you are having sweatings? It is good in Poona . . . no smelly sweatings.'

Sanjay, who lived in the slums not far from Tanjiwadi, had only a notional idea of what he should charge me for any given job, exercising a personal inflation rate that fluctuated wildly by the day. After a while I developed my own inverse scale and we generally calculated a happy mean. On the other hand, most pleasingly, he soon nominated himself as my business adviser in any dealings or negotiations with a third party, picking a path for me through the financial minefield that greets any Westerner on his arrival in India. Undoubtedly the most resourceful man I have ever met, Sanjay could produce whatever we needed, at whatever time of day or night, and for that we were often to be extremely grateful.

Across the tiled landing at Ashoka Villas lived Mrs Chaturashringi and her teenage daughter Leelatai. Mrs Chaturashringi was to become a surrogate mother to me and given half a chance, I think, might have become a genuine mother-in-law. Many were the evenings spent in her cluttered sitting room, which smelled so strongly of incense and the rather curious boiled-egg whiff of garam masala. We would chat about any number of topics over cups of Darjeeling tea – for Mrs Chaturashringi was widely read. Then we would nibble at the latest recipe in my introduction to Indian cooking served to us under the shyly smiling gaze of Leelatai, presumably to demonstrate her skills as a hostess.

Mrs Chaturashringi had been to an English Medium school, that is to say, one that taught all its lessons in English, and she was, as a consequence, a dedicated Anglophile.

'So tell me, how is your dear Queen?' she asked me that first evening as I consumed plate after china plate of spiced peas and potatoes.

'Well, fine, I think. Yes, fine. I haven't heard from her for a while.'

'We had always planned to go to the Mother Country, you know, my husband and myself and Leelatai. Sadly he passed away I think just about ten years back. We shall never go now I wouldn't fancy . . .'

'Oh dear . . . Yes, I'm sorry about that . . . Umm . . .'

'Life must go on of course.'

'Of course.'

It seemed that being a widow in India was not an enviable position. More often than not a husband's family quickly lost interest in their daughter-in-law, leaving her to return to her own parents or make her own way in life. Some families insisted that she shave her head to denote her widowhood and shun social situations. Occasionally there was still the reoccurrence of the outlawed tradition of *sati*, the Hindu practice of a wife throwing herself on to her husband's burning funeral pyre. Thankfully Mrs Chaturashringi's in-laws had remained on friendly terms with her and thought the world of their granddaughter whose education they funded. She also received a small income from them and added to it by privately tutoring well-off students who looked unlikely to meet the requirements of private school entrance tests. This did not, however, impinge on her main pursuit in life – the search for a husband for her daughter. Daily she, and a seemingly rather less interested Leelatai, scoured the Matrimonial Lists to be found within the pages of the *Maharashtra Bugle*. Here parents of both boys and girls advertised for suitors: 'Intelligent Bsc, looking for young intelligent girl. Must have good teeth.' 'Punjabi girl 24, good domestic skills looking for union with suitable income earner. No caste bar.'

One day soon she would certainly make a 'good catch', Mrs Chaturashringi knew it. Indeed, she looked at me most thoughtfully as I bid them goodnight on the landing and unlocked the door of my new home.

6

Osho

Ashoka Villas was a handy place to stay and with its friendly neighbours, medically trained security staff and its proximity to the ashram and the railway station, I was to be very happy there.

Four or five tiring days later, after being ferried in Sanjay's rickshaw all about the town in search of household items with which to furnish Ashoka Villas, I was able to admire the comfortable surroundings of my flat. In the kitchen there was now a small gas ring and aluminium saucepan bought from one of Sanjay's very good friends in the bazaar near the fort. Exotic embroideries hung across the windows and on the floor lay a large number of highly decorated cushions on which I would now be able to loll and watch the endless cricket on the small black and white television set that Mr Rentaparti had lent me when he had brought round the lease to sign. We had celebrated the occasion with great slugs of Superior Challenge, which, at half past nine in the morning, duly lived up to its name.

When he had finally lurchingly left, I had slumped down on my one kitchen chair and reflected on my rapid change in circumstance. Barely weeks before, the lachrymose Neeta had been waving me off from the gates of the school and now I had a new home and a new job. Now that I had a moment to consider my situation I suddenly felt full of enthusiasm for my new life. The Superior Challenge had no doubt been partly responsible for my sudden euphoria, but I knew at that moment that whatever little I had to offer in terms of teaching skills I would be happy to make available to the children of the ashram.

Blundering into the bedroom for a pre-prandial siesta, I had collapsed with these thoughts on to the rock-hard bed that provided the only furnishing. I was sure that in time I would get used to it, as I would the quirks of the plumbing in the bathroom. Disaster had threatened the fabric of Ashoka Villas a few days after my arrival when I failed to notice for a little while that the cold water tap of the wash basin also mysteriously operated the valve to the lavatory cistern. It was only when its plastic lid floated past me across the floor that I made the connection. Apart from that I was very pleased with my new accommodation. It was ideal really. Yes, really ideal.

Well, nearly ideal. There was only one drawback, a drawback that I discovered a few days after arrival: Ashoka Villas was only a healing crystal's throw from Osho.

One fine morning, as they nearly all were in wintertime in Poona, Mrs Chaturashringi pointed me in the direction of Koregaon Park, 'a particularly beautiful area of our town' that I was absolutely under no circumstances to miss. Past the 'School for the Blinds', a large, dusty Victorian building, the shutters of which seemed permanently closed, and the neighbouring 'Cataract Club' which I thought for an absurd second catered for devotees of cascading rivers, I turned right and soon found myself in a pleasant, broad and perfectly straight road. On either side high, solid walls and thick foliage above blocked out any clear view of what appeared to be large impressive buildings behind. Between the walls and the cobble pavements were carefully manicured beds full of brightly flowered bushes which had been recently watered. The most extraordinary thing, however, about this particular avenue was that it was almost devoid of traffic except, of course, for a couple of dozen rickshaws parked a few yards from their card-playing owners outside the gates of a large privately owned hospital; with a low rumble, a man was pushing a small hand-cart along the road, his biceps bunching as he ran it up and over some well-maintained sleeping policemen. His vehicle was piled with what looked like bars of soap, although I supposed they couldn't have been as he was eating one.

What a relief it was to be away from the roar and the smoke for a while; indeed it was quite a shock to the system to find this oasis of calm – a bit like stepping out of a nightclub and into a seminary.

Pleased not to have to have all my senses on red alert for once, I slipped into something of a reverie as I wandered along. It was therefore only slowly that I became aware of a most curious phenomenon. The world around me seemed slowly, insidiously, like a dye seeping across a cloth, to be turning maroon. Believing myself to have slipped into some curious, fanciful daydream, I pulled myself together hurriedly.

It was true. I now found myself in the midst of dozens of drifting people, all of them dressed in long, flowing maroon robes. Almost without exception, European or North American, the men had long, flowing beards and the women had long, flowing pre-Raphaelite hair. There was even on my right a long, flowing waterfall, slipping shinily down a marble wall and disappearing into a slatted grille in the flowerbed. Most of the figures were either making their way from one set of solid, black, double gates guarded by a long, flowing figure seated at a desk on a tall stool, on one side of the road, to another set on the other, or vice versa, or were standing in groups stroking their long, flowing hair. Predominantly, though, they were hugging.

As I passed the two black gateways I glanced in. After the noise, dirt and conflicting smells of the bazaar or the slum it was a new world. Winding paths stretched away between Japanese-style gardens and down these walkways wandered hand-in-hand dozens more pairs of strange maroon forms. It was almost silent but for the murmuring of their conversations and the babble of a water garden far off to my right. Closer in on my left, almost immediately inside the entrance, was what looked like an enormous bandstand surrounded on all sides by mosquito netting. Perhaps I expected to see the glint of giant brass instruments and massively puffed cheeks but instead all I could make out was a large empty throne on a plinth. It was surrounded on all sides by kneeling silent figures. Had I not noticed expensive watches and designer sneakers peeking from below the robes, I might have believed that I had been transported into some fantasy kingdom and that these patient subjects awaited their King and Queen who would arrive in a train, regal rather than locomotive, with their inevitably charming and beautiful princess. Tripping and slipping off the side of the pavement and bending my ankle to a sick-making angle brought me back to my senses.

Bemused, I carried on down the road, occasionally glancing furtively behind me. The maroon effect was diluted but was still much in evidence as I approached a small parade of day-to-day shops set back from the road. Walking across a colourful mosaic terrace, I stepped into a tiny shop, sandwiched between a 'Ladies Hairdressing Saloon' and 'The Imperial Hosiery'.

All the products were displayed in long glass-fronted cabinets that ran the length of the narrow room. An elderly woman in a lumpy, constricting sari paced up and down with an enormous bunch of keys, waiting to find out which of them she could now release to my safe custody. A toothbrush, toothpaste and a small bar of yellow soap were all released and I put them on the counter by the big, chrome till just inside the door. As I paid with crumpled orange ten-rupee notes, I looked up at a large, gilt-framed photograph over the till. From it a man in a robe and a loose turban, with a grey-white beard and large, dark, luminous eyes, was gazing at me penetratingly. He looked just like an Indian guru.

'Who is that, please?' I asked of the two pretty girls behind the piles of sandals and scarves that were heaped on the counter. One girl looked at the other in astonishment and the other pressed her hand to her mouth; then they both rocked with unnecessarily loud laughter. The lady with the keys huffed and turned on her heel to pace back down the corridor. As neither of the girls were going to be in a position to give me an answer for quite some time and I was beginning to blush, I turned away and found myself in front of a long, flowing white man in his early twenties.

'You have not been to Osho before? You do not understand what is Osho?' he asked in what was, I thought, a Dutch accent. (I actually did ask him later where he came from but he only replied, with a certain disdain for such territorial exactitude, that he was a 'child of de world'.)

'Come, I will tell you all about Osho. You can take some time from wandering this earth? Take some time to give your soul a good scrub. You will see how clean you can become.'

And with that, our two faces a perfect contrast of certainty and bewilderment, he took me to back to the terrace, which turned out to be a wooden-tables-and-benches-herbal-teas-and-sawdust-bread-rolls type of place. My new friend, as he assured me he had now become, was called Ved, which apparently meant Knowledge; he had once been called Dirk but had changed his name when he had given up his past life five years before, jettisoned his imported jeans in favour of a maroon robe and 'spiritually joined my worldly being to Osho'.

'So, how do you survive? You know, what do you do for money?'

'You know, Will, when you receive the spiritual nourishment that is to be found here in Osho, you need for little else. You know?' He smiled at me beatifically and muttered something about a trust fund left to him by a grandfather who had made bits for radiators in Rotterdam.

'But all that is not so important. Come, Will, come sit with us.'

So he sat me down amongst dozens of other maroon figures and told me all about the Bhagwan Shree Rajneesh, or Osho as he preferred to be known – the man in the picture. The Bhagwan had died in 1990 but had made his name, in this life, as, amongst other things, a 'sex guru'. He had followed no particular religion or philosophy, tradition or creed but had suggested that regular copulation was a sure-fire way to find Enlightenment. This theory had proved very popular.

In 1981 the Bhagwan had set off to America to set up a commune in Ohio. Eventually the wild stories of goings-on became too much for the farming folk of the mid-West. In a blaze of publicity, he was ejected, for tax evasion, from the USA but not before he had amassed an enormous number of followers and seventy-odd Rolls-Royces. The cars stayed but the disciples followed and they set up business again in Poona. Many, like my interlocutor Ved, came to follow the last of the Bhagwan's doctrines: the Mystic Rose, modestly described by its deviser as the greatest discovery on the path to Enlightenment since the Buddha's *vipassana*.

Although not immediately as attractive as some of the more physically oriented practices, the Mystic Rose still had its devotees. Not too complicated to tackle, it required only that the participant laugh solidly for three hours a day for a week, then cry for three hours a day for a second week and then do nothing for three hours for a final week. Though the indolent and wealthy followers of the commune certainly could, unfortunately for them most Indians would never possibly be able to afford the time to follow this route to illumination.

With plenty of time on their hands, the Baghwan's followers spent most of it complaining to each other about their ailments or congratulating themselves on their spiritual progress; most appeared to be the wives of Italian bankers or kids out of college with the family credit card. A lot, of course, were just washed-up middle-aged, middle-class hippies. As work did not cast its limiting shadows over the commune there was always plenty of time for self-examination, time to compare notes with the other devotees of the guru's teachings:

'*Cara, cara, bella*, how are you? I feel so wonderful; three hours of Buddhist meditation this morning and now, this afternoon, I am going for my Ayurvedic massage. It will be lovely, isn't it?

'I did the meditation too but it is terrible for my piles. I think it is the cold floor.'

'But you should take some of my painkillers, then you feel nothing. I take three and I meditate no problem.'

'Oh, OK, I get you, sounds good but is it homeo? I like homeo, only homeo, homeo—'

'Well, it is quite, I think . . . but anyway they certainly make you feel pretty relaxed, baby.'

'Hi, guys! How you all doing? Good? Cool, I just feel so good right now – you know, like a natural high, you know what I mean? I just got this little bubble of happiness just swelling up inside of me and it makes me feel so floaty, you know what I mean? Cool. God, I wish I could share it with you guys. You know, just grab a little bit of it and sprinkle it all around you people. I just wanna share a bit of all this goodness, you know? Hey, get away from here! Get away! God, don't you hate these kids that come in begging all the time? Why can't they leave me alone? Someone should keep them out. Jeez!'

'Yeah, you're right. Yesterday one of them came right up and touched my hand and she was so dirty. I nearly grossed out and, you know what? I'd just had my jasmine rub.'

'Oh, that is so bad; I hate that. Are you OK? Yeah? You sure? You're not just saying that? OK. Listen, I gotta go. Sorry. I got tantric at three and then aroma and then gems at five. You guys wanna do cocktails at my hotel tonight, about seven?'

'That would be so nice. Byeee, love you honey, mmm, mmm. Hugzzz. OK, bye now.'

Upon which a great deal more hugging took place and then everyone settled back into another fruitful afternoon of navel-gazing and I made my flabbergasted but not greatly enlightened way back to Ashoka Villas. This was not, however, the last time that the 'Osho effect' was to make itself felt in my Indian life.

Sanjay, whose knack of appearing just when I needed some advice or some transport was not, I suspected, always totally altruistic, was waiting outside the gates of Ashoka Villas when

I appeared that evening in search of something to eat. On his invitation, I doubled up and climbed on to the back seat.

'Aakash, Aakash! Ohh very nice, Mr Williams!' He rubbed his hands together and started to fiddle with the controls of the autorickshaw. 'Oh Drupad! Aakash – a very nice restaurant I think?'

Drupad, a silver whistle to his lips and waving a large stick, was preparing to wave us on our way, although, as far as I could see, the street was empty but for a bullock and cart and a couple of cyclists.

'Oh, yes, very nice *karna* there. No problem there.'

'My cousin brother is working as waiter there. Oh very nice – there you will like very much.'

'Is it . . . ? It won't be too expensive . . . You don't think?'

Sanjay inspected me as if to consider what might be my budget but he seemed to be more confident of my buying power than had been Maria-Helena von Würfelwerfer.

'What are you saying?' he exclaimed. 'There is no question. It will be perfect for you.'

'Yes, yes, perfect,' agreed Drupad. 'Near the hospital. Peep-peep-peep!'

Well, that was a relief I supposed.

We leapt forward with a small wheelie and then stopped. Furious revving ensued.

'Doctor Irani always eating in Aakash. Very nice doctor. Hysterectomy! Peep-peep-peep!' Drupad shrilled as he disappeared in a cloud of black smoke.

Sanjay proved, not for the last time, to have made an excellent choice. Aakash Garden Restaurant, only ten minutes from the station and next door to 'Pantaloons – India's Family Store', was announced by an illuminated sign that read 'Salivation Guaranteed'. Inside the green gates was a small, half-covered courtyard lit with dangling strings of egg-size light bulbs. Casting feathery shadows, a large tree grew in the middle of the restaurant and was surrounded with chairs and tables, covered in green-checked tablecloths and decorated with small vases of pink carnations. At one end an open kitchen bubbled, sizzled and steamed, the chefs sprinkling sweat and swear words into their concoctions as liberally as they did herbs and spices. Next to it, in a small storeroom, a group of young waiters squatted in permanence in front of a huge, never-shrinking pile of onions, which they peeled with small, sharp knives – a Sisyphean task which they seemed to find deeply upsetting.

'Welcome, good sir. Welcome, good sir! You are most welcome.'

From the greeting that I was given by a rotund man with stringy rake-over hair and an exhausted dinner jacket, I took it that I was being well received.

'So you have come from Osho, I think. Yes?'

No.

'Oh . . . no? Oh! Well, never mind. Come, let us find you a fine table.' Turning, he scanned the largely empty restaurant. 'Yes, I think so.'

He waved at another group of waiters who had been laying some tables at the back of the courtyard and they rushed to smooth and stroke and tidy a table near a large, blaring television.

'Come. Sitting please.'

I complied.

Taking my hand again between both of his he shook it repeatedly as he bobbed back and forward, bowing at the waist as if standing on a pitching deck.

'My name is Dikshin Doegar. Thank you.'

'Oh, well my name is Will Randall. Thank you.'

'Mr Rambo! Welcome to my restaurant. Welcome. Now what is it you like to eating? Veg? Non-veg? Non-veg, I think. Good. Today you are permitting I will choose for you? Good. Let me see! What is nice for Rambo tonight?'

He plucked up a menu and held it in front of him as if he were about to sing an aria. Stentorian, he read out a long list to a scribbling waiter. Snapping it closed, he bowed low which appeared to be the sign to 'Ready, Steady, Go' for the attendant staff who set off at high speed in the direction of the kitchen.

Throughout the course of the meal, which was remarkably good, waiters, who clearly wished to make the task of eating my meal as easy as possible, surrounded me on all sides. They tucked in napkins, moved ashtrays, poured glasses, pushed bowls closer and pulled others away. Food was expertly served on to my plate, the serving spoon hanging interrogatively in the air in front of me. Enough? Soon, thanks to all this attention, I had to pause. Puffing slightly, I sat back briefly in my chair and immediately there were four enquiries as to my welfare and the general standard of the food. Should I not resume my task, surely one of them would offer to finish it off for me – to save me the effort.

During the evening, the restaurant filled up steadily and by the time I left there were no empty tables. Undoubtedly it was a popular place but it was with some relief that I escaped the slightly claustrophobic attentiveness. Due to my culinary ineptitude, though, I was to become a regular diner at Aakash. Sometimes I ate alone in front of the old television that pounded out endless Bollywood films – most of which seemed to have been filmed on the side of a Swiss mountain – but more often I was invited to dine with one of the many groups of middle-class businessmen who made up the main percentage of the clientele. Employed by day in the middle management of international companies, at night they sat and ate and drank quantities of disinfecting IMFL (Indian-made foreign liquor) whisky and swore foully at the waiters as a demonstration of their financial superiority. Nothing was good enough and dishes were endlessly sent back for more spice or less salt. Beers were ordered and needed to be 'medium-cold' or 'a little bit warm'. More often than not when the temperature was tested with a podgy, hairy hand, it was sent back to the refrigerator with a large portion of invective.

Although this was clearly a social institution that I would be able to do little to change, I tried, for my part, to be as polite as possible to the members of staff serving at table. This seemed to be appreciated, as before long they would reserve a table for me, keeping back last dishes of anything that they knew I particularly liked. Neatly folded, the day's copy of the *Maharashtra Bugle* was produced soon after my arrival and in it I followed the local stories of the moment: the debate about compulsory motorbike helmets; the activities of a group of pioneering prohibitionist women intent on eradicating illegal liquor from the slums, oh, and, of course, the cricket scores.

Before long I was on first-name terms with the waiters, who slowed between tables to air their thoughts on any number of national and international subjects, and to give me my first rudimentary lessons in Hindi. Complicitly, we also shared a certain mistrust of the tubby Devashva, the eleven-year-old son of Mr Dikshin Doegar. At the beginning of each evening he would sit his not insignificant bottom down at the table that was reserved for him and, pausing only to issue abrupt orders to the staff, would plough his way through dish after dish ferried to him from the kitchen. He paused only to wipe his nascent moustache with the back of his hand.

So it was that my new existence took on an ordered routine. Swept up as I was in the mad whirl of Indian life, with its endless kaleidoscopic fascinations, I had hardly any part of my mind spare to consider what I had left behind. My future in England was freeze-framed, like a photo lost in the back of my wallet, until I returned home. It was, for now, as I crossed the slum, or the river, the bazaar or the brown, parched park of the central cricket *maidan*, as if I had never lived anywhere else.

7

Dear Maradona . . .

Finally settled at Ashoka Villas, it was time to turn my attentions to my new students.

Much of the first week was spent finding my way about Tanjiwadi and Sanjay proved to be my enthusiastic guide. On the back of an enormous, deafening motorbike, an Enfield Bullet, I had my internal organs rearranged as we thumped in and out of the tiny little lanes that threaded their way mysteriously through the slum. Each area seemed to have its own personal identity, although, to my eye, this shambolic housing settlement spread without any delineation across the city, and people would introduce themselves as coming from 'Tanjiwadi slum' in the same way that a Londoner might announce that they were from South Kensington. Even more strangely it seemed that this identification with a particular area was the source of some considerable pride for the inhabitants.

Healthy competition was widespread and cricket teams and football players would meet and compete as they do in any other part of the world. The difference of course was that the teams would all meet on the same uneven, naked piece of earth. By the time I had spent only a few days in Tanjiwadi I had already begun to recognise that the people who lived there were immensely proud of their sense of identity; even here there were local heroes to be admired, the local team to be supported. Here, too, where there was so little, there still existed a powerful sense of that strongest of human desires – the need to belong.

Much though I would have liked to just slip, unnoticed, into this community it was not going to be quite that easy. Indeed, initially, the reception that I received in the slums was mixed. When Sanjay and I had blasted into one of the small courtyards and lurched to a halt, he would kick down the stand and I would climb unsteadily off the bouncing, squeaking seat. Immediately, women lying almost prostrate on the ground, their folded legs tucked up underneath them as they did their washing, would slap the wet clothes heavily together. Pulling back the ragged curtain in front of their doorways, hung to keep away the crowds of flies, they would disappear inside, pushing their youngest children ahead of them, as the milky-blue liquid ran away into the gurgling, stinking drain.

Quiet groups of suspicious young men leaned against gaunt, dusty trees and each other, holding hands as was their habit, their arms on comrades' shoulders. My appearance caused suspicious looks; sometimes they would nominate a spokesman by prodding one or another of them in the back and whoever was selected would call over enquiries to Sanjay who would reply cheerfully, pointing at me. His smile was not always returned but I was always closely inspected. Shopkeepers and tradesmen dotted around the area seemed, more than most, to be willing to proffer some sort of friendship. Seeing what they considered, sadly wrongly, to be well-lined pockets they would offer tea and a seat on the carpet inside the tiny shops that sold a jumble of packeted foodstuffs and household goods. Once I was settled they would demonstrate their wares with grandiose sweeps of their arms.

Initially, though, I could not say that I felt exactly welcomed in my new world and, not for the first time, wondered whether this had really been a good decision. So at the end of the first week I asked Charuvat what the local people had been saying. What did they think of me? Perhaps they wondered why I was there?

Well, he explained softly, I needed to remember how tenuous

life in the slum could be. When their homes could be razed to the ground at any moment they were permanently aware of the temporary nature of their security. To my concern he explained in his halting but careful English that many locals were mistrustful of anyone who appeared to be doing something for nothing. Here where there was so little, people could not afford any charitable generosity other than small acts of kindness for neighbours and friends. It seemed inconceivable that anybody would be willing, or able, to offer their services for free.

Perhaps they thought that I was a missionary masquerading as a teacher, but really there to spread the word of one offshoot or another of the Christian church? For the many devoted Hindus and Muslims this reeked of some Western plot: a religious colonialism to be strongly and rightfully resisted. Either that or I was acting for childless couples in the West, poised at any stage to snatch an unsuspecting toddler from the bosom of their family so that they might be brought up by strangers thousands of miles away. More outlandishly, it was suggested that I was a surgeon in India to remove the organs of unsuspecting children, only then to smuggle them away on ice to Europe or America. I laughed uneasily – sticking plasters made me feel giddy. The slum barons – the *zamindars* – who thrived on the extortion and rent payments that they raised from this poor and often ill-educated community, spread a lot of these rumours. I shouldn't worry, said Charuvat, when they get to know you they will soon accept you. Anyway, the developers were much more of a threat to our security than the *zamindars*, who, in Tanjiwadi at least, were relatively tame and to date had left the ashram alone. No, he shook his head; it was the developers that worried him. OK, that's all right then, I had replied rather doubtfully, but for several nights after this revelation I woke sweatily wondering what a *zamindar* looked like.

Despite these concerns, I quickly slipped back into a profession that I remembered with pleasure I had always, well, nearly always, loved. These children were going to make it easy –

ready, as they were, to return whatever I offered with interest paid in smiles and laughter. Admittedly some of the younger ones occasionally looked at me with suspicion when I tried to engage them in one silly game or other but Pushprendra Prakash and his older brothers and sisters quickly welcomed me into their world.

Initially I had terrible problems remembering the children's names as there was no point of reference. In England, where I had always prided myself on learning names quickly, my task was made much easier by the fact that I recognised the names; I did not have to learn David or Fiona, I just had to apply them to the right people. Here, though, I had to learn the name first and then remember its owner. And when they possessed names as tongue-tripping as Pushprendra Prakash I got myself into a hopeless muddle.

By coincidence, the children seemed to divide themselves neatly by age into two groups. This, of course, was not done precisely as many of them had no real idea how old they were. Very often their birthdays were fixed on the date that they had arrived in the ashram, yet it did seem that there was a natural division. Harshada agreed to look after the under-sixes. Abhishekh would help her when he had time spare from his studies and they both seemed to derive great pleasure in taking the children through numbers and alphabets, songs and games.

Fourteen youngsters sat in front of me the first Monday morning of term. We none of us knew what to expect but it became quickly clear that we were all intent on giving it our best shot. My class did still possess a fair age range, the youngest about nine, two or three of the older children in their mid-teens.

Prakash, as he had to be known for short, was probably the oldest. If my arrival and introduction to the ashram went smoothly, it was thanks to him. A tall, strong but kindly boy, he possessed a maturity that was very comforting, for if there was ever any need for me to delegate then he would automatically take charge, astounding me with his sensitivity to the requirements of any situation. Each morning he made it his responsibility to seek out lead-swingers and skivers who, quite by mistake, had got involved in playing with kittens or the neighbour's baby and just had not noticed the time. If ever I was wanting for anything, then it was Prakash, a popular local figure, who went looking for it in the curving, winding alleys of the slum. When it was time for me to go home at the end of the school day he would hurry off to look out Sanjay. Chastising the poor man, who was more often than not sipping tea at the shack with its giant bubbling cauldron on the edge of the rumbling road, he would urge him to hurry to pick me up.

His dependability was always admirable. Not that he was priggish in a I-hope-to-be-civil-servant-when-I'm-older-sir kind of way. He simply realised that in the world into which he had been born, self-reliance was a vital skill. No doubt he had learnt this during the first seven years of his life during which he had had to survive by scavenging for scraps in the battered, yellow town skips. Charuvat had rescued him from one and had brought him home to Harshada. Having no recollection of his own parents, he was devoted to them both.

It was natural, therefore, that it was he who volunteered to start with the introductions that very first lesson.

'My name is Pushprendra Prakash . . .' With confident ease, he reeled off the short speech that he had given me when we first met. When he reached the end he smiled at me. 'It's OK, Billbhaiya?'

'Great, very good.' The others clearly thought so too as they produced an energetic burst of applause.

'So you're fourteen. OK . . . So what do you like to do?'

I had written out a number of questions which, if not exactly sparkling conversational gambits, would at least test the level of their spoken English.

'I like to eat food very much!'

A gentle giggle signalled the general agreement of the class.

'Good. So . . . Let's see. What kind of food do you like? What is your favourite food?'

I thought of a dozen of my favourite dishes.

'Well,' he paused, his cheerful face now drawn down into a confused frown. 'Well . . . just some food, *Bhaiya*.'

'Oh, yes. Sorry, right. Well, anyway, next question. Umm . . . where do you live?'

'I live in Tanjiwadi in Poona in Maharashtra in India.'

'Good, fine. And where is India, then?'

'Where is India? What do you mean, Billbhaiya, where is India?'

'Show me where?' Flicking it open, I spread a colourful map of the world, which I had bought in one of the upmarket English bookshops near Koregaon Park, wide across the floor. Simultaneously, all the children rocked forward on to their knees and elbows, hands cupped under their chins, fascinated by the curious, incongruous shapes of the different shaded landforms.

All but one.

'Bharat.' The boy who still sat upright looked me proudly in the eye as he used the Marathi word for India. 'Bharat is a very nice country, aren't you thinking so, Billbhaiya?'

'Yes, it certainly is . . . Err . . .'

'One of the best countries? Do you think?'

'Yes! What is your name then?'

'My name is Sahas.'

Sahas, Prakash's closest friend and ally, was a striking-looking fellow. His hair always immaculately parted and combed smoothly backwards, his poor clothes always neatly worn, he took great pride in himself and his world. Honest, too, he possessed an innate, noble sense of what was right and what was to be done well. Like all the children of the slum he needed to be a pragmatist but he had a dreamer's imagination too. Often I would find him, his arms folded, one foot cocked up on the low wall that surrounded the yard, his eyes narrowed, his back straight. One day an explorer, another, a brave sea-farer or a soldier, he would gaze out across the river into the hazy distance imagining some adventure far away beyond the dirt and dust of Tanjiwadi.

'US, where is US, Billbhaiya? That is a very nice country too, I think . . . ?'

Now, he too leaned forward to look at the map.

'Maybe one day I will be going to America . . . Or UK. UK is your place I think?' He glanced up at me questioningly. 'Where is UK, Billbhaiya?'

Sahas appeared as unimpressed with the small pink blob as Prakash had been with my name.

'Yes . . . maybe I will go to US.'

'I think they are some very beautiful actress in America?' shrieked a pretty girl sitting next to him.

'Please be quiet, *Bahan*. I am sorry, Billbhaiya. My sister is a very silly girl.'

To his great chagrin Sahas had a real sister, Tanushri, who was, I suddenly realised, the little girl to whom I had given my food on my first visit to the ashram and who had thanked me so movingly. Their childhood, like that of Prakash, had been disfigured by unhappiness, made all the more poignant by the fact that they had once known a normal family life. When their uncle in Poona, to whom they had been sent from the country to lodge by their parents, had been unable to find sufficient rupees for the rent, they were all turned out of their home. The kindly relatives had decided to chance their fortune in the eastern state of Orissa, where their aunt by marriage had relatives. Sahas, then only ten, had turned down the invitation to go with them and instead, taking the five-year-old Tanushri by the hand, was determined to return to the family village. They, of course, had no money – just the package of provisions packed for them by their disconsolate aunt.

During their first few months on the streets of Poona, they had both held tight to the hope that they might, one day, return to their small house – nothing much, a single room cluttered with aluminium cooking pots and bundles of carefully treasured belongings. Smoothly swept, the shiny cow-dung floor had been their playground and their bed. There they had been safe, they had been at home.

Sahas had thought that they might make their own way by train or bus, or even hitch rides on the bullock carts that plodded along the sides of the roads that snaked out through the hills surrounding the town. Tanushri had been very young, though, and they had saved no food or money, having to survive day-to-day by begging and running errands, avoiding, all the while, the fat, stinking men who prowled the night wanting to touch and feel.

Eventually the young brother and sister had been too tired to make their trip, half-forgetting, as time wore on, in which direction they should have headed. Just as Sahas was beginning to despair about ever being able to lift themselves from this hand-to-mouth existence, by great good fortune they had been pointed to the door of the ashram.

This huge change in their luck had briefly resurrected the hope that, in time, they might be able to return home, but some months later their dream came to end when news arrived, delivered by one of their neighbours, a bone-thin old farmer, that their parents had died in a typhoid epidemic that had emptied the little community. Reaching inside his sweat-stained cotton shirt, the equally destitute but honest villager pulled out his closed fist. Slowly, he opened his fingers, and there, in the dirt-creased palm of his hand, Tanushri saw, through tear-blurred eyes, a pair of small gold earrings, the family's only pair, that their mother had wanted her to have.

She fiddled with one of them now as she smiled at me, slapping her brother playfully on the leg.

'No, it's true, Billbhaiya. I have got pictures. Look!' Out of the pocket of her faded dress she pulled a small folded piece of paper, which she smoothed out on the flat of her hand to reveal a rather scrumpled pop singer. Reverentially, she positioned it on North Dakota.

'There, you see!' she cried. 'Her name is Maradona!'

'Don't you mean Ma—?'

'And sometimes she sings with no clothes!' She released a surge of giggles and pounded the floor with her small fists, so funny did she find this idea.

Everyone else looked mildly bemused.

'Well, right. Anyway, Sahas, where do you live?'

'I live in—'

'Billbhaiya, is it true in America—'

'Hang on, Tanushri. We were just talking about . . .'

Finally this excitable, charming, nutty little girl had us all thumping our heads against the rough plaster walls of the dim classroom; pretty and sweet-natured, she was irredeemably scatter-brained; often she seemed so *distraite* that I was not at all sure whether she was following the same lesson as the rest of us. Sometimes, her replies to my questions were so incongruous that I was sure she spent much of her time in her own private world. In common with her brother and perhaps, to a certain degree, all the children, she loved to dream. For dreams were, after all, for free.

Her fantasies, however, were not those of her brother. Rather than dreaming of heroic adventures, she was happier in a world of catwalks and movie premieres. She kept a scrapbook of exotic cuttings gleaned from old magazines, which she had found in the heaps of recycled paper that were salvaged and stored in huge bundles near the gates of the factory. Whenever she had a moment she was to be found poring over them, imagining herself, no doubt, in the glare of the flashbulbs.

Eventually, after I had managed to convince her that I would answer her questions about the world of film and fashion – but sometime after the lesson – and Sahas had spoken to her quietly and firmly, I succeeded in asking all the children to introduce themselves, which they did with varying degrees of confidence.

'Right, now you can all ask me any questions you like, you know, about me, my life in UK, err . . . *the* UK.'

Hands stabbed the air, some, on second thoughts, retreating almost immediately to laps. Others strained for the ceiling desperate to take part. No matter if a question had come to mind or not.

'OK, go on then, err, Unmesh, it is Unmesh, that's right, isn't it?' I picked up the seating plan that I had scribbled down on the back of my list of questions. Unfortunately Tanushri had turned it round to take a look and had now muddled me completely. By chance, this time I was right.

'Yes. Well, Billbhaiya,' the boy paused thoughtfully, 'So do you have a car?'

'Well, not now, I don't. But before I did.' Not that I really wanted to go into my motoring history, which had been about as chequered as a Formula One finishing flag.

'I see.' The tone was earnest. 'What engine was it?'

'Well, I don't know, really. Petrol?'

'I see. You had fuel injectors?'

'Weeelll . . . ?'

'You know how it works. Look . . .'

Shuffling on his bottom, Unmesh moved round the circle, flicking through a small booklet. Bespectacled, slight and rather tentative of speech, Unmesh was the boffin of our group; he was forever taking things apart to see how they had been put together. Normally he succeeded in restoring them to their original state. His beloved notebook, stuck permanently in the pocket of his shorts and attached by a piece of rough string to a greasy, much-chewed piece of pencil, was full of jottings and figures all written in a concise, firm hand. He bubbled over with enquiries, questions, conundrums to solve and facts to remember. More often than not, it was he who was able to provide a sensible explanation to a problem that had left the rest of us stumped.

His sister, Kundanika, who although only a year older than her brother towered above him, now scooped him up and returned him to his original place.

'Sorry, Billbhaiya,' she whispered politely as she dusted the small boy down, folding his collar more neatly. Kundanika was a great organiser, as I have noticed some people are destined to be. (Sadly, it seems to have played no part in my astrological plan.) A sturdy mother-figure at the age of twelve, she delighted in pushing and prodding the little ones to and fro, out of bed and into line, ensuring all the while their safety and happiness. Morning or evening she could be found with two or three hands in each of her own, soothing a hurt or laughing away a minor dispute. Occasionally, I felt physically stunned when I remembered that Kundanika and her little brother had witnessed their father murder their mother, that they had seen their mother burst into flames after she had been soaked in kerosene: a wife murder that went all but unmentioned in the Indian press and that occurred at a rate of more than one a day in Delhi alone. The children's father had been imprisoned – although, statistically, this was by no means a foregone conclusion – and his relatives rejected the children as inconvenient reminders of their daughter-in-law. One of the policemen at the courthouse lived in the Tanjiwadi slum and had taken the children to the ashram. Their father had never come to reclaim them. It seemed, after all that she had seen, extraordinary, impossible, that Kundanika could carry on with such equanimity, such poise and sense of duty.

'That is fine now, Billbhaiya. Sorry for interruption.'

Happy now with her brother's appearance, she let her hand rest softly on his shoulder, smiling tenderly as she watched him sketch out some new fantastical design. Serene, rarely ruffled, she was an influence of calm, forgiving gentleness on the younger children – but even she occasionally tired of the endless antics of Dulabesh, the joker in our pack.

At that particular moment, Dulabesh was standing on his head.

Distracted by Unmesh's injectors, I had not noticed him place his forehead on the tiled floor and then flick his legs up smartly until they were resting against the wall. He grinned a curious upside-down smile and then, rather impressively, folded his arms.

'Come on, Dulabesh, down you come!' As so often, I had trouble keeping a straight face.

'Oh, Billbhaiya, I am just looking at the world from underside!'

I tilted my head a bit to see if this could actually be done. I am still not sure.

'No. Look, come on down!'

'*Tike*, OK!' He slowly lowered his legs and then somehow

managed to stand up straight in one movement. He turned to the class and bowed slightly at the waist, beaming a bright smile. Winding an imaginary crank handle, producing a funny ratcheting noise from the side of his mouth as he did so, he lowered himself cross-legged to the floor.

Had Dulabesh simply been a show-off, one of those boys who always has to be the centre of everyone's attention, one of those kids who can do disgusting things with various of his joints or who can make vulgar noises with one orifice or another, then he might have become rather irritating. But as it turned out, Dulabesh's liveliness was contagious; if he was present then we all seemed imbued with more energy, more enthusiasm for the tasks before us.

Slight, indeed taller only than Unmesh, there was such get-up-and-go, such oomph, such delight in his face whatever he was doing that it was difficult sometimes to realise that this little figure of fun had also suffered terrible things. Originally from Calcutta, he had grown up in a happy family home, but at the age of four, wriggling his hand out of his mother's to watch a performing dog, he had simply lost his parents in the crowded Howrah Railway Station as they were making their way home one rush hour. Mistaking an interstate for his own home-bound train, he discovered himself travelling further and further into the night. Running up and down the corridors, pushed between legs, stroking familiar-looking saris, he searched for his mother's scent and his father's shoes but when he looked up he found only the faces of strangers. He had been trying to get back ever since.

One day, after he had just finished a gymnastic display that involved several flip-flacks and the use of the back of the irritated Beckham as a vaulting horse, he told me solemnly that one day, he had decided, he would head back home. But we knew, he and I, as he held my sleeve and cried, that 2000 kms and several years stood between him and his goal. The normally laughing, happy Dulabesh was only one of thousands of dispossessed children, carrying more than their fair share of grief, who through no fault of their own found themselves orphaned, separated from their families and left to fend off hunger, thirst, disease and the pimps and perverts who made up the phantoms of their nights. Depressingly, even if they managed to get themselves established in later years, with work, a home, a family, the inadequate diets of their early years – 20 per cent of all Indian children are seriously malnourished – meant that they were far more likely to suffer from serious illness in older age and a significant percentage would die prematurely.

Fortunately the high spirits of the children meant that I had little time to dwell on such dismal statistics. Progress continued apace. Once I had managed that first morning to ascertain the standard of the English that they could speak or understand, it was easier to organise a timetable. In the mornings we spoke English, sometimes we just chatted about their hopes and dreams, what interested them about the world and what they would like to know more about. At other times, we imagined ourselves in a variety of different scenarios, which we would act out in short sketches. Some of them were practical: 'In the restaurant', where they acted out the roles of both the waiters and, with greater enthusiasm, the customers; 'At the garage', 'Lost in the street' or 'In the bank'. Others were more surreal: 'In a spaceship' (Unmesh's design, of course), 'At the fashion show' (Sahas scarlet as he stomped down an imaginary catwalk while Tanushri gave a running commentary on his make-believe costume) or 'An expedition to the North Pole', which involved a degree of perplexity at the idea of skiing down snowscapes or even the idea of being freezing cold. We practised reading and writing too: menus, directions, space charts, and so on. Abhishekh helped to teach mathematics, Hindi and Marathi and we all learnt more about the history and geography of India and the wider world from a children's encyclopedia that I borrowed from Mrs Chaturashringi.

Religious education, the teaching of the extraordinarily complex Hindu faith, with its three million gods (at last count) and almost as many impenetrable rituals, was provided by the local, immensely respected and popular Brahmin priest, the spectacularly entitled Sadhu Professor Shri Vishnu Rangarajan. The Professor lived locally in great simplicity, his religious writings and a brass-bound chest of faded orange robes his only belongings. With great joy, the local population provided food and daily necessities for their 'guru', their spiritual leader, and he in return came regularly to instruct the children in the teachings of the great works of the Hindu faith: the *Bhagavad Gita*, the *Mahabharata*, and the writings of innumerable theologians.

Grey hair twisted into a large knot on his head and the three stripes of sandalwood paste and holy ash across his forehead, combined with a less than spotless robe and necklaces of wooden beads, gave him an air of the utmost authenticity; his science-laboratory thick glasses with their tortoiseshell frames and greasy lenses, a look of great scholarliness. Above all, though, he was kindly and on the days that he was expected the children would stand at the gates of the ashram with small gifts awaiting his arrival. As soon as he entered, leaning on his thick wooden stave, they would form a queue to kneel before him and touch his bare feet; that greatest and most moving sign of Indian respect. Then, seated quietly in a circle around him, they would listen in an atmosphere of enchanted awe, as he started to speak. His voice, a clear murmuring stream of sound audible above the noise of the daily passage of people and traffic in the lane outside, transfixed them as he recounted one or other tale of magical adventure, of colossal events, as the gods arranged their universe.

Although I was never to be a Hindu, not being Indian or born in India, the Professor always treated me with great courtesy and friendliness.

'We fellows are teachers all the same,' he would tell me elliptically when often he would stay to take part in our lessons.

'Tell me then, Mr Williams, so when were you born?' he asked me soon after our first meeting.

I told him the date and year.

'But what time precisely, please?'

For not only was the Professor a religious leader, a specialist in 'aura cleansing' and a practising herbalist, he was also the source of the most important information available to Indians. He was an expert in the stars, in horoscopes, in predicting auspicious days, and people planning a wedding or a business transaction, an arrival or a departure, would visit him from all round the town. For many, the timing of these events was crucial; everything needed to be aligned so that the event might take place at the best possible moment to ensure the best possible outcome (in what was surely not the best of all possible worlds). Such superstitions were not the obsession simply of the poorly educated; even Indira Gandhi, the (as it transpired) ill-fated Prime Minister, had surrounded herself with holy men, diviners, who might ensure that her every decision was taken at the most propitious moment. When Queen Elizabeth II visited the former colony for the first time, the pilot had to land the plane five minutes late to avoid certain catastrophe.

The Professor, therefore, clearly thought it necessary to check that I had not appeared in this world at an inopportune moment.

'Yes, I need to know at what time in the day. This is most important.'

'Two o'clock in the afternoon.' I remembered this with some pride, my mother having complained that my brothers' separate appearances in the early hours of the morning had been 'extremely tiresome'.

'I see. *Ek* minute, please.'

One minute ticked by rather slowly as he reached into a pouch at his chest hidden in orange folds and pulled out a badly mauled booklet. Removing his glasses and sticking the two arms into his thick hair, which gave the impression of a puppet peering over the top of his head, he peered at the long columns of numbers and squiggles. His face darkened.

'Well?' I enquired with faltering cheerfulness. 'What does it say then, you know, in your book? Everything OK?'

I laughed. He did not.

'You said two in the afternoon?'

'Yes . . .'

'Hmm . . . Two in the afternoon UK time?' The Professor was well travelled, having attended and lectured at seminars across the world.

'Yes, that's right. No, sorry. I was in Germany at the time. I mean I was born in Germany.'

'Oh, I see. *Ek* minute.'

Another timeless sixty seconds elapsed as he rustled the pages of the fraying almanac this way and that.

'Oh, fine, very fine.' He sat back on his folded legs, slipped on his glasses and smiled at me with transparent relief. Despite my probing enquiries he refused to tell me what might have been my outcome if my appearance in this world had taken place in Hammersmith rather than Hanover, but only smiled as he tucked his book away, ready for his next consultation.

In the afternoons, formal lessons at an end, the children drew pictures, made models from junk collected in the street, went on walks, followed treasure trails. Often I would give them some small task to accomplish in the evening, a list of words to learn or a letter to write:

> *Dear Maradona,*
> *I think you are very beautiful . . .*

With great pride every morning, they would demonstrate how well they had learnt their lessons or how carefully they had written out their work. Most days, when it was time to bid them farewell, I would receive some small gift, a picture drawn in chalk, a new design of paper dart, something whittled out of a piece of wood. Soon my rooms at Ashoka Villas were brightly decorated with artwork and handicraft. Unmesh's design for fuel injectors, which he had torn from his book at the end of our first day together and handed to me wordlessly, intrigued many a visitor to my bathroom.

More often than not, after lessons were over, we would go out on to the patch of waste ground and play impromptu cricket, with a stick, an exhausted tennis ball and an old plastic oil container for stumps, or the strange tag-cum-rugby game of *kabbadi* which left me exhausted and bruised, fit only to collapse into the back of Sanjay's rickshaw. If it was too hot we would just sit in the shade of the rough boundary wall and share sips of super sweet sugar cane juice bought for five rupees in a grimy glass from the rickety stall at the end of the alley, with its clanking press and its poster that cruelly advertised a 'European-style Amusement Park' – tickets for which were far beyond the means of the local population.

One afternoon, shortly after my arrival, when the black coke pollution seemed to sit more heavily than usual on the slum causing it to choke and grumble, a chauffeur-driven car came to a silent stop at the gate of the ashram. An elegant lady stepped out, announcing herself as the proprietress of the engineering company housed in the modern office building that shone on the other side of the busy Bombay Road.

Surprisingly, although this lady was to play a vital role in my life in India, I do not believe I ever addressed her by name. As a person, despite her public role, she was intensely private and so I do not propose to name her here. It is enough to say that she, like a number of other people of her financial means, was willing to give freely in order to improve the lot of others. Trite though this might sound, if it were not for the likes of her, India would find itself with even greater problems to confront. Later I was to discover that her generosity sprang from personal tragedy, but now I was just struck by her kindly, gentle demeanour, the softness of her hands and voice, the straightforward integrity with which she went about helping other people – a real fairy godmother.

She had heard of the good work of the ashram and was willing to offer the old-fashioned bungalow, in the grounds of the modern office block, as a classroom. The large, airy room was ideal, roomy enough for the children to work in groups, according to their age. There was a new blackboard and some picture books, some slates and chalks. She would be happy to allow them to use this place indefinitely on the understanding that the classes should be available to some of the other slum children as well. It was heartily agreed that they would be most welcome. Everyone was most pleased.

But, and here the lady's kindly face became suddenly solemn, we needed to realise just how precarious our present situation was; she had been informed by her personal assistant, who had gleaned the information from the secretary's grapevine, that the businessmen-owners of the land on which the ashram had been illegally built had made an application to the bank for a loan and already had intentions to develop the area. In the strange time frame of India, I already knew that something which had seemed impossibly distant for so long could suddenly become imminent; of course it might never happen either but I remembered how solemnly Charuvat had told me of the possible crisis. The only way to prevent the arrival of the bulldozers would be to buy the land ourselves which would require a surprisingly large sum of money in this overpopulated city. The elegant lady would be fundraising for our cause amongst her rich industrialist colleagues. As our part of the bargain the children were to perform a play or a musical piece, something impressive that could provide the centrepiece of a theatrical evening to which she would invite suitably sympathetic and wealthy friends. She was going to see if she could find an appropriate venue.

Beyond the purchase of the land, we needed eventually to find ourselves financially independent, no longer having to rely on the day-to-day donations of kindly neighbours. Charitable acts play a large part in the spiritual and daily life of India and, from top to bottom, in the street and in the home, regular kindnesses are much in evidence. Sadly, it took no time at all to realise that there was still a vast vertiginous canyon of need that could never be filled from individual pockets. The ashram needed to become self-sufficient. Lump sums donated by our audience would, we hoped, build enough capital to provide an annual income, which would cover the ashram's running expenses. The children, their charm and their intelligence were naturally our best advertisement. It was vital, she reminded us again as her chauffeur held open the car door, that we acted quickly because the lack of regulation over these 'illegal' constructions meant that no permission would be required for their destruction.

'And, please,' she gazed upon us fondly, protectively. 'Make sure you stay out of the way of the *goondas* because I fear they will be making their presence felt soon.' She wished us well and stepped back into her air-conditioned car, which swept quietly away down the bumpy track.

'It is such a pity nobody here is knowing how to organise an entertainment like this,' mused Charuvat.

'Yes, shame,' I agreed. 'I directed the school play once when I was in England but it was a complete—'

'Oh, you maybe doing one drama here, Mr Williams, that will be being very nice!'

Only on my way home in the back of the rickshaw, bouncing between the bench seat and the metal strut above my head, as Sanjay weaved his magic through the snarled and snarling traffic, did I remember the horrors of my forays into amateur dramatics. The empty stage, the endless silences – apart, of course, from the odd thump and groan backstage as someone collided with something in the terrifying penumbra. Opportunities for ridicule popped out at every turn, guaranteeing self-enforced social exclusion for months to come – the appearance of an unwilling young actor glaring back into the wings from where he had been shoved by a burly, heartless teacher, the precarious sets, the unexplained blackouts, the farcical, booming voice of the prompter and the strained smiles of the parents, particularly the fathers, at the end of the performance.

With an embarrassment that brought a blush flashing to my face, I recalled my own appearances on the stage: my schoolboy Friar Laurence who forgot to give Juliet the vital sleeping draught and therefore provided every opportunity for a happy ending. An obstinate Romeo insisted on falling on his sword anyway, and suggested afterwards that I should have done much the same myself.

My motorbike messenger in a modern-dress student

production of Molière's *L'École des femmes* had whiled away the time, until his brief and only appearance in the last act, at the theatre bar. He had then arrived (illegally) on a swerving pizza delivery motorbike, taken out a couple of courtiers and delivered his message. Due to the ill effects of several pints of strong lager, he was then seen roaring back out through the auditorium in the direction of the Gents before ever having the chance to listen to the return message. Fortunately, nobody noticed. The production was in French.

No, never would I get involved in theatricals again. Although, of course, it was for a good cause. Anyway, what on earth were we going to perform? Randall's *Hamlet*? *Oliver*? The setting was much the same. Dulabesh as the Artful Dodger. Or perhaps *The Sound of Indian Music* with the children appearing as the Family von Charuvat and featuring me as the lonely goatherd? Beckham and his inamoratas could make a guest appearance as my flock.

Laughing out loud, I frightened a motorbike, which was conveying homeward a family of five, children on laps and handlebars, their pretty mother riding side-saddle pillion. Unfortunately I caused it to swerve violently into the path of an oncoming camel. Sanjay weaved on through the traffic, as I hid inside the black hood of the rickshaw.

A play? No, it was impossible, quite unimaginable.

8

One Very Dumb Fellow

With my Indian directorial debut lurking worryingly in the back of my mind, fortunately there were plenty of other distractions. Abhishekh had been across the road to the factory a few days after the arrival of the elegant lady and had been shown by a smartly uniformed guard around our new 'school'. It proved to be very much to our liking. The premises comprised a wide-fronted, slightly dilapidated, low building, the top two-thirds of which was constructed entirely of wood which had probably been painted white at the time of its construction. The non-stop zoom of traffic had guaranteed that before long it had adopted its present colour, a remarkably authentic smoke grey. Smooth wooden steps led up to a narrow veranda that was piled with cardboard boxes, old filing cabinets, antiquated computers and other sundry junk. Inside was an enormous storage space and on all sides were piled huge amounts of papers, records, files and computer readouts, all thick with dust that was traced by the footprints and the regurgitations of several generations of rodents.

Above us, neat rows of naked light bulbs created a pleasingly symmetric pattern across the ceiling interspersed as they were by rusting fans. On the wall just inside the door was a bank of Bakelite light switches, one of which the guard flicked on experimentally with the end of his baton. Puffs of smoke, such as one might hope to see at an upmarket magician's show, shot out of the top of the electrics box just above the switches and absolutely nothing lit or turned. The guard shrugged, turned and clump-clumped his way down the steps and back across the car park to his air-conditioned office.

In one corner was an old porcelain sink with a tap that produced, after some considerable hesitation and a few bronchial gasps, some brown sludge and then a quite contented flow of bright water. At the back of the room were what appeared to be the doors to a large cupboard, but when we opened them we discovered a smaller room which, apart from a dozing black and white cat, was entirely empty.

Over the next few days we shifted all files and records into the empty room and set about cleaning and redecorating the main area. Harshada and the older girls squatted down on the rough wooden planks of the floor and scrubbed their way backwards to the front door, repeating the process two or three times until the planks looked as if they had just been sawn. They had to return to this task a few days later after I accidentally flipped over a dented tin of the home-made white-wash that we were using to brighten the room. They did so with a good-natured zest that rendered my apologies all the more useless. Embarrassed, I backed into a leathery old man dressed only in a white singlet and dhoti, that curious arrangement of cloth wrapped around the waist and hitched up between the legs, a cross between a skirt and festoon curtains. Electrician to the slum, Jyotish had come to fix the light switches. With the aid of some thick rubber gloves and nimble fingers that retreated hastily at the smallest crackle, he pulled open the scorched box. Armed only with a handleless screw-driver and a few pieces of silver paper which appeared to have come from a chewing gum wrapper, he poked and jabbed away until everything was in working order. Health and Safety inspectors were, in any event, unlikely to worry us.

As requested, I made up a list of our requirements and presented it to the elegant lady. Soon we had new piles of chalk and boxes of pencils and pens, all inscribed with the name of the company; for the younger children there was a blackboard on one wall, pallets of paint, puzzles and jigsaws, for the older ones, exercise books and several hundred second-hand paperbacks. We were set. On the very first day, when all the children and I crossed the road and walked up the steps for the first time, there was a palpable feeling of pride.

Kundanika, talking gently to the children, arranged them in seated lines and, as they closed their eyes and brought their hands together in prayer, they became quite still as in a melodious whisper they all started to recite a prayer.

> *'Oh my God, we love thee,*
> *We thank thee for all we see.*
> *Oh my God, let me be*
> *The best I can in praising thee.'*

And so a school routine slowly took shape and soon we were comfortable in our new surroundings. As we had agreed with our benefactor, we were joined by a number of the slum children and although some ran away, horrified by the vague order of the lessons, most stayed. They joined in smoothly, as many of them were already friendly with the children of the ashram, and came with us on our first official 'school trip'.

Sanjay provided a bus that had been saved in the nick of time from a wrecker's yard and a kind fruit seller had donated a few dozen bananas, which we converted into sandwiches for lunch. It was only when the children boarded the bus in a state of great excitement that I thought, for the first time in a long time, of my last school trip, an outing which had resulted in this whole adventure.

For these children, a day out and about was a rarity: the slum was as isolating as it was nurturing. Each of the windows in our vehicle was stuck permanently open, but the result was pleasant and the younger children enjoyed making faces into the wind, their eyes closed as they caught the breeze. We crossed over the river and down from the bridge where I could see women beating piles of laundry into wet, white circles of suds on long flat stones at the sluggish river's edge. As we neared the fringes of the town, the areas of open land became more and more widespread, until there was nothing more than a few shacks and a lot of goats.

High, ornate iron gates opened on to the winding driveway that led to a large open-fronted house bordered with a deep veranda – one of the many palaces belonging to the Aga Khan. Couples walked quietly around the fringes of pretty flowerbeds and there was an atmosphere of quiet reverence that contrasted starkly with the noisy hooting of the road beyond the entrance. It was here that one Mohandas Gandhi, the Mahatma, the Great Soul, and his closest associates had been placed under house arrest by the British, and here too where his wife and secretary had died. Their tombs stood at a little distance from the palace in the shade of a wooded grove.

Even Tanushri and Dulabesh became strangely quiet when we walked through the rooms that the great man had inhabited for nearly two years. We fell silent when we looked at the thin narrow white bed on which he had attended his wife, silent too when we looked at his modest possessions preserved in glass cabinets, wire-rimmed glasses and his wooden sandals – flat planks with uncomfortable pegs to slot between your toes. Sahas stood, visibly emotional, on the threshold of Gandhiji's bedroom murmuring the lines of the great man that were inscribed on a panel by the door:

'An infallible test of civilisation is that a man claiming to be civilised should be an intelligent toiler, that he should understand the dignity of labour and that his work should be such as to advance the interest of the community to which he belongs . . .'

Sahas looked at me questioningly and I did my best to simplify the English for him.

He smiled.

'Very beautiful, I think, Billbhaiya?'

I nodded.

Almost without remembering to breathe we filed through the simple, unadorned rooms until the last of our party reached the restoring sunlight. Dulabesh practised walking on his hands across the spongy grass, surprised by the green stains that it left on his hands and knees, while Kundanika lay down in the shade with the little children until, too restless in this wonderful new space, they jumped up again and raced each other down the neatly tended lawns The older boys chose to sit on a bench and sketch pictures of the palace whilst Unmesh pestered them about the architect, the building materials, the dimensions and specifications, and confused them with any number of other impossible questions and theories. Generally speaking, good-natured chaos reigned.

That afternoon we moved on to the ruined fortress of Shaniwar Wada on the edge of the bazaar in the middle of town, but first we had lunch in the shade of an enormous feathery tree. Sanjay appeared clutching the box full of banana sandwiches and the children drank from plastic bottles of water raised high above their mouths. There was much to stimulate young minds at Shaniwar Wada – giant spikes on the door designed to impale overeager invaders and an area outside on the edge of the humming bazaar where the Peshwar rulers had ordered that their enemies be trampled to death by beautifully decorated elephants. Here too the young children enjoyed this unusually large space to play and ran around in circles in a swirling, screaming game of tag before throwing themselves prostrate on the ground pleading for mercy from their opponents. An officious policeman had waved Sanjay on, his battered vehicle thought to be lowering the general tone of this national monument. Sanjay had had to move promptly rather than pay a fine, as bribes were popularly termed, so we agreed, Charuvat and I, that we would lead the children through the bazaar to the end of Laxmi Road and meet Sanjay at the dusty car park.

Zigzagging our way through the old town, we were all fascinated by the shiny, flashing, colourful stalls and shops. Two of the youngsters, Vijay and his younger sister Himaja, each held one of my hands as we stared at the beautiful rolls of cloth, the jewels and the bangles. A seller of bamboo pipes played a duet with his mischievous monkey. Vijay laughed when the monkey took a swipe at his owner for playing a wrong note and Himaja drew a little closer to me when it started skipping around on its long lead, its hand held out for baksheesh. Vijay dragged me down a side street, past shops selling 'Shirtings and Suitings' and then down another and another, left and right, down alleyways that seemed almost roofed in from the sky, all the while following a man above whose head floated a cloud of balloons and dozens of bags of pink candyfloss on sticks, and under whose arm was a clutch of silver paper kites. Only after a while did I realise that we had lost the others far behind in the depths of the bazaar. Haplessly, we turned this way and that in an attempt to backtrack to the main road, but it was impossible, the great carnival of the marketplace kaleidoscoping into one great inescapable muddle. Laughing, shouting, welcoming faces on all sides began to blur. The noise began to become intrusive, the din preventing me from getting my bearings, not allowing me to find my way out. To make matters worse it was beginning to get dark and the children were already tired. Suddenly I became obsessed by the sickening conclusions that the slum barons, the shadowy *zamindars*, would draw from my nonreappearance with Vijay and Himaja.

Somehow we stumbled on the place where we were supposed to meet Sanjay and his charabanc. It was deserted but for a man selling popcorn from a bag seven foot high. I ordered three portions for cheering-up purposes and we sat down on the pavement under a large hoarding advertising in bulging colour 'Ropey French-Cut Breifs'. We waited . . . and waited. Then, miraculously, out of the bluish gloom appeared the minotaur eye of an autorickshaw – at its helm was Sanjay. He looked grave as we climbed aboard and charged me twice the normal fare back to the ashram. Initially, he and Charuvat had decided that they would wait for us – no doubt throwing their eyes heavenward at the lack of sense of direction of their English friend as they slid back in their seats. Unfortunately for Sanjay, the uniformly hungry police – and as many of them lived in the slums, they did need to supplement their risible salaries substantially – seemed to track his every move and were soon demanding that he move on or fork at some much-appreciated baksheesh. He and Charuvat had, instead, driven back to the ashram to deliver the rest of the children and our knight astride his three-wheeled steed had returned to rescue us.

Sanjay hurried to the Professor the following day to have his general alignments checked because that night his stars had certainly not been in the ascendant. Hardly had we pulled out into the white-water traffic when a khaki-clad arm started to wave furiously while its partner clamped a silver whistle to a pair of furiously peeping lips. Releasing a stream of Marathi with such vehemence that I was left in little doubt about its probable content, Sanjay stamped on the brake and brought us to a bucking-bronco halt. It looked at first, when the two young policemen approached, as if it would be a simple case of 'fifty rupees and goodnight – oh OK, twenty-five if that is all you have got' until one of them spotted me.

Acting as if I might be on the way to assassinate the Prime Minister, he gestured at me to get out of the rickshaw, which I did, leaving Vijay and Himaja to gaze in consternation through the side bars of the machine at the two policemen who were gazing in consternation at me. One of them began to question me in what I think was Marathi. Whichever language it was it had the effect of making me sweat profusely. It also reminded me keenly of an unpleasant incident involving some French *gendarmes* on the Belgian border. That particular stand-off had resulted in me having to remove all, absolutely all, my clothes in the electrical generator room of the *douanes*. I had only narrowly avoided a probing, surgical-gloved investigation.

Looking at Sanjay in despair, I reached very slowly for my wallet, aware that at any moment the young policeman's rather rusty twelve-bore shotgun might be swung in my direction. Despite the tenseness of the situation I could not help thinking how odd it was that the end of each of the two barrels was plugged with a red plastic stopper – perhaps to keep the rain out. Fortunately Sanjay put on a magnificent display, which involved gesticulating open-handed at the little children and then clutching his heart, kneeling in supplication in the dirt before the retreating officers and then flicking his fingers dismissively at me whilst tapping his temple in disbelief.

Deciding that there must be easier opportunities to earn their living that evening, the two policemen disappeared into the crowd.

'Oh, you see, Mr Williams, it was most easy,' Sanjay replied with a flamboyant rev of his throttle when I enquired how he had procured our deliverance. 'I am just telling this police wallah that these two children, they are my young children. Then I tell them that you are one crazy man from the Osho and you are one very dumb fellow – just getting lost in the bazaar. They look at you and they are straight away believing me. Yes, they are saying, he is one dumb fellow too! Ha, ha! Yes, ha, ha!'

'Mmm, yes, I see, ha, ha, ha!'

That evening at the Aakash Garden Restaurant, which I reached late but much relieved, all seemed to be quite normal. I read the *Maharashtra Bugle* as usual and discovered that the Prohibitionist Ladies of Poona were threatening direct action, that the police were going to be on holiday so that motorbike riders would be able to leave their helmets at home without coming to any harm and, of course, that England had lost another cricket match.

In one corner Devashva, Mr Dikshin Doegar's son, was tormenting a sleeping customer by tickling one of his hairy ears with a piece of palm leaf. The waiters looked on impassive, impotent, as the boy reappeared from behind a pillar each time the unfortunate man nodded off. Now was my chance to remonstrate with him, something I had been hoping to do for some time, as his doting father seemed to pay little attention to his regular bad behaviour. Unfortunately, just at that moment I was introduced by my waiter friend Kamal, with some business deal no doubt in mind, to Ali Baba, the jeweller of Koregaon Park, who was sitting at a table opposite me. This dark, dashing merchant from Kashmir with carefully curled moustaches was alone, bereft of any of his forty thieves, as he called his drinking friends, gazing disconsolately into his 'peg' of 'Royal Stag' Indian whisky and bemoaning the extraordinary nature of the European mind.

'You know, my friend, you know, I just cannot understand the way you fellows are thinking. Every day I have white ladies from Osho. They come in my small shop to buy. Very good. Very nice. I show them beautiful necklace and bangles. They like. I like. So then we start to bargain. I ask a price – let's say two thousand rupees. Of course I want to sell at maybe one thousand. Maybe if it is beautiful lady not so much – maybe nine hundred, eight hundred. Then, can you imagine, the lady says: "No, I know Indian bargaining. I won't pay two thousand rupees, only sixteen hundred." So then, of course, I must bargain a little bit. It is the way. So then I sell at one thousand eight hundred! What can I do?'

He shook his head and bought me a drink.

'You must come to my shop sometime. You will be most welcome.'

I thought that I probably would.

'And can I ask? One more thing. Why do you use paper, you know, in the toilet? It is very strange. What is wrong with water? Much better? More cleanly? What are you thinking? Very strange European people . . . Anyway, you can come, you are always my guest.'

9

Wilbur the Pig

Boat Club Road is a wider, quieter, more refined street than most in Poona and runs parallel to a strip of river on which, if you were brave or hardy enough, I suppose you could boat. Many of the buildings on either side date from before the war and, although grimy, still hold the character of a time gone by. Others are modern, with clear-cut lines, although those still under construction are given a surreal, wonky appearance by the roped-together bamboo scaffolding in which they are clad. As I approached one late afternoon, men scampered along the skinny poles with buckets of white-wash and cement carried on their heads, shouting, waving their arms, smoking, eating and drinking – in fact, doing just about everything but holding on.

Despite the astonishment I had initially felt doing nothing more than walking down the street, I seemed to have now fitted in quite happily to Indian life. Indeed, I was occasionally rather disdainful of new arrivals at Osho as they shrieked and jumped at everything that happened differently from the way things were 'back home'. Soon, of course, they too became inured to the seamier side of the street and for the main part seemed to cope by ignoring or overlooking everything that struck them as unpleasant. At least I felt that I was doing my best to engage with the world in which I was now living.

On the right about halfway down stands a large, almost ceremonial arch and against it on one side leans a small kiosk-cum-sentry's hut. Through the archway is an elegant area of garden surrounded by large houses, each with its own individual sentry's hut. I was always a little bemused by this insistence on visible security, particularly because, as in the case of Drupad, the defenders of homes and livelihoods were generally not in their first youth and, more often than not, were asleep.

There was a faint stirring from the uniformed figure the day that I first arrived for my yoga class. I had progressed quite well with a small booklet entitled 'Yoga for Children – a Teacher's Handbook' that I had found in the classroom. Apart from one worrying occasion when I thought I might have to call upon the assistance of my neighbour, Mrs Chaturashringi, and her daughter to extract me from a complicated position, during which my knee had locked at a crucial moment, I believed I was getting the benefits of yoga. Consequently, I decided that I should pursue it rather than allow it to sneak off quietly as so many of my past interests had done. So I had answered an advertisement in the *Maharashtra Bugle*: 'Yoga for standards from beginning to master. Classes for Lady and Gentlemen or Lady and Gentleman separate.' Fortunately there was a session – one designed for lady and gentlemen – that started in the early evening and meant that I could attend it directly from the ashram.

Mrs Bindra's apartment was spacious and spotless. On a grand piano at one end of the large drawing room stood a picture of a very tired-looking Mr Bindra who had moved on to his heavenly abode a few years earlier. This, no doubt, with some relief as Mrs Bindra was a woman of inexhaustible energy. A shy maid opened the door but was almost immediately ushered out of the way as Mrs Bindra bounded on to the scene.

'Ah, you must be Randoz!' she cried, dressed in a thick, pea-green, towelling tracksuit and matching large *bindi* mark in the middle of her forehead. She flexed at the knees a few times and did something strange and painful-sounding to her wrists as she asked me what it was that I was doing in India.

Without pausing for any possible response, she continued, 'So perhaps you are very good at yoga? I have been doing it ever since I was a small girl. You know sometimes it is almost a way of life. I really don't know where I would be without my classes and, of course, without my wonderful master, Ivor Patel.'

At that moment there appeared from behind a screen that stood at an angle in the corner of the room a slight but wiry man in his sixties. Gandhiji himself would have approved of his style of dress: a plain white shawl arranged rather too carefully over his powerful shoulders matched his smart loin-cloth but, unlike the Mahatma, whose scalp had been clean-shaven, Ivor Patel was the proud owner of a long and rather straggly beard, and thick, lengthy curls of hair which were bunched on the top of his head; the hirsute ensemble looked as if it could have benefited from a good scrub. Somehow despite this he managed to emanate a sense of great serenity. He did not address me directly, but instead smiled and made his way to the far end of the over-decorated sitting room. With an extraordinary fluidity of motion he sat down cross-legged on the intricately patterned mat that had been laid out for him by the maid. Slipping off my clean socks and shoes and leaving them in a tidy heap by the door, I was beginning to feel anxious about the whole experience. I felt stupid, dressed as I was in totally inappropriate gear. Now, before it was too late, I began to wonder, as I often do, what sort of lurid excuse I could dream up to leave again. There was no point me being here, anyway; I was wholly unsuited to these sort of gymnastic capers – I could hardly touch my toes let alone tie myself in knots. Just as I was formulating the unlikely reasons for a house fire at Ashoka Villas and a sudden vision thereof, which would necessitate my imme-diate departure, the doorbell rang again. The maid hardly bothered to move as Mrs Bindra bounded for the door once more and opened it to a gaggle of overenthusiastic women dressed in similar outfits to their hostess. From the puffing and fanning it seemed that they had jogged their way to the class. They all looked rather puzzled at my presence but to a woman brought up their hands in greeting which I returned rather proficiently.

'So I think we are all ready, Mr Patel?' suggested Mrs Bindra uncharacteristically gently.

'But surely we are waiting for that nice English girl who was here before?' An elderly lady with thick glasses and a headband that appeared to be inside out sought support from the other ladies who were already sitting. They nodded their agreement and rearranged themselves.

'Indeed yes,' interjected Mr Patel with a twinkle and to our general surprise, 'yes, I am very much hoping that she will be coming along to join us. She has so many possibilities. Yes, yes, really fantastic possibilities . . .'

Mrs Bindra blushed beneath her headband and seemed about to say something when the doorbell rang again. This time the maid seized her opportunity and wrenched the handle back.

'Sorry, sorry, always getting lost; it's all so confusing here – what with the traffic and everything – I just don't think I will ever get my head round it, do you know what I mean? Gosh, sorry, Mrs Bindra. Has everybody been waiting for me? How absolutely awful, I'm *so* sorry!'

A twentysomething blonde girl also dressed in sporting attire was fizzing round the room kissing in the rough direction of the rather baffled ladies that were waiting.

'Well here I am, and ready, absolutely ready.' She sat down with a bit of a bounce on a spare corner of mat.

For the next hour or so I was directed by Mr Patel to stretch and twist my body into positions that nature, or even nurture, had surely never intended. My rather lackadaisical approach to the exercises shown in my beginner's guide seemed to be of absolutely no use here. I waited with great concern to hear some part of me pop or click, for me only then to discover that the joint was no longer useful or would no longer return to its original position. Eventually, after having been instructed to lie as flat as I possibly could on my back on the really very comfortable carpet, I had to be gently woken by a solicitous Mrs Bindra with the offer of a cup of jasmine tea.

'Isn't it such fun, simply marvellous? I feel so much better, don't you?' Before I had a chance to answer, the enthusiastic and very pretty English girl took a sip from a plastic bottle of water and carried on. 'I come here for a month every six months just to see darling Mr Patel – even though he is a bit naughty, isn't he? He says some of the most outrageous things, you know, just when you're getting in position! But he is so masterful, isn't he? I just get back home feeling so refreshed. Which way are you going?'

We crossed Boat Club Road and she chatted on merrily.

'Of course, I find India very difficult to cope with some-times; you know, it can be so hot, so many people. I do feel useless, you know, but I'm not really that kind of person . . . err . . . In fact you see I'm an actress. You know, I've done a couple of seasons in rep and one with the National but even so, you know. Pretty good . . .'

'Oh, yes. No, very good!' I was much impressed.

'You see, the trouble is we don't spend a lot of time in the real world. We tend to surround ourselves with art. India can be such a shock to the system. Are you with me?'

Well, as I watched her spring pneumatically up on to the high pavement, I thought I probably was.

A small herd of donkeys came slipping and sliding round the corner, their bony bodies hardly remaining upright as they came cantering towards us over the tarmac. Fenella, my companion, shrieked most realistically and I was caught halfway between throwing myself gallantly in front of her or setting off as fast as I could in the opposite direction. Fortunately, despite their erratic progress, the animals managed to divide themselves either side of us and made their clattering, uncer-tain way on down the road.

'I'm not sure I'm terribly good at coping with all this, you know!'

'No, well, I'm not sure that I am either. Quite tough some-times, isn't it?' I agreed soothingly.

Fenella sighed again as we passed a group of women who, wielding hefty sledgehammers, were breaking stones from an enormous pile that had been dumped on the pavement. Their bright saris and gaudy jewellery glittered even more than normal against their sweating skin. Further along the road, a man dressed in a vest and tablecloth skirt was indolently pouring liquid tar from a watering can as if tending to his prize roses.

'Look at him, lazy thing! Oooh it makes me so cross.' She scrunched up her face in a most affecting way. 'Perhaps I should have a word with him, do you think so, Randoz? By the way, where does a name like that come from?'

Sighing, I explained the problems I seemed to have with my name. I also offered her a lift, suggesting at the same time that direct intervention with the road gang was probably ill-advised.

'Oh, I suppose you're right. It does make you cross though, doesn't it?' She looked back crossly, fetchingly, like a modern-day Joan of Arc. 'Oh well, "The quality of mercy" et cetera, et cetera, you know.'

'Oh yes, "To be or not to be",' I replied rather feebly.

Fortunately, Sanjay was still lurking around talking to his friends and waiting for my reappearance. Fenella and I both climbed aboard. Sanjay, who could hardly believe his eyes, smiled at me enthusiastically and muttered about 'Madame from England, very beautifully I think,' as he yanked the starter lever of the autorickshaw. I could see him glancing repeatedly in his rearview mirror, gazing at her with a mixture of rever-ence and lust, although I was under the distinct impression that his hormones had a galloping upper hand over his respect.

To my surprise Fenella asked to be taken to the Blue Diamond – by some distance the smartest hotel in town. She invited me in for a drink, which for a variety of reasons I accepted. When we arrived Sanjay enquired whether he should wait and I, for a variety of similar reasons, told him that I did not want to keep him from home any longer than was necessary.

'I do feel badly about staying in a place like this, you know, but I find it all so difficult to cope with otherwise. Do you think that is terrible of me? I do feel awfully guilty about it most of the time,' Fenella admitted as we stepped into the white-marble cool.

A couple of the *sanyasins* from Osho wandered ethereally through the lobby rubbing essential oils into themselves, audibly 'omming'. They were quite clearly not feeling guilty about anything at all.

We took the lift to the top floor.

'So why are you in India, Will?' she enquired genuinely as she propped herself up on some pink pillows and I perched on the edge of the bed. 'Are you on some sort of spiritual quest too?'

'No, not really . . .'

I went on to explain to her how it was that I found myself living in India and I took pleasure and no small pride in telling her about the ashram, the children and what it was that we did there. It was then, suddenly, that I remembered our planned production. Here I had a professional within – well, almost within – my grasp! Anyway, um, did she have any good ideas about, you know, some sort of play?

'Well, it depends if you want to do something Indian or European, doesn't it? Hey, why don't I call you Wilbur? Wilbur – like Wilbur the Pig! Like in the children's book. Oh, what's it called? You don't mind Wilbur, do you?'

'Oh, no. Absolutely not!' And strangely, just at that moment, I didn't. I would advise against anyone trying the same again.

'So let's think then . . . well if it's Indian, let me see. Oh of course! It's got to be the Ramayana, I mean really, it's got to be your first choice. Nice big cast, lots of songs and music, yes, movement and dance. You've got love, emotions, action, excitement, the works. Now that's what I would definitely go for. It'll be absolutely marvellous, Wilbur.' She patted the bed next to her enthusiastically. 'In fact I'm quite tempted to give you a hand – oh, if only I didn't have to go back to London! I've got a great new part in a great new show with Ken.' She drew a hand to her chest at the thought. 'What a shame, how exciting, sounds fantastic. God, wish I could get involved, sounds really amazing.'

'The Rammy – what did you say?' I asked, uncertain whether to shift a little further over to ensure I got to the bottom of it.

'The Ramayana – it is one of the central stories of the Hindu religion. Surely you know it? The story of the fight between good and evil, between Rama and Ravana, the capture and rescue of the beautiful Princess Sita. Gosh, it's so stimulating, so thrilling, so theatrical. You're going to absolutely love it.'

'I see, so what exactly do you do when you put on a play? I mean how should I start? I mean, I mean, well I mean – are you sure you wouldn't like to stay?'

'I'd love to get involved, honestly I would. But you'll be fine, I'm sure you will.' She stroked my hand in the most comforting way. 'You know, our work doesn't come up all the time and I really have to make the most of all my opportunities. You will let me know how it all goes, won't you?'

'Yes, OK, but I really don't think I know what to do.'

'Just feel it, Wilbur, just feel it.' She seemed to move closer in a spirit of artistic camaraderie. 'Just feel it.'

Then, just as I was about to move over a bit further in the hope of closer creative involvement, the emotion of the moment suddenly appeared to become too much for her. Seemingly exhausted she flopped back on the bed and closed her eyes.

'Now I think I will have to have a rest. So lovely to meet you, Wilbur. Good luck with everything. I am sure that it will go swimmingly. Goodbye. Goodbye.'

'Oh, right, goodbye then. Thanks. Bye?'

There appeared to be no further movement from Fenella so after a bit of toing and froing and hard thinking, I gave up and let myself out of the hotel room door.

Never mind.

So yet again I found myself about to embark on a venture for which I was singularly ill-qualified. However, as I now appeared to be making something of a habit of it, I felt strangely less apprehensive than I had before.

Having spent as long as I could walking the air-conditioned corridors and boutiques in order to avoid the heat and dust clouds of the afternoon, I made my way through the gilt and glass doors and out into the palm-tree-shaded courtyard where I was not greatly surprised to see Sanjay asleep in the back of his rickshaw in the shimmering heat. I woke him gently by rocking his machine.

'Wi*iii*lbur, oh, Wilbur, stop, stop!' Fenella came storming through the front doors, dressed in a white bathrobe, a bath towel twisted on top of her head. She appeared to have had the time to apply some curious greeny brown unguent to her face before she realised the importance of finding me again. 'Oh, thank goodness for that. I thought you might have left and that I wouldn't have been able to get hold of you again. Quick, quick, come back upstairs to my room – I've got something terribly important and exciting to ask you.'

'Oh, righto!'

We hurried back inside to the great surprise of the doormen and, not least, of Sanjay who looked on bleary and bewildered but, I thought as I was yanked into the lift, rather admiringly.

Pushing me into the room she closed the door behind her with a flourish. A terry-towelling, verdant Cleopatra, she looked at me breathlessly.

'I completely forgot to ask you – can you act?'

'What?'

'Can you . . .' she was breathing hard now. 'Act?'

'Act?'

'Yes, you know, act.' She spread her arms and took a couple of little steps to left and right. 'ACT!'

Yes, well, why not? In reality, I admit, apart from my afore-mentioned theatrical disasters, I had only really ever appeared as the handle of a teapot and, rather reluctantly, a hedgehog in a couple of plays at primary school. But if I could direct, surely I could have another go at acting? There could not really be anything too much to it. Anyway, why did she want to know?

She stroked my chest in her enthusiasm.

'This is fantastic,' she murmured.

I could only agree.

10

Let's Go Fly a Kite

Near the Osho Commune, in the small parade of shops, was a bookseller specialising in 'Mystical and the Spiritual Books'. Owned, somewhat surprisingly, in this male-oriented commercial world, by a mother and daughter team, the high-ceilinged room was a maze of different piles of books stacked horizontally according to their category. Thanks to our daily power cut, light came only through the front door and a small grille high up in the back wall, so, as I hunted along the shelves, the younger of the two women approached me with a torch, aiming it so that I could see the names on the spines.

'*Chai*, Mister? Or perhaps some coffee?' asked the older woman who was seated on a stool behind a low table, two legs of which I noticed were made up of piles of books. I wondered what would happen if I wished to purchase one.

'Well, perhaps some tea would be nice.' I had grown by this stage to enjoy the tiny cups of horribly sweet mud-coloured liquid, although more than one cup at a time had a racing effect similar to that of those tiny cups of coffee that are served up to shaky, pale, chain-smoking women in Parisian cafés.

Reaching under the table, where a number of incense sticks were burning, she lit a small gas ring and expertly balanced on it a small brass saucepan with a long black wooden handle.

'Just one minute, please ...' She adjusted the flame. 'So

please tell me, Sahib, what sort of reading material are you looking for?'

'Well, actually I was looking for a copy of the Ramayana.' Fenella had fired me with enthusiasm.

I sat down on the low stool that was pulled out for me. It was extraordinarily uncomfortable.

'Oh, the Ramayana, that is most interesting. You are interested in our holy writings? You are a scholar from England perhaps? From one of your fine universities? You know, of course, of our university here in Poona? You know we call it the Oxford of the East? Perhaps you have given lectures here?'

'Well, yes, no, no, no' was my lame response in reply to the barrage of questions, though I need not have worried too much because the old lady had already turned away and was arranging a wooden ladder against the wall. Her daughter holding it steady by sitting on the bottom rung, she climbed up with remarkable agility to a shelf above the front door. After a few 'left, right' directions called down to me over her shoulder, so that I might shift the beam of the torch about to help her find what it was she was looking for, she removed what appeared at that height to be a large cardboard box. Somehow she succeeded in tucking it under her arm like a washing basket and descended again.

'This one, I think you will be liking very much. A most beautiful edition and I think I can make a very nice price for this one.' Regardless of the price, I wondered how I would ever get it home. On closer inspection, I realised that it was obviously a volume of some antiquity, bound in leather, the surface of which had become rough with use.

'It is certainly very beautiful. So what, so what sort of price would you think this would be selling for?'

'Well perhaps we can discuss the price afterwards. I am sure you would prefer looking first.' I recognised the sales technique: Sanjay had taught me well. Make sure that the customer was interested and then get down to extensive bargaining.

'No, really, how much do you think this would be? Perhaps

it would be too expensive for me?' This anyway was a question I already knew the answer to.

'Oh, no. I don't think so. Let's see.' She slipped on her glasses. Pulling a desk calculator towards her she stabbed a few buttons idly as she wondered where she could start off the bidding. She hit the 'Clear' button and then punched in her chosen figure and, turning the calculator about, slithered it across the table towards me.

'Sixty thousand and five hundred rupees?'

This was luckily going to be no contest.

'No, I think that will be too difficult for me.'

'But please have a look inside. You will agree it is the most beautiful volume.'

She started to gently turn the pages.

'It comes from one of the ancient palaces, you know. We are so lucky to have it here. We do not really want to sell it – but of course we know that you would look after it very carefully in your university.'

'Err yess . . .' I coughed in a suitably professorial fashion. Actually, it was beautiful, richly illustrated with painted, gilded, fabulous engravings of weird animals and gods.

Oh dear, here I was again. Since I had arrived in India, I was forever trying to extricate myself from complicated business dealings. Where was Sanjay when I needed to be rescued?

This time, however, I realised I was in luck.

'Oh, what a shame! Of course this copy is in Hindi. Unfortunately we will not be able to use that. I must have a copy in English.'

'But you will be able to translate it for your students!'

The ironies of this conversation were beginning to become too complicated.

'No, I must have something in English, please,' I said as firmly as possible. 'Maybe something simplified, something for children?'

Masking her disappointment reasonably successfully, the lady turned to her daughter and said something in Hindi –

possibly slightly dismissively – before busying herself with the brew under the table. The young girl took back her flashlight and disappeared off to the back of the shop while her mother ladled out the cups of tea.

There seemed to be no shortage of versions of the Ramayana as she returned with a pile of a dozen or so different-shaped volumes of varying thickness. Despite my protestations that I needed an English version, some were in foreign languages and alphabets, some annotated, some illustrated, but the copy that caught my eye was one entitled *The Children's Ramayana* – a paperback of forty or so pages seemed a lot easier to grapple with than the six-hundred-odd that I had seen in the tome placed in front of me earlier. It was also the cheapest copy there – probably the reason that I felt left duty-bound to come away with a number of other books, all suitably erudite for a confirmed academic but destined to bore me silly. They were wrapped up in sheets of the *Maharashtra Bugle*, the good wishes of the shop owner thrown in for free.

After I had acquainted myself a little better with the story of the Ramayana, I realised that Fenella had been quite right about the fantastic possibilities of the play – though some of the events of the story were going to cause us some significant technical challenges.

Casting the play, on the other hand, was relatively straightforward – the younger children, who spoke little English and could read none at all, could be employed as a rent-a-mob; the advantage of their age too was that they appeared to be willing to do anything, however ludicrous, without so much as a blink of embarrassment. The secondary characters were drawn from the quieter youngsters and, depending on how communicative or reticent they were, I awarded them smaller or larger roles.

There were only really four major parts to be worried about: Lord Rama, all-round good chap, saviour of the universe; Princess Sita, his sweet but not overly bright wife; Hanuman his faithful assistant, his Robin to Rama's Batman, but with a greater sense of impish fun and without the tights and the exclamations. Then of course there was Ravana, King of Lanka and evil incarnate.

Abhishekh, the oldest boy by at least two or three years, declared himself unavailable for selection – 'I don't think it's my kind of thing, Mr Williams, I'm always being a little embarrassed in front of other people.' Despite this the characters all seemed to fall into place relatively easily. The cheeky Hanuman could only really be played by Dulabesh who although a little young was mischievous and energetic. His gymnastic antics would be well suited to the role of the monkey king. Kundanika, although the oldest girl and, as ever, willing to do anything to please, was altogether too quiet and softly spoken to play the part of the princess. She was also about three inches taller than any of the boys and would certainly be more useful helping to organise and possibly control the younger ones. So it meant that pretty and sweetly spoken Tanushri, however sleepy, vacant and on occasions silly she might be, would play Sita. Sahas was the obvious choice to play Lord Rama because he seemed to possess an innate nobility; he was capable of melancholy on occasion, certainly, but his simple ability to behave with dignity in any situation and above all his resolute air of bravery meant it was perfectly believable that he might take on the evil forces of the universe.

The wicked Ravana was considerably more difficult to cast. Tall and domineering, he needed to tower over his enemies in order to be able to dish out his evil powers, and none of the children in the ashram was markedly taller than any other. This Ravana was also so feared and hated that I was not sure that any of them would be happy to play the Devil who would attempt to destroy the beloved Lord Rama.

Problems of height were solved by the scientifically minded Unmesh who, having studied the book that I had brought back from the shop, had come to me with a design demonstrating a hideous representation of Ravana and a side-on view showing a small person sitting on the shoulders of a larger one. As it was he that had designed this particular arrangement, I suggested that he might like to play the top part, to which he agreed happily, rushing away to tell his friends the news. Three minutes later he came back to me and apologised, saying that he was really sorry, but he wasn't sure that he could play the part after all as he didn't think that Ravana would wear glasses. Laughing, I reminded him that he would be disguised and so therefore need not worry.

'Oh, yes, good, that's no problem. So you are liking me making a new drawing?'

I assured him that I would and he disappeared out into the yard with his pad tucked under his arm, sitting down in the shade against the rear wheel of the elegant lady's white limousine.

It turned out to be the mild-mannered Prakash, the most affable and least domineering of all the children, who volunteered to play 'the Legs'. Thanks to his great good nature, he did not mind playing the villain of the piece if it meant helping out; solidly built and strong, he also had the added advantage of being able to carry little Unmesh for the duration of the performance.

Rehearsals were to take place in the yard outside our new classroom and I was beginning to feel quite the part – the great director. But after our first rehearsal session, an unmitigated disaster which took place after lessons, I very nearly abandoned the whole project.

One little boy appeared at the rehearsal with a kitten under his shirt which mewed incessantly to remind us all how sweet it was, and although I did my best not to stroke it too, it seemed to have the most dominating role in the proceedings. Eventually we all gave up and watched it prance and skitter around the wooden floor of the classroom, chasing balls and climbing up chair legs until it, like us, rolled up and had a snooze on the thin straw mats on which we had been acting. It was all very frustrating.

We tried again.

The older actors amazed me by their diligence and had seemingly learnt all their lines within a few days. This was partly because they took the same approach to our play as they did to their studies: dedicated, serious and tenacious. But it was also certainly true that because the Ramayana itself was so much a part of their upbringing, their task was made much easier by their prior knowledge of the tale; the titan struggle between Rama and Ravana was a story that they had heard from their earliest childhoods.

These children were no cynics, they had not been spoilt by an excess of 'opportunity', and were willing to take the story on all its levels: an exciting adventure story of superheroes battling one another across the continents, a story full of romance and comradeship, a tale of exciting battles fought, heroic deeds undertaken in the shadow of the dark forces; as they grew older, however, they also came to recognise within the story many of the great issues which they themselves would have to countenance as they grew up in the India of the twenty-first century. Good and evil were clearly delineated for them. Certainly in the ashram the values that they held had been inculcated in them from an early age, and there was remarkably little rancour about the often strict discipline and limited possibilities of their lives. This translated itself into a willingness to work long hours to get their performances right. In a world where not a great deal was certain and, for many of them, little had been permanent, they seemed perfectly happy to try to accommodate my ever-changing ideas, willing to try out my suggestions, however impractical, just enjoying the atmosphere of camaraderie and the sense of belonging.

Extraordinarily, the little children, although they tired much more quickly than the older ones, were pleasingly compliant – keen to make sure that this was a success. They were disciplined and polite when I attempted to explain something, unselfconscious when I asked them to do all sorts of ludicrous things – all in stark contrast to the vain, self-obsessed, self-important youngsters I had most recently taught at home.

After that first rehearsal, as I sat on the roof of the ashram and watched the children flying home-made kites, I imagined the effect this world might have on some of the pupils at my last school. How would they respond if I could air-drop just a few of them – Black Marker Pen and some of his mates, for example – into the Tanjiwadi slum? With a grim smile, I imagined their retching reaction to the smell and the dirt, the food – or the lack of it – and the heat. When they realised that there was nobody to hold their hands, let them off their most recent misdemeanour, dole out their pocket money, 'my allowance', or buy them the latest gear, would they collapse, give up – cry? Or would they be impressed by the standard of self-survival set by these children, their industry and their enthusiasm? Perhaps they would be able to realise their talents and rediscover strengths that had withered or had never bloomed in the choking ether of British society, through which they blundered anaesthetised, blinded, by commercialisation?

Gazing down at Beckham, who, tail in air, was grumpily but copiously ejecting the end product of a great deal of vegetation, it was impossible to tell.

Closing my eyes, I leaned back against the low wall that separated the roofs of the two ashram buildings. My directorial debut had taken its toll and, as so often when it was this hot, I began to drift away.

Somewhere out of the clouds of my dream flitted childish, crayon images of home – bright green fields, houses with square façades, symmetrical windows and carefully tiled roofs. Friendly animals, cats and dogs and tortoises and hamsters, poked out from behind expensive cars. Children with toys chased one another down well-ordered streets, and loving couples with blue eyes and pink cheeks kissed each other in comfortable bedrooms – all in a happy kaleidoscope of pictures which suddenly before my dreaming eyes seemed to rip and tear as if clawed away by revealing fingers. When the last curling ribbon fell away, I could make out a new scene of immense activity: human beings toiling, crawling one over the other with relentless effort, twisting this way and that, all seemingly in an attempt to find their way into a faint light that glimpsed in at the sides of the dark, stifling scene. The picture stretched into a distance that my brain could not adjust to, but strangely, and I still remember this discovery now, every human figure had its own distinctive face.

Across my consciousness passed a mysterious shape. So close did it fly that I felt the air waft the sweat on my forehead providing me with the briefest relief from the heat of the afternoon. Suddenly, returned to the world, I woke to discover the tangled remains of two kites lying beside me, the grimy strings draped across my chest.

'Hurrah!'

Dulabesh was leaping from one foot to the other, performing a little triumphal dance by swinging his arms high above his head and then down below his knees.

'Hurrah, Billbhaiya! Look, we are taking one kite from Shivajinagar! It is a nice one! Hurrah!'

Turning on my side and giving my face a brief rub with one hand, I watched as Unmesh, his tongue sticking out in his excitement and his intense concentration, set about disconnecting his kite from the downed 'enemy' much as a falconer might a rabbit from strong claws. Shivajinagar, the chosen foe, was the slum that lay across the way, on the other side of the midden that passed as a municipal waterway, the thick, black sludge that oozed its way between these two parts of town.

Looking up I could see that there were a dozen or so kites, all of the same twig and plastic bag construction, flying on either side of the divide. Red plastic bags from the enemy camp, blue from ours, they stood up in the wind like the heads of so many hooded cobras, their bodies long twisting tails of ribbon made from strips of matching plastic. Small boys and girls weaved their bodies this way and that, teasing invisible lines in a hope of bending their craft across the path of the enemy. Once they crossed then the rush was frantic. Spooling grey string heaped on the ground as hand over small hand they tried to pull the entangled kites over to one side or the other. The winner landed his opponent's on his own side, often narrowly missing toddlers who were just happy to throw up a wispy broken bag and watch it waft over the rooftops and weeping, suffocating trees.

Unmesh had naturally devised his own flying machine, constructed from thick black plastic stretched over a frame of old umbrella spokes. With its two separate strings, it could perform lethal acrobatics. Now, holding it by the top, he lifted it into the air and watched it blow away from him. Quickly he turned and began to guide it into the burning sky.

'Well done, Unmesh. That was a bit of luck!'

Unmesh gave me a small, rather annoyed frown over his shoulder as he steered his fighter into battle. Clearly luck, as far as he was concerned, had nothing to do with it.

'Did you have nice dreams, Billbhaiya?' Kundanika, accompanied by Sahas and Prakash, had just climbed up the little ladder on to the roof. Below them I could still see Beckham watching the acrobatics with some disapproval as, with practised lips, he tried to fit a whole swede into his mouth at once.

The girl smiled at me and I laughed, still yawning.

'Yes, very nice dreams thanks.'

'What do you think about when you are dreaming, Billbhaiya?' Sahas asked seriously.

The darkness of earlier started to creep in again but I forced it back out.

'Oh, nothing in particular. Just about home, family, friends. I mean . . . err . . . not that much, um, lots of things.' I was aware for a change of my faux pas. Anxious not to leave the silence hanging, I carried on, 'So, well, I was going to say . . . So what do you dream about?'

Sahas paused, frowning.

'Well, sometimes I dream of travelling away. You know, to be going to other places. Like you, Billbhaiya. Going to magic places.'

'And you, Kundanika? What do you dream about?'

'Oh, I dream of a husband and some happy childrens. That I would like it very much. A small nice house for us to live in the country. That is my dream.' Quickly she looked away, embarrassed at being so outspoken, but her words seem to carry weight with the two boys too. We sat for a while in silence as Unmesh cruised the sky above us and Tanushri looked on in admiration.

'I feel a kind of joy when we talk.'

Sahas seemed surprised that the words had come from him, seemingly out of nowhere, but he looked me straight in the eye nonetheless and nodded once hard. At the moment the simple phrase sank in, I felt as if I had won a million pounds, or been knighted by the Queen or both. My face flushing deeply, my skin tingled.

'No, it is true,' enjoined Prakash. 'We are liking you very much.'

For some reason, I could not listen, not out of modesty – far from it. Perhaps, although I am not sure, it was from a fear that somehow I might fail them, disappoint them – that they would lose their faith in me and, consequently, in some curious way, themselves.

Dulabesh had somehow managed to crash-land his kite behind enemy lines and was now teetering along a rusting metal pipe high above the sludgy ooze. Soon he had crossed to the other side and, dodging a larger boy, had disappeared down one of the side-alleys; as if he now suddenly found himself in a cartoon, he kept appearing at doors and openings, lanes and side streets, pursued by an ever-swelling group of children. Just when I thought we had lost him, he darted from behind a shabby cloth and began to head back across the pipe, kite in hand. Although the 'opposition' baulked at the idea of following him across the dangerous bridge, they soon equipped themselves with an impressive range of projectiles with which to try and wrong-foot him. Two-thirds of the way across, an old thongless sandal caught him a clip across the shoulder and he looked for a moment as if he might tip into the thick, probably dangerous, manure below. When, finally, he righted himself and scampered back home, the huge sense of relief that I felt made me realise, all of a surprising sudden, how much store I now set by the future success of these children.

'So,' Prakash had continued as I watched, 'we are hoping that our playing will be very nice for you.'

'Our play, you mean?' I corrected gently. 'Yes, I hope it will be too.'

11

Rolling!

'Silence, silence please!'
'Ready . . . rolling.'
'And action!'

'And the sentence of this court is that the prosecution will be sentenced to imprison—'

'Cut, cut!' bellowed the megaphone that pointed from the canvas chair in the corner of the room and the short, chubby legs in tight trousers folded and unfolded themselves in exasperation beneath it. 'Oh no! Oh no, Mr Williams, you have goofed again! Randall has goofed again.'

The diminutive director addressed this last damning proof of my incompetence to one of his assistants seated by his side, notes in hand. The latter nodded enthusiastically and, as the director waddled over to my Judge's desk, I was sure I could see the sycophant who hung on his every word start to write down the 'g' of 'goof'.

'Now Randall, please try to remember you are sending the defendant to prison – only the defendant.'

'OK, Ravi, I'll get it right this time, don't you worry,' I replied and sneezed as one of the horsehairs of my wig tickled my right nostril. I could hardly see the director in front of me for the sweaty slick of make-up that was pouring off my forehead. To further confuse my dulled mind, I could not help thinking that there had been a dreadful mistake with my name and that the two or three hundred people crammed on to the tiny courtroom set all thought my name was Randall – Randall Williams. Although, now I thought about it a bit more, it did have a certain ring – I tried it again under my breath with an authentic American accent.

'Starring Randall Williams . . .'

The beheadphoned soundman looked up sharply in my direction and I suddenly remembered the tiny microphone hidden in the folds of my robes. I gave him a little wave and he raised an eyebrow in return.

'Ready now, Randall?' demanded Ravi grumpily.

'Ready,' I replied as I turned my attention to Sanjeev, the Bollywood superhero who stood in the dock. At that moment he was having his stick-on moustache attended to by a paint-brush-wielding technician. This proved troublesome for the cheerful make-up man as Sanjeev insisted on smoking a cheroot at the same time.

'Are you ready now, dear Sanjeev?'

'*Do* minute,' came the inevitable reply. After a couple more puffs, Sanjeev held out his cigarillo as a conductor might his baton and immediately, as if from nowhere, a hand holding an ashtray appeared to receive it. Sanjeev blew out his remaining exhaust and as a couple of minions fanned away the remaining smoke, he rearranged one eyebrow into a 'do-your-worst-villain' stare.

'Remember, Randall, you are an evil man – evil. Let's see it – horrible, horrible. I want to see it in your eyes.' Ravi came up close, aping an Indian Quasimodo to better see the chilling effect that I was about to provide. Sadly, all that he did see in my eyes was a large amount of foundation diluted only by my sweat and his spittle.

'Yes, oh yes! Keep that. Keep it! Great! OK, ready!'

'Silence please!'

'Rolling!'

'Clapper. Scene 32. Take 13.'

'Action.'

'And the sentence of this court is that the prosecution will be sentenced to imprison—'

'Cut!'

Fenella had presented me to a delightfully eccentric lady in the coffee shop of the Blue Diamond whom she introduced, I suspect more for her benefit than for mine, as 'the finest, the most influential casting director in the whole of Bombay – no, India!' The lady smiled demurely and asked me about my acting experience. She seemed only mildly interested in my performance as a teapot handle but I think was quite amused by my interpretation of the reluctant hedgehog which I re-enacted for her there and then.

'I think Ravi would be most interested to meet you. Come, we will fix a date.' Pulling out her mobile telephone, she speed-dialled a number as she removed an earring.

After a couple of minutes of whispered chat she turned back to me.

'He will be here in a minute.'

It transpired that the film – an historic epic, the story of an Indian freedom fighter who struggled bravely against the British and was finally condemned to life imprisonment by a heartless British Judge (possibly to be played in this instance by Randall Williams) – was actually being filmed 'on location' in Poona. The director appeared, rather as I had hoped, in a long white limousine and parked what he could of himself on one of the café's *faux parisien* chairs. It became clear from the muttered conversation and the glances in my direction that my eligibility for the role was being seriously discussed. I thought it might be diplomatic if I made my excuses for a couple of minutes to let them discuss it more openly. Just as I was clearing my throat and gesturing vaguely in the direction of the loos, the casting director pointed at me and, turning to the director, said, 'So what do you think, Ravi?'

Pause.

I looked at him as winningly as I could manage.

Ravi, leaning on his elegant cane, appraised me through his dark glasses – or at least I presume he did – and replied as might a Mafia don, 'You think I would be here if I wasn't interested? But can he look evil, this is what I am needing to know?'

We were not yet to address one another directly.

'Of course he can! Can't you, Randall?'

'Oh yes,' I replied with as ghastly a grimace as I could muster. It actually quite hurt.

'Yes, well we can work on that . . . Car will come on Monday morning. Discuss all finances with err . . .' He waved at the charming casting director as he lumbered to his feet and rolled out across the cool marble floor.

'He is a most wonderful man – one of the finest directors in Bombay, no, in the whole of India,' she said loudly enough for the departing Ravi to hear, as Fenella winked at me.

It was true; I discovered later that Ravi was indeed the master of that particular art – the Bollywood blockbuster.

That morning the car duly arrived and I found myself sharing the back seat of the sleek saloon – how proud Sanjay would have been – behind a uniformed driver and sitting next to a man, whose name, as was so often the case, was complicated and unfamiliar to me but who introduced himself as one of the 'executive producers'. I was – indeed am – not certain what this involved but he was clearly important as his girth was very nearly the size of Ravi, the director. The contrast between this form of travel and the normal thundering, machine-gun ride that I was used to was significant and, I thought guiltily as I slid down in the leather seat, I was enjoying it very much. Travelling like this in cool, sound-proofed silence, I hardly ever feared for my life.

As we arrived at some traffic lights, an inevitable arm reached out, its hand extended, while the other one clutched a drowsy, snotty baby to the breast of a smudged sari. The traffic lights were slow to change and as the seconds went by the slender hennaed fingers of the hand slowly clenched, and the fist turning over slowly, tapped apologetically on the darkly tinted window. In the air-conditioned capsule of the car I wriggled uncomfortably as the executive producer snorted.

'You know, ten years ago no beggar in the road would have

dared to come up to a sahib's car.' He shook his head. 'And now they are ready to get knocking on the window – how long, how long are you thinking, Mr Williams, before they want to break this window – smash it? Where will we be then? I ask you and I tell you: we will all be going to hell. Oh yes. My goodness yes.'

To my enormous relief the lights hesitatingly chose to change and with the rumbling roar of expectant traffic building behind us we moved smoothly on, the bodywork of the car just clipping the now outstretched hand and knocking it away as its owner disappeared in a haze of heat and choking fumes.

The three days' filming that I had been contracted to do on *The Legend of Rajah Singh* were all to take place at a disused library building that had been converted, with considerable craftsmanship, into a British courtroom in Lahore, now in Pakistan. It consisted of a main room about the size of a tennis court, open at one end to an entrance hall which had been converted for the purposes of the film into the public gallery. In the grounds tents had been erected to house the various departments required in the film-making process – make-up, costumes, props, and an enormous canteen, from which emanated the most delicious odours all day and most of the night. At a little distance from the hoi polloi stood the air-conditioned Winnebago that housed Sanjeev, the star, and his entourage. From the moment of my arrival in this whirr of activity I felt immediately dispossessed of my body, unable to control what became of me – a little like being prepared for an operation in hospital after you have been slipped the pre-med.

In India generally, and here perhaps most specifically, there appeared to be three people for every job, and everyone, in a country where employment made a great deal more difference than whether you were going to be able to go to the pub on Friday night or not, was very keen to prove that they were indispensable. Gangs of young men brawled over who was next to apply powder to my glistening forehead, and hands roamed my body, fortunately entirely appropriately, as I was disrobed and costumed by a dozen figures – one for the shirt and one for the trousers and one for the little waistcoat done up with a chain. Finally, after a low-level stand-off about who was to tie my shoelaces, I was accompanied like a boxer to the ring, brushes brushing my shoulders, shoes and wig as I walked on to the set.

If outside had been pandemonium then what was happening on the 'stage' was pure choas. Hundreds of people scurried around with wires, lights, stands, weights, and giant reflector panels of polystyrene and silver foil. The fringes of the room were quite dark due to the intensity of the lights but it was from here that all the directions seemed to come in quickfire Hindi, the voice strangely Dalek-like through the loudhailer. Every time an instruction was delivered, one section of the room would jump and scurry with exaggerated attention to detail, glancing into the gloom to check that this was exactly how things should be done.

Guided by expert hands I found myself seated at a huge expanse of desk some feet higher than floor level. From here I had a magnificent view of the rest of the room that was a whirl of activity, technicians vying physically for room to complete their allotted task. Such was the bedlam that for a few minutes I was ignored and began to enjoy the spectacle. I was brought back to the realisation of my responsibilities by the sudden appearance of a sheaf of papers in front of me.

'Your lines,' a disembodied voice informed me and I snatched them up in alarm.

Fortunately there were relatively few, for it seemed that I was to spend most of my time on screen just looking evil. There were, however, enough to remember for them to be a nuisance – particularly as these days, as I am painfully aware, due to a less than studious approach to personal well-being my retentive powers are not what they might be. However, I was able to resort to a tried-and-tested formula that I had used at school – or was it university? In front of me on the desk in order to provide additional judicial authenticity had been laid a blotter, the paper stuck at either end into the red leather holders. If I slid my script under the blotting paper, the bottom of the page first, I could slide it out and downwards with my thumbs. Admittedly it did mean that I would have to read the script upside down but I thought I would be able to manage.

All the bustling activity was suddenly cut short by the repeated shrill and sustained shrieking of 'Ready, ready? Ready now?' from a sidekick in the darkness. Silence and stillness fell almost immediately over the courtroom. Until that moment nobody had given me any instruction at all about how I was supposed to act – but it was presumed that I knew because before I could raise my concerns the soon-to-be well-worn liturgy of 'Silence, rolling, clapper, action' was trotted out by those responsible and filming commenced. As I had absolutely no idea what to do but could see that the camera seemed initially to be pointed firmly in my direction, I attempted to be as magisterial as possible, all the while trying to inch down my script which appeared to have become lodged under the blotting paper. I need not have worried unduly because as soon as the hero had sashayed his way to the dock there was another megaphonic call to 'Cut'.

After a seemingly endless period of waiting, during which countless bits of equipment were moved about the place, we were ready to start again.

'So now, Randall, this is your line, you say it straight to camera and remember evil. I must have evil. You are an evil Britisher trying to crush the will of the Indian people. You are a horrible evil man. Yes.' Ravi the director finished with such venom in his eye that I was beginning to believe him. He walked slowly backwards across the set never losing my gaze. 'One practice then. And action.'

With a last final effort I was able to dig out the top of the script which inevitably tore straight through the middle of my line. I managed to piece it together and read it out in a voice that would have made Count Dracula's blood run cold.

'And the sentence of this court is that the accused will be sentenced to imprison—'

'OK, that's great, Randall. Let's do it! Ready?'

'Silence please, rolling.'

'Scene 32. Take 1. Clapper.'

'And action.'

'And the sentence of this court is that the accused will be sentenced to imprison—'

'Cut, Randall, why don't you do it the same as before?'

'But I did . . .'

'And why are you looking down at your trousers? Don't be looking down, be looking up!'

'Well . . .'

'OK, ready?'

'Umm . . .'

And so it went on . . . and on.

It seemed, however, in spite of my permanent difficulties and fumblings with the script and the general confusion that the stopping and starting caused me, that Ravi was more than happy with my performance because at the end of the second day he reappeared from behind his megaphone and came to find me as my wig was being tousled over by a number of wardrobe assistants.

'Nice work! Nice work, Randall! I think you captured the role of the Judge most satisfactorily. We are all most happy.' He then paused and looked at me over the top of his dark glasses. 'I am right in thinking that you have many children? I mean you are knowing many children in Poona? I am correct?'

I explained to him the work that I had been doing in the ashram and he nodded enthusiastically.

'Yes, yes. Correct. That is exactly what we want. You understand tomorrow we are shooting your arrival at the court-house and we need some crowd scenes with many children. Every audience likes to see many beautiful children. Can you bring us maybe twenty or thirty children? Then they can be in the crowd scene and they will be very pleased.'

Short notice was never something that appeared to be a problem in India but I explained to him that I would have to ask Charuvat whether he was happy for the children to appear in the film.

'There will be no problem,' Ravi smiled. 'I am sure that he will be very happy for them all to attend.'

It was an endearing quality of Indians to impress upon me *faits accomplis* without the slightest knowledge of any complication that there might be. 'Of course we can pay some small money to the ashram for your services. Please ask him if it is possible because we have important things to do tomorrow. We hope very much that they can attend.'

In fact when I went to the ashram later that evening not only were all the children agog to know what I had been doing but when they also found out that Sanjeev was the star of the movie they all pleaded with Charuvat to let them go. With a gentle smile, he gave in to their entreaties and the following morning they arrived in a war-torn bus commandeered by Sanjay from an unknown source. I stepped with some embarrassment from my chauffeur-driven car and was immediately surrounded by a group of grinning faces. Eventually with great excitement they disappeared into the costume tent only to reappear a little later on dressed in only slightly more ragged clothes than those that they had worn when they went in. The properties department had produced a marvellous old Bentley in which I was to arrive and the crowd was to boo and whistle me from behind some craftily disguised plastic metal railings.

I was much more at my ease as I had no lines to remember or wig to irritate me, so, on instruction, I stepped as ceremoniously as I could from the back seat. Instead of greeting me with shouts of fury, the youthful crowd, jumping up and down with excitement, bellowed friendly salutations.

'Hello, Billbhaiya, you have a very nice car. You, you are looking very nice today. You are very beautiful.' Dulabesh, who had climbed on to Prakash's shoulders, was laughing ecstatically and Tanushri was leaping about at the front, waving frantically, no doubt in an effort to get into the frame.

'He is our friend, very nice man from England,' they shouted to the cameraman, the bemused technicians and the rest of the crowd – much to my delight and much to the frustration of the film crew.

'Cut!'

When finally I had explained to the younger ones that they were not to recognise me and were certainly not to treat me in a friendly fashion, they went very seriously about their task. Equipped as they had been by the props department with a variety of out-of-date vegetables and fruit, they shrieked their disapproval as their missiles came whistling through the air.

Next on the film schedule was the arrival of the hero. The crowd seemed to be so in awe of his status that when he appeared handcuffed from the prison van they could only gape with undisguised admiration. Generally, though, the effect was good and we were about to pack up for the day when one of the technicians noticed on the video monitor that one of the small boys was holding a rather too obviously anachronistic ball point pen and autograph pad.

Finally the scenes were in the can and the children changed back into their everyday clothes. They were still wildly excited by the experience. Pleased that they had enjoyed themselves so much I waved them off, telling them as they went how much I was looking forward to seeing them the following day.

Once rid of my judicial attire, I sought out the company accountant who was sitting on a small camp chair on the veranda of the old building, a large brown briefcase on his knees. We renegotiated my fee, a sum that we had already agreed but which he was hoping to adjust at the last minute – slightly downwards.

'But I am very sorry, Mr Randall.' Here at least was one person who seemed to have properly worked out my name, although I was thinking of having my first and family name swapped around by deed poll ... 'I am most terribly sorry but I have only ten-rupee notes. This bloody bastard *babu* at the bank only gave me bloody, damn ten-rupee notes – but this is India. What can you expect? Everyone is so damn useless. Oh dear, I am getting myself all in a pickle. Bloody bastard.'

He hunted about despondently in his briefcase, shrugging and shaking his head.

'No, they're fine. Everyone is not . . . No, don't get yourself in a pick . . . Honestly, look, don't worry, it's OK.'

'Really, I am hoping that this will not be causing you too much inconvenience.'

Upon this he finally selected and withdrew enough bricks of the orangey brown notes to fill up a couple of white carrier bags. He handed them over to me with an unhappy smile and bade me farewell. I thanked him and made my way towards the gate of the library compound. He came rushing after me.

'Oh, sorry, sorry. I am completely forgetting – Ravi has asked to be talking with you again. Would you please meet him at the Blue Diamond Hotel this evening at eight o'clock.' Surprised and intrigued I agreed that I would.

I met the director fresh from his shower, enveloped in a huge white towelling dressing gown. He greeted me as an old friend and invited me to take a seat and a glass of whisky. This was a treat that I had not experienced for some time and accepted gratefully, even though I was somewhat taken aback by the quarter-pint measure he sloshed into a hefty crystal tumbler. Tinging the glass cheerfully now and then, I battled through it.

'So good of you to be here, Randall. I hope I am not inconveniencing you too much?' I waved my hand grandly as if to say that it was of no matter that I had cancelled something considerably more important than another game of cards with Mrs Chaturashringi and took another sip of fine Scotch.

'We are all most pleased with your work. Yes really. It has been a real pleasure to work with you. I hope you have enjoyed working with our team?' I nodded and smiled a little too eagerly. 'We were wondering – you see we have a new project – whether perhaps you might be interested in working with us again?'

The alcohol and the plush surroundings seemed to have

made me rather lordly. I nodded with a stately lowering of my head.

'Let me tell you a little about our new project. It is set in modern times – a sort of romantic comedy. It is the story of one big Indian family: the grandmother, her children, and their children. The grandmother is very keen that her last remaining daughter is married and she is trying everything to make this happen. One day an Englishman, a little older, a teacher but good-looking and kind-hearted, comes to stay with them in the house as he is a friend of her brother. They fall in love and then they are married in a big Sikh wedding.'

'Err . . . yes, I see, what would you like me to help you do?' I rather imagined myself as an evil foreign businessman, or playing some other unpleasant and distinctly unglamorous role.

'But you will be playing the part of the husband-to-be. The film is entitled *An Ideal Wedding* – of course it is for the audience to decide whether this is the case or not. We will be filming for one month on location in Chandigarh and of course we will fly you there and we will be staying in one very nice hotel.'

'Wow, brilliant, that sounds amazing, definitely, I would really like to do that.' Not thinking twice, I rushed in. This fault, once perhaps correctable, is, I fear, with me to stay. 'That sounds fantastic. When does that start?'

'Well, we are finishing up here in two days' time and then I am meeting my new film crew in the Punjab next Monday – so in five days' time. No problem for you I think to get there?'

'No, goodness me, absolutely no problem at all, sounds amazing, I would really like to do it.' I drained my glass with enthusiasm. 'Of course, I could get there earlier if you want?'

Ravi smiled broadly, hitched around his bathrobe and even removed his sunglasses in order to underline the intimacy of the moment. He refilled my glass almost to the brim with his finest malt. I took it and drank greedily, my head spinning with the excitement of suddenly becoming a film star and the not negligible alcoholic effects of the whisky. I knew it had been a good idea to come to India. I knew there had to be more to life than simply being a schoolteacher. This was my big break – what I had always been destined for. I drank again.

'That is very good news. I am really very pleased that you are going to be available. We were all the little concerned that you would be busy.'

'Busy? Why would I be busy? No, and anyway acting is my life. What I have always wanted to do – ever since primary school. I have always thought that that is what I wanted to do.' I was beginning to burble.

'That is good because we all thought that you would be busy working in the orphanage. But if you are free and available that's great. We can start immediately.'

'Oh no!'

How could I have forgotten?

Unforgivable.

I felt sick with embarrassment that my head could have been turned so quickly. Of course it had mainly been the whisky – no, that was a terrible excuse. How thoughtless of me. Staggering to my feet, I took one last sip of my drink and looked one last time around the lavish furnishings of the room. Not sure what to say, I mumbled my excuses and headed for the door. Ravi proved to be surprisingly sympathetic.

'Look, we all understand you are doing a very nice job in the ashram. We don't want to interrupt the work that you are doing because we think it is very important, but we would be very happy for you to appear in our film because we think you are a good actor and,' he tailed off rather lamely 'we don't have any other European actors that we know.'

'No, I'm sorry, but my priorities are with the ashram.' I tried to staunch my disappointment and guilt with expressions of noble sentiment.

I wandered towards the door and opened it.

'Well, if you think there is any way you can arrange it, then we will be very pleased. Goodnight now, Randall.'

That Monday morning I made my way by autorickshaw to

the ashram as normal, taking with me the photographs that I had been given of the film-making. The children adored them, poring over them, pointing one another out and laughing fit to do themselves an injury. I told Charuvat how I had been offered an alternative role for a whole month but that I had turned it down because I was busy with the children. I failed to mention that I had almost accepted without giving them the slightest thought . . . The gentle man looked flattered but also surprised. This was surely a very good opportunity for me, wasn't it? Couldn't I go and do the filming and then return? Abhishekh could take over in my absence as long as I left him a few ideas. The children would be delighted if I was to appear on the movie screen again. As Sahas told me, they were already very proud of me. Touched, I explained I would have liked to but I wanted to be there with them and, anyway, unfortunately, it was now too late as the filming had already started. No, he replied, I would still be able to go if I wanted. There was a flight that evening that would take me to Delhi and then a connecting flight on the following morning to Chandigarh. How did he know that, I asked? I was certain that he had never been able to afford to fly – it seemed useless, therefore, to have a working knowledge of the timetables. He smiled his soft smile, stroked his beard and pointed across the wasteland to the bridge. On it sat a shiny Mercedes-Benz. Ravi had appeared at the ashram the evening before, his redoubtable person causing no little consternation. A deal had been struck.

As was so often the case, the vast, hugely complicated machinery of life in India, hidden from view, seemed to encapsulate me, trapping me within it and, like a weightless astronaut, I rarely seemed to be able to propel myself unaided in any one direction or another.

Grinning, I had climbed into the back seat, promising to write to the ashram and assuring Charuvat that I had not forgotten about our play. Dulabesh flipped up into a one-hand handstand, waving me goodbye with the other. The others kicked their half-inflated football high into the air with glee and Beckham booted his stall and snorted with disgust.

12

I'm Getting Married in the Morning

Screen kisses always seem to be so effortlessly performed, the couple involved oblivious to everything that is going on around them apart from the wind in their hair and the sweeping music. This is so deceptive. Kissing on camera is a remarkably stressful pastime even if the beneficiary of my own amorous efforts was an unsettlingly beautiful Indian starlet. The proximity of a large camera, the heat, the remembering of the lines, the variety of instructions, to say nothing of the three hundred eyes monitoring my every effort meant that the whole episode was one from which I took some time to recover.

Due to the strange, unchronological nature of film-making, scenes were filmed according to practicality, rather than according to the true unfolding of events. So, although this scene of white-hot passion would appear halfway through the film, it had been left to the final day of shooting. This extended wait, an exquisite sentence hanging over me, had done little for my nerves. Nothing, though, was as alarming as the moment, seconds before the scene was to be filmed, when I discovered a small notice on the back of a packet of breath-fresheners that I had, naturally, been feverishly consuming: 'Excessive consumption of Brilliant Breath may have a laxative effect.'

Some of my fellow actors had already disappeared back to Delhi and Bombay, their job done. How different our farewells had been from the rather tentative, strangely shy introductions that had been made on my arrival. I had been greeted with an odd mix of timidity and a whiff of suspicion. On the first evening Ravi invited the cast to dinner in a restaurant in the strange grid-like city that is Chandigarh. Conversation had been awkward. The actresses, some of them household names, busied themselves serving the food then engaged in conversation of their own, chattering quietly about family, make-up, recipes and clothes, while the men sat mainly silent passing the odd compliment about recent film performances. (Nobody had yet had an opportunity to admire my performance as the Judge – the film would not be released for several months.) To my great surprise these actors were remarkably quiet, restrained individuals – not at all the prima donnas that I had expected them to be.

Our meal finished, we left the restaurant and were wandering back across an area of scrubby parkland to the vehicles that had been sent to pick us up when we were suddenly accosted by a group of excited girls speaking heavily accented classroom English. They must have worked quickly because from somewhere they had produced autograph books and pens. Circling us, they methodically ensured that they had picked up all the worthwhile signatures. Most of their requirements did not include me but one small girl dressed in a smart, light grey *salwar kameez* found herself standing unavoidably in front of me.

For the sake of politeness, she proffered her pad and pen.

Hot with embarrassment, I scribbled a rather wild version of my name on the pink page. Deftly, I stepped out of the light when I saw her inspect what I had written, and then frowning, look back at me, utterly mystified. She moved over to her friends, all delighted with their own inscriptions and showed them my addition to her book. They shrugged collectively and glanced over in my direction. Well, you never know, he might be someone interesting, they had clearly decided and advanced towards me en masse demanding that I signed the remaining books. Naturally, I could not refuse and, I think, signed the last one with a certain flourish.

Luckily, I had had my introductory training course in film acting on the set of *The Legend of Raja Singh* and had begun to understand the mainly chaotic nature of the whole process. Occasionally nerve-popping focus was required when I found myself on camera but for the main part I was relatively comfortable with my new life. In fact, in many ways, being a movie star was my life.

Most of the plot, a mix of domestic and matrimonial wranglings, took place in a large 1950s upper-middle-class house on one of the wide boulevards that stretch out towards the country from the city centre. Day and night the house was almost as busy as the street outside – endless streams of people, furniture, equipment, food, costumes, journalists and 'special visitors' poured in and out of the building and, despite the seeming chaos of the situation, progress was slowly but surely made.

It was now that I began to discover that film acting, aside from the financial attractions, of course, is not always the glamorous pastime it might appear to be. Very often, too often, I was required to appear bleary-eyed at seven in the morning only to discover that I was not called upon to participate until mid-afternoon. Inevitable as this soon became, it was not to become any less irritating. After years of being directed by the ringing of school bells, this hanging about was difficult to cope with. Many hours of enforced inactivity was very frustrating. Many of my fellow actors and actresses, used as they were to these extended periods of waiting, managed to occupy themselves, listening to headphones, knitting, eating, sleeping or flicking through celebrity magazines on the off-chance that they might find some mention of themselves. As this last option, at least, was not open to me I became increasingly exasperated and spent my time sending the one available postcard at the hotel – of the hotel – to the children at the ashram and to friends and family at home until, one empty afternoon, the actor who was playing my friend and future brother-in-law, an intelligent, kind man called Pawan, asked me whether I would be interested in going halves on a game of Scrabble. I readily agreed although my frustrations were not much diminished by his ability, stroking his moustache thoughtfully as he did so, to thrash me on every occasion. Still, it was better than twiddling my thumbs and waiting for something to do.

Finally the indoor filming came to an end. It had been a relatively smooth operation despite, on one occasion, a blackout caused by a cow that had chosen to chew its way through the power cables that ran from the generator lorry into the house to power the thirsty camera lights. This had resulted in gasps of concern from the younger actresses and a large moo of surprise from the electrified cow.

What became much more confusing and complicated were the shoots that took place on outside locations. A huge quantity of men (and apart from the actresses, they were all men) and equipment had to be ferried around the town in a convoy of lorries, vans and cars. It always amazed me that despite the often semi-hysterical tone that these movements provoked, each change of scene seemed to be accomplished without hitch.

That was, of course, until we came to the wedding scene. The heroine of the film, having decided that if she wishes to avoid eternal spinsterhood there is no possible alternative to getting hitched to the *firang*, the foreigner – me – agrees to be wed. As was the custom of the characters, the ceremony was to take place in a Sikh temple, with all the attendant glitz and pizzazz that this particular ceremony engenders.

In an outer suburb of the town, on the side of the dusty, noisy Delhi Road, stood the chosen *gurudwara*, or temple. As our flotilla of vehicles approached I could see minarets, ornate archways, open windows and a large white dome shining in the early morning sun – for this was to be an all-day 'shooting'. Once we had all processed through the small archway and into the enclave of the temple, the peaceful calm of the interior of the courtyard was in pleasantly sharp contrast to the pandemonium of the countryside around. Most concerned that I should not commit some disastrous religious blunder, I stuck firmly to Pawan's side and asked him to clarify anything that I might not have understood.

The crew dismantled the contents of a number of lorries, tying, as they did so, handkerchiefs of all varieties of colours and designs around their heads. For without our heads covered none of us could gain entrance to the temple.

'What am I going to do, Pawan? I haven't got any handkerchief or hat or anything,' I muttered to him as a group of turbaned, long-bearded men dressed in long, white robes approached. These were the priests who oversaw the day-to-day running of the temple and whose agreement had been given for today's filming. Ravi appeared from his limousine sporting a superbly colourful silk handkerchief on his head and approached the priests, bringing his hands up in front of him in salutation. He smiled most agreeably. After a few minutes' discussion he turned to me and, beckoning me over, introduced me to the wise men. Without an excess of welcome they greeted me and asked in excellent English for my name which I gave them – Will not Randall. After a few more questions about my home and my background, they moved away a little to consult. Pawan and I edged back under the shadow of the archway, as the day was already perspiringly hot.

Negotiating was definitely Ravi's forte but he did now appear to have hit some sort of bargaining wall, because from where we were standing we could see him scratching his head through his handkerchief as if a significant problem had been laid in his path. Pawan assured me when I murmured some concern that I really need not worry as, and I had been told this many times before, 'everything is possible in India'.

My attention was distracted by the arrival of Vishnu, the excitable betel-nut-chewing wardrobe master.

'Come, come with me, Mr Williams! Quickly, quickly, quickly! Costume ready now.' Vishnu had an extraordinarily muddled understanding of time restraints. If he had hours to spare as he clearly did now, he would get himself in a terrible panic. If something were needed immediately he would take an exasperatingly long time fiddling and messing about, as if everything had suddenly become too much for him.

'This way, this way please!'

We disappeared into a makeshift tent of bed sheets that had been erected in the corner of the courtyard. Inside I found laid out for me the most exotic outfit that I think I have ever seen. Baggy, cream silk leggings held up by a drawstring at the waist – the original pyjamas – were covered down to the calf by an elegant long tunic, the *kurta*, made of a soft, smooth cream material and embroidered elaborately around the collar, cuffs and either side of the hidden clips that held it closed down the front. Around this was tied a pink sash and on to my feet were slipped a pair of highly decorated leather sandals with toes that turned up at the end in a most authentic fashion. Vishnu had managed to provide a full-length mirror and I took a rare opportunity to admire myself.

'Now pleased to be sitting down!' He produced a plastic chair and, as if dunking my head below the surface of a swimming pool, he pushed me down by both shoulders.

'And now! And now the *pagri* – the turban!' he exclaimed with all the enthusiasm and showmanship of a great magician. He withdrew from a leather trunk a narrow strip of cloth, red spangled with white and black circles, some fifteen foot long, and proceeded to loop it around his arm with all the practised ease of a cowboy looping his lasso. This proved to be a cunning deception as Vishnu, a Hindu, had about as little idea as I did of the technique required to keep my headgear in place. Thirty minutes later I reappeared from the makeshift tent with a pile of material on my head that resembled not at all a turban and should have carried some form of health warning as a potentially dangerous weapon, bristling as it was with several dozen pins that would have been better suited to holding down hats at Ascot.

It seemed, however, that all Vishnu's efforts might well have been in vain, as Ravi was looking very serious – or as serious as a man with a spotty handkerchief on his head is able.

'Oh dear, Randall. I am afraid they have a problem with you. Yes, quite a big problem. I am afraid that it is your entire fault. You have goofed again.'

My heart leapt with incredible speed into my mouth before it sank back towards my curly sandals. I glanced over at Pawan, who to my surprise was smiling broadly. Had I inadvertently committed some terrible blasphemous transgression? No one had said anything to me before now. Concentrating hard, I tried to keep my poise – not least because any untoward movement on my part meant that, at any moment, my whole headgear might come collapsing down around my shoulders in a shower of tinkling metal pins.

'Mmmm . . . err . . . oh, dear! I'm sorry, I don't think I really know . . . How have I goofed? I mean what have I done wrong?'

Despite the awkward situation in which we clearly found ourselves, Ravi permitted himself a small smile as he wiped perspiration from his sunglasses and rearranged his handkerchief.

'Your beard; that is your problem, your beard.'

'But I don't have a beard!' I rubbed my fairly cleanly shaven chin just to make sure.

'No, yes, that is exactly the problem. The priest is saying that if you are going to be married in this temple then you cannot do so if you do not have a beard.'

For of course it was perfectly true that not only all the priests but also the now sizeable collection of men who had come to observe the proceedings were all more or less bearded and turbaned.

'Oh Jesus, I mean God, err . . . golly, so yes, I see what you mean. So you mean they won't let me in if I haven't got, err . . . don't have a beard? Well, what the hell are we going to do?'

This, I could see, was going to be quite a major problem, particularly as this was the finale of the film – the happy ending.

'Well, it seems pretty straightforward to me. There is only one thing to do.' Ravi waved over the shrinking Vishnu who, although he did not speak good English, had worked out from the anxiousness of our tones that something was amiss and that he might well be responsible. He nodded in some confusion as the director issued him a string of instructions in Hindi and then sped to a car where he rather brutally woke the slumbering driver.

'Yes, there is only one thing to do.' Ravi turned on his heel and headed for his fold-out chair that had been erected near the generator lorry. 'We will have to stick one beard on you!'

'Ha, ha, ha, you're joking. Ha, ha, ha, you are, aren't you? You're not? But will they let me in with a stick-on one? Will that be good enough?' I asked rather doubtfully.

'Either that or he will have to get his wallet out!' laughed Pawan.

'What do you mean?'

'What do you think?' he replied, rubbing thumb and forefinger together.

'Baksheesh in a temple?'

He smiled.

I knew. I knew. This was India.

Miraculously, Vishnu reappeared with a large variety of beards ranging from the rather effete Charles I model to the positively Rasputinian and I suppose that any one would have done had it not been for the fact that in all India or, at least, all Chandigarh, there was not a single blond beard to be had. Finally, Ravi struck what I presume was a financial deal with the priests who proceeded to throw open the doors of the temple to him, his cohorts and his clean-shaven Englishman. At about two o'clock in the afternoon filming eventually started.

Five times is the required number of turns around the altar containing the holy book, the Granth Sahib, before a Sikh wedding ceremony is complete. In fact we only completed three, the priest not allowing us to complete all five because we would then have been properly married. Sujatta, my beautiful bride-to-be, said that she did not think her father would appreciate the surprise news that her daughter had suddenly got hitched to an Englishman.

After the beard stand-off, things had gone relatively smoothly but, as I made my way up into the temple chamber pausing briefly to wash my feet in a ceremonial footbath, two large Sikh men, sitting cross-legged just inside the door, looked up at me, looked at one another and shook their heads. They stood up smiling, came slowly over to me and, taking me gently by either arm, led me out on to the wide veranda that surrounded the temple. We were followed by ten or so other men who gently bade me sit down on a low wall that ran around the edge of the building. In the same way that the equivalent number might have attempted to repair a car engine, so they set about trying to patch up my turban. Vishnu's effort came off quickly with only the odd 'Ow' and sucked finger and then the lengthy process of winding, tucking, pulling and twisting commenced. It soon became clear that everyone, apart from me, had a better idea of how it should be done than anyone else. Fairly early on it was forgotten that I was in fact an animate object. After about half an hour I re-appeared, my head feeling rather as a rugby ball might on its reappearance from a scrum. I was convinced that the turban was tied much too tightly and that this would, more than likely, have some damaging effect on my upper brain but a quick check in Vishnu's mirror confirmed that they had done a magnificent job. Feeling quite the part, I made my way back into the central room in order to take my wedding vows.

That over, in the topsy-turvy, non-chronological world of making films, Ravi, who had now regained his customary good cheer, announced that we would now be filming my arrival at the temple. Unbeknownst to me, custom had it that the groom should arrive on horseback – the warrior come to take his bride. As a result a horse had been hired for the occasion and he and his owner were waiting in the shade of a derelict building when we reappeared from the temple. Plodding towards retirement, the animal, decked out in rather tatty golden-red brocade, paid little attention to the toings and froings of the lighting technicians but instead chewed ruminatively on a bright red carrot.

Attempting to convince his owner by nuzzling him under the arm that he had just about had enough of the whole charade, he was disappointed to discover that he was completely ignored. A business deal was being struck with an acquaintance in the crowd. Frustrated, the horse pawed the ground with one hoof and snorted with derision as I approached.

Finally, he decided, it was just simpler to get on with the job and the sooner it was over the quicker he could call it a day. The shot of my arrival, complete with ceremonial sword, a parasol carried behind me to keep me shaded, and my greeting of assembled guests and family, went surprisingly smoothly – apart from a nasty moment when I attempted to dismount and caught the curly turnover of one of my sandals in one of the intricacies of the saddle. Leaving one of my feet behind me, I had to be helped down by a couple of the other actors to the good-natured amusement of the now sizeable crowd of onlookers.

It seemed as if we might almost be finished for the day when I was approached by an elderly man. His grey beard neatly rolled and fixed in a net, as was the habit of the older generation of Sikhs, he greeted me formally and requested in English a photograph of his young grandson sitting with the groom on his horse. The five- or six-year-old looked anything other than enthusiastic about climbing aboard, but was eventually hoisted nervously on to the saddle in front of me and did manfully well at producing a smile. Unfortunately, as this was unofficial business, the owner of the horse was distracted by further ongoing negotiations and had only one eye open to my antics.

Beaming down into the camera lens, I, too, was only half-aware of the fact that the horse's attention was unfortunately not focused on the photographer. Hardly had I heard the click than we were off. A cart, piled with fresh fruit and vegetables and pulled by a donkey with a woebegone expression, was rumbling its way past the entrance to the temple grounds. We felt like royalty as the crowd parted and the horse with a winsome whinny, surely not heard from it in quite some time, set off in pursuit of a healthy dose of vitamins and minerals. Horrified, but not nearly as horrified as the young grandson on the saddle in front of me, I gripped the reins and yanked. This always – and I knew this from several spaghetti Westerns – would cause our mount to come to an abrupt halt, sparks appearing from his hooves. Sadly, when both the reins came away in my hands, it became clear that they were for show only. We gathered pace.

In the full knowledge that it was being pursued (and rather as I used to react when I saw blue lights flashing in my rear-view mirror), the donkey could not decide whether to slow down or speed up. Frightened, it decided on the latter option and broke into a medium-fast trot. This, of course, was no match for our steed, eyeing hungrily as it was from beneath its embroidered headdress food fit for a wedding feast. With a little shake of its mane, it broke into a canter on the potholed road. Both of its riders emitted a small shriek as we surged forward. Only once we were alongside the cart did the horse realise that it was going to be impossible to eat from the stall while it was still on the move. Aware that the donkey was now well into its stride and had no intention of pulling over, our charger gave up in disgust, stopping dead. This, to my horror, had the effect of projecting the small boy out of his position in the saddle in front of me, and he thus sailed effortlessly over the somewhat startled horse's nose. My reactions were far too sluggish to think about trying to catch him by the seat of his pants but, to his great good fortune, and possibly mine, as I now noticed that we were being pursued by a large, excitable crowd, he landed in shocked silence on a large but soft pile of okra. The tasty Indian vegetables held him comfortably in their grip. Before I had a chance to confirm his safe landing my steed turned and, head bobbing with disappointment, we trotted smartly back to its whistling master.

Feigning an inability to understand the high-speed, top-volume complaint that the horse's master seemed to be aiming at me, I disappeared, unravelling turban in one hand, loosening pyjama trousers in the other, into my dressing room. Quite a little while later, when things seemed to have calmed down, Vishnu and I peered out through a crack in the sheet walls to see Ravi disconsolately counting rupee notes out on to the flat of the horse-owner's hand.

My equestrian antics over, I was pleased to return to the hotel which, I discovered to my delight when I climbed out of the white limousine, had been transformed into the set for the wedding reception. Thousands of tiny lights were garlanded through the trees of the garden and lavish flower arrangements had been positioned either side of a long walkway through the grounds. At one end, furthest from the hotel building, long trestle tables had been decorated with white cloths and cleverly arranged sprigs of foliage. At the other, on a low platform, stood two golden thrones. These were beautifully adorned with garlands of marigolds and jasmine. Away on one side was a large modern-looking discotheque with a huge set of speakers. Laid out on the lawn was a shining parquet dance floor.

The order of ceremonial events meant that my new bride and I were to sit in the two thrones, receive gifts and generally be admired. During the festivities a Bangra group was to perform a number of hearty, air-punching Punjabi dances. I could see them running through a couple of last-minute rehearsals, dressed in their exotic gold and blue costumes; turbans for the men and pretty headdresses for the girls, they clapped and shouted, swirling in intricate forms across the floor, clearly enjoying themselves immensely. It became apparent, to my relief, that I was not required to say anything during this particular scene and so I made my way towards the bar that had been constructed on the set. The good news was that this was not just a prop and very promptly I was served a lavish cocktail by a waiter, who, I suddenly realised, was Vishnu our costume wallah in a white shirt and bow tie disguise. Fortunately I was already in my new costume – a black braided suit and another turban that could have stepped straight out of the Raj – for I could see Vishnu was serving himself copious quantities of vodka which he appeared not to require diluted. He would surely soon be incapable of tying his own shoelaces let alone my headgear.

I soon discovered that Vishnu was not the only person who had every intention of enjoying himself. Once the scene of the bride and groom receiving their presents was finished, the camera was aimed at the dance floor and the Bangra dancers and the rest of the cast and crew, suitably attired, danced until the early hours of the morning. As I weaved my way down the avenue of flickering lights towards my bedroom I recognised the figure of the Vishnu, his bow tie under his right ear, slumped in my throne.

Two things were certain the next morning. First, thanks to the vodka I felt awful – as if my internal organs had shrivelled to a third of their normal size and were now stuck to the inside of my rib cage. Secondly, the only remaining scene to film was 'The Kiss'. Despite the attractiveness of Sujatta, my leading lady, my general enjoyment of the pastime I would be called on to perform, as well as a certain amount of practice and experience in this domain, I could not help feeling a little nervous about kissing in public. In this case the 'public' numbered well over a hundred and would all be totally focused on my every move.

I realised then that the directors had sensitively left this particular scene until last, allowing me and Sujatta to get to know one another over the preceding few weeks.

The scene itself was really very romantic. My beloved was to stand on the balcony overlooking the town, the wind in her long, lustrous hair. She would be in tears because she believed that I was about to leave her and return to England. I was to appear through an archway, express my undying love for her, ask for her hand in marriage and then give her a great big smacker on the lips. Easy. At least it might well have been had there not been a huge audience all of whom had eyes on stalks, waiting to see quite how the white man would tackle the whole situation, waiting to inspect his technique. I noticed that a number of special guests had appeared during the course of the day and wondered whether perhaps tickets had been issued. Roll up! Roll up!

The white man was also wondering quite how he would perform and also realised shortly before he stepped through the archway that he had in fact finished the packet of breath-fresheners . . .

'Action!'

Coming in as confidently as I could manage, I walked over to Sujatta who seconds before had applied glycerine drops to her eyes, which gave her the most genuinely tearful air. I mumbled through my lines and attempted to give the impression that I was interested in her replies. The moment came; I took a deep breath and leaned forward. In fact it was all incredibly easy – I don't know why I had been so concerned about it. In fact it was quite good fun – well, very good fun. They had said not to rush it – to make it look natural. No problem.

Well, this was fine. I suppose that this was the life of a romantic hero . . . We would probably have to have two or three different takes. Film acting really was my life.

'Cut!' called the cameraman.

I was right.

'Oh, sorry, Randall. I am very sorry.'

'Don't worry. No problem. I know we always have to do a few takes. What was the problem? Something to do with the lights?'

'Err . . . Yes . . . Correct. That is kind of correct. Well, you see we are having one small problem. You see when we are watching you and when you are turning your head for kissing . . . then . . .'

'Yes . . . then what?' I asked nervously, looking round the roomful of poker-faced technicians.

'Well, you see, umm, one problem . . .' The poor man, a good friend by now, seemed overcome with embarrassment. 'You see, there is one blinding light reflecting from your balding head and no one is seeing any kissing at all!'

13

The Play's the Thing

Cosseted and cocooned as I had been in my five-star luxury, it came as something of a shock to return to the ashram. I had bidden farewell to Sujatta at Bombay Airport – kissing seemed so much easier out of the spotlight of the spotlights – and had taken the train back to Poona. Ravi seemed pleased with my performance although it was with some trepidation that I awaited the first screening. Fortunately, as with so many things, the date of the film's release seemed to be obscured by such a haze of other Indian imponderables that I was able to temporarily forget about it and concentrate on my return to Poona. Back at Ashoka Villas little seemed to have changed and I was greeted by Drupad at the gate with a gleeful cry of 'Appendectomy!'

Mrs Chaturashringi had thoughtfully opened the blinds to air the apartment, placing flowers on the entrance table and a plateful of *idlis*, those soft elliptical rice cakes, and vegetable curry on the sideboard in the kitchen. Sanjay, whose memory appeared to be elephantine, was waiting at the gate as the sun battled its way through the pollution the following morning. He seemed so pleased to see me that he almost forgot to charge me when we arrived at the edge of the slum. The weather had got noticeably hotter in my absence – or I had adapted too quickly to the air-conditioned comforts of my hotel bedroom – and I struggled sweatily across the concrete bridge that divided the ashram from the main road.

I was assailed by smells that I had successfully forgotten about, and the mosquitoes and flies zoomed up to give me more than a passing welcome. I sighed, wondering whether I was really capable of going back into this desolation – not least because I felt swamped by guilty feelings, appalled that there was such an enormous gulf between the riches of the world of films and this small community who, amongst hundreds of thousands, millions of others, were struggling to feed themselves healthily.

Even my warm welcome at the Aakash Garden Restaurant the night before had left me with little appetite. Kamal, delighted by my short account of the antics on the set of *The Ideal Wedding*, handed me a copy of the *Maharashtra Bugle*. On the front page were several depressing columns reporting the recent destruction of a Delhi slum, which did nothing at all to raise my spirits – if it could happen there in the faraway capital, what was to stop it happening here? Ali Baba tried to cheer me with an account of the activities of the Poona Prohibitionists, who had begun to drop leaflets at the restaurant on a regular basis, despite the feeble protestations of Mr Dikshin Doegar. Despite myself I did manage a small smile when he told me of the latest absurdities of the Oshoites, who had organised a naked rave which had been invaded by eager local youths and equally enthusiastic policemen. The party-goers had finally been bundled into the back of an unmarked van dressed only in the maroon robes that they had not been able to stand up in. But finally memories of these pampered few and their fey ability to waft through India had only served to make me angrier, stepping lightly as they did from limousine to air-conditioned hotel suite, seemingly blissfully unaware of the hardships all around them or at least studiously ignoring them.

I had gone home early, revolted. My sense of disgust had not been much improved by Devashva who, suffering from a surfeit of Chicken Pasanda and Thums Up, a poisonously sweet fizzy drink, had thrown up gushingly on the sandalled feet of a group of inebriated managers from the Kellogg's Cornflake

Company. In hindsight, I must have been in a distracted frame of mind not to have appreciated the moment.

However, as soon as the first of the small children ran up to me squeaking their hellos and their good mornings I realised how happy I was to be back. The experiences and excitements of my newfound movie career paled into insignificance in the face of so much tangible humanity, genuine kindness and generosity of spirit. I felt content simply with the friendship and the feeling of communality in which I was honoured to be included once again.

Ironically of course, the children were fascinated to hear about my adventures in Movieland, and they pored over the bad photographs that I had taken, trying to catch a glimpse of the world I had inhabited around the smudges of my thumb and the dark shadows of the camera case. In many ways it was quite extraordinary that they should have expressed such interest because, as far as I knew, none of them had ever been to the cinema, and although some of the neighbours owned television sets there was none at the ashram. Such was the power of the Palace of Dreams, however, that they yearned for the opportunity to lose themselves in the sumptuous sets, exotic costumes and beautiful stars. They marvelled at the pictures of the Bangra dancers, the wedding outfits and the pictures taken by Vishnu, unbeknownst to me, of the departing ceremonial horse and its unwilling riders.

Unfortunately, although the younger children were innocently unaware, a very serious threat to the continued existence of the ashram had reared its corporate head in my absence. As the elegant lady had forecast, the owners of the land had finally decided that it was time to make it pay. Already, to my horror, they had begun to build a high brick wall around the only small area that had not yet been built on by the slum dwellers – the children's play area. In some cases the wall was built so close to the façade of the existing shacks that the occupants hardly had room to slide out of their front doors.

Goondas, the heavies employed by the developers, had already driven to Tanjiwadi with bundles of leaflets explaining the reason why the population would have to move. Written in Hindi and English, and perhaps by design extremely confusing, they served little purpose in an area that was largely illiterate other than to spread the fear of homelessness. Resilient as ever, the occupants of the slum were putting up a stiff resistance, canvassing politicians who after cursory expressions of interest disappeared behind disingenuous secretaries and sheaves of unanswered letters.

'So perhaps now is the time for us to do our theatre? Perhaps we can raise money to buy the ground if it is successful?' Charuvat had clearly been giving this some thought while I had been away and remained splendidly optimistic. What was, on the other hand, also clearer was that Charuvat was clearly looking to me with my newfound experience in the performing arts to make sure that it became a reality.

For some reason the prospect of this venture filled me with even greater dread than 'the Kiss' had done. Perhaps it was because of my experiences in the past, the realisation that there were countless things that might go wrong, that the line between success and head-in-hands failure was an infinitesimally fine one, but perhaps, predominantly, it was the fear of letting everyone down, the grim realisation of how extraordinarily important this venture was to my new friends. Feeling in need of some moral support, I went to see the elegant lady.

The *chowkidar*, a rather more youthful version of Drupad, pressed a button as he saw me arrive, greeting me with a pseudo-military salute as a sleek metal gate slid backwards. I walked into a formal courtyard and admired the range of beautifully maintained classic cars and motorbikes. Maybe thanks to some clever communication between the front gate and the house, a maid in a Victorian uniform opened the front door, just as I stepped on to the doorstep. I waited for a few minutes in the shining hallway and soon the elegant lady came softly down a sweeping staircase.

'So you found my residence with no problem then?'

Bidding me follow her into a spacious, brightly lit office that looked out on to a tidy tropical garden on the banks of the same river that only half a mile upstream flowed past the wasteland, where the children of the ashram used to be able to play, she invited me to sit in a large, leather chair and we waited a few minutes while the maid served us tea.

'You have a beautiful house,' I ventured with rather inadequate conversational verve.

'Yes,' the lady sighed. 'But empty now.'

A brilliant student, she had married young to a fellow Parsee, a boy who had great dreams, and together they had built up one of the largest civil engineering companies in India. Soon they were well provided for, happy with a young family, a son and a daughter. In their turn, the children too had glittering academic careers and with great pride their parents looked forward to welcoming them into the firm. Indeed, their son had just come from his father's office, when, like countless others every year on the roads of India, he was killed in a motorbike accident. His father never recovered and died barely two years later of a broken heart. Since these tragedies, she and her daughter, now married and a mother, had taken up the reins and although life had changed out of all recognition it still had to go on.

It was in memory of her son that she had become increasingly involved in charitable organisations. The ashram, though, she confided to me, was her favourite. Her son had so loved children, had been so wonderful with them.

'Have you decided what it is that you will do?' she asked, changing the topic quickly before the memories became too painful.

'Well yes, I have been giving it some thought. I was thinking about putting on a production of the Rammie, Ramy Annie something . . .' I bumbled. 'Sorry I am not quite sure how it is pronounced.'

'The Ramayana?' She leaned forward in her seat to better understand. 'Don't you think that will be a bit too complicated? I mean it is twenty-four thousand verses long?'

'Is it? Yes, yes I know, but we will be doing a simplified version, you know, a few scenes.'

'Well, if you think it's possible – it sounds like a big under-taking to me. But then of course you're the expert.'

'Oh no, I wouldn't really say that . . . But, by the way, how long do you think we have got to, umm, rehearse?'

'Do you think a month will be long enough? In light of what I hear from my contacts the developers seem to be getting ready to move and this, I admit, is beginning to worry me. Also, I think that it would be nice to put on the performance before the beginning of the holidays. The last Thursday of this coming month. That's what I had earmarked. I have had to prepone a little.'

'Prepone', in Indian English then, meant to bring forward as opposed to postpone. Inexplicably pleased to discover this word, I was sure I would now use it as much as possible.

The elegant lady opened up a thick, leather-bound desktop diary.

'That's right. We asked the Professor to look into it and he pinpointed that as an auspicious day, particularly in the evening. I have to fly to Delhi a couple of days later and so I will be out of station. As well, one other thing is that the school will not be available during the holidays and many of my friends will be going away.'

'The school?'

'Oh, I am sorry. Didn't I tell you? I have arranged for you to use the theatre at St Olive's, one of our private schools. I am the chairman of governors there. It has a very nice big theatre and I think that it will be very good for your spec-tacle.' She paused. 'There was just one thing that they asked if you could do . . .'

'Yeeesss?' I asked, sensing danger.

'I'm sure you won't mind. The headmistress of the school, a very nice lady, she was asking me whether she thought you would be interested in giving a short speech. We agreed next Friday.'

'Speech? What kind of speech?'

'Oh, nothing too serious. Just a little talk about your plans for the play?'

'Who for? A class or something?'

'Well, actually I think it is for the parents and all the teachers. Next Friday is parents' meeting.'

Never mind. I should have seen it coming.

'By the way,' I got up to leave, 'about these *goondas*. Do you think they will really turn up? I mean . . . you know . . . they sound pretty nasty.'

'Well, who can tell? But you must remember these men are from a slum somewhere too. They are just trying to feed their families too.'

'Hmm . . .' Rather unconvinced, I agreed that they probably did have difficult lives too. This did not mean that I was looking forward to discussing their problems with them.

We agreed on a few further points and she promised to pop along to some of the rehearsals and to provide us with any assistance that we might need. She pointed out, however, that it would be good for us to be able to demonstrate how resourceful we were and how little we needed to rely on the charity of others.

'Maybe . . . I was thinking it will be better if you can make as much of the equipment you are needing as possible. You know you can make things from recycled materials and so on.'

'Oh, yes, sure, the children will enjoy that. It will be a bit like *Blue Peter*.'

'Blue Peter?'

'No, sorry, no, nothing . . .'

14

Play Up and Play the Game

My loins were girded for the continuation of our rehearsals but before we threw ourselves back into the theatrical fray, I thought there was time for another worthwhile excursion – and what could be more worthwhile? We were going to watch the cricket.

Greener than any grass in the whole of the rest of Bombay, the outfield had been smoothed to a perfect flatness and bounded by a perfectly arranged oval rope. The wicket, a browner-shaded rectangle which had been surgically clippered out of the centre, was finished at both ends by neat pairs of white stripes and the six solitary sentries of the stumps, waited patiently for something to happen. The whole cricket pitch was calm, empty and peaceful. I wondered how far I would have to travel to find an equal area of unpopulated land. Several thousand people lived on an equivalent-sized piece of land in Tanjiwadi. Pigeons, taking a break from the hustle and bustle of city life, swooped down in circles, picking out loose grass seed from the faint cracks that stretched along the length of the wicket.

This calm was most peculiar in a city of such extraordinary activity, but it was made all the more bizarre because this empty field was surrounded by twenty-five thousand frenzied Indian cricket supporters. Whilst his English counterpart might have contented himself with a packet of sandwiches, a flask of warm tea, the radio and his own personal scorebook, not so the Indian cricket fan who had arrived at the stadium with enough food and water to last not only the day but probably the entire test match. We were well equipped too. Harvada and the girls had spent the previous two days cooking and preparing enough provisions to sustain us for the day. Cricket was a festival all of its own.

Although all the girls, apart from the motherly Kundanika who had accompanied us in order to ensure we all behaved, had stayed at home, the cricket ground being almost entirely a male domain, they seemed excited about the prospect of our trip as they waved us off from the ashram in Poona. Sanjay had somehow procured what I have always wanted to describe as a charabanc. Knowing him to be something of a bus enthusiast, I complimented him on it.

'I am hoping for Ashok bus!' he hollered above the noise of the argumentative gears. An Ashok Leyland, more specifically, one of the very many successful vehicles built in India out of Indian-Western partnerships, which included Maruti-Suzuki and Hindustan-Isuzu.

'But none is available so they give me this TATA machine. Not so good but OK.'

'So it's TATA for now, eh Sanjay?' He did not reply but looked at me quizzically in his mirror, as he let out the clutch without a word and the flowers in the vase that was stuck to the dashboard swung jauntily as if in a spring breeze.

The dawn rose with deceptive gentleness. Although the Ashok's engine did not really allow for much conversation as we thundered through the rocky plateau that separated us from the big city, I could tell from the expression of the children's faces that this was going to be a memorable day for them. Some of my gains from the world of motion pictures had managed to secure a couple of dozen tickets for a one-day match between England and India to be played at the wonderfully named Wankhede Stadium – the centre, today, of Indian sporting aspirations and dreams and the Bombay heartbeat of India's obsessive fascination with the game of cricket.

My experience of cricket went only as far as a few games

for my local pub side (having successfully avoided any real
sporting interaction till the age of about twenty-eight when I
was suddenly tackled by a morbid and nostalgic longing to
recoup lost opportunities). The Butterleigh Cricket Club had
been a very sociable affair, games being played and the
outcome confirmed before evening opening time. Most of our
opposition teams, home and away, were made up of the
customers of other public houses. Due, I presume, to my ability
off the field rather than on it, I had been promoted to the position of chairman of the club after a couple of years. This post
was almost entirely ceremonial and seemed to include little
more than an early inspection of the tea and ensuring that the
beer barrel was set up on the side of our pitch, which lay,
reasonably flat, on top of a rolling hill. It was, of course, tacti-
cally vital that it be put in position early enough for the ale
to have settled before the game began.

I was neither specifically a specialist bowler, nor batsman,
nor fielder, which I suppose made me an all-rounder and there
had been certain successes. Probably my most memorable day
on the field had been against a team of morris dancers from
further down the valley. They had held a pre-team meeting at
the Butterleigh Arms and this seemed to have left them in a
weakened state. Making the most, too, of the liquid refresh-
ment up at the pitch had meant that when, to my astonishment, I managed to hit the ball down towards the hedge at the
bottom of the outfield, three fielders pursued it. One lost control
of his own velocity while the other two undertook an
impromptu brawl over who should throw the ball back to the
lurching wicket keeper. My haul of five wickets was, I admit,
eased by the necessity of a number of batsmen to lean on their
bats in order to remain vertical. In an attempt to reach one of
my wider deliveries the wild stroke of a bearded bohemian
resulted in him sitting down uncomfortably on his own stumps.

Much though I enjoyed the social side of the game I was
often a little bemused by the rules which often meant that I
ended up sounding like the well-known tea-towel: 'When-
you're-out-you're-in etc.' I had learnt long before that it was

quite pointless trying to explain this most eclectic of games to visitors to England who to begin with had no idea what I was talking about when I started to refer to googlies and runs, and gullies and slips (which anyway meant underpants to French people) and legs and chinamen – unless of course they were Chinese and then they just got offended. After a little while, it usually became quite clear that they could not have been less interested. Thereafter, they were only rather appalled at the announcement that all this was going to go on for possibly the best part of a week.

So, despite my significant successes on the field, I found myself very much the amateur as I sat among several thousand people who spent huge quantities of time poring over statistics, checking on scores, discussing outcomes and acting out scenes from the field, in parks, alleyways, on pavements and beaches. Hero worship in India made the media-fuelled excitement about football players in my own country pale into second division insignificance. Players appeared on platforms with politicians and, of course, on television to titillate viewers in a hope that they might be more open to buy any number of products – cars, paints, motorbikes, beer and, rather inevitably, soft drinks.

In just a few moments the man that they called 'the Little Master' was about to appear through the little white gate, and not since Roman gladiatorial times had the public made their support known with such fervour.

Even if there had been no match to watch the antics of the audience were spectacle enough. Somebody appeared to have sold three times as many tickets as seats but as everyone in the crowd had been used since birth to living in close proximity to his fellows, nobody seemed to mind an invasion of personal space that in Europe would have been enough, almost instantly, to have caused a fight. Everyone appeared to be extraordinarily good-natured, everyone here for the game rather than for the alcohol, for the swearing or for the possibility of being able to injure somebody else. In the stand almost directly opposite a small musical group was tuning up

– a variety of brass instruments, drums and strings jangled and sparkled in the bright sunshine.

Boys picked their way delicately through the crowd. Wooden trays, tied up with string, hung round their necks, from which, like Dickensian match sellers, they sold any variety of refreshments: samosas, newspaper cones of nuts, cardboard pots of ice cream dripping vivid yellow unguent. Men yoked and balanced by twin milk churns, that swung backwards and forwards and from side to side, occasionally dipped their ladles into them to fill up small paper cups with sweet lemonade. Others dragged huge kettles of tea along the ground, the spouts plugged with a wadge of leaves or paper to prevent sloshing or cooling.

Distracted by the colourful displays all around me, the roar of the crowd crept up on me by surprise and by the time I had turned back to look at the pitch the noise was deafening. India, it appeared, was to field first and as their heroes strode confidently out on to the pitch their supporters increased the volume of their approval by the second. Strangely lonely, two helmeted Englishmen took their positions and one of the two umpires, dressed in pork pie salesmen's outfits, signalled that play was to begin. Almost as suddenly as the noise had swelled, it fell away again until the first bowler ran towards the wicket and, as he did so, the noise, like a new mounting wave, increased again until as the ball left his hand it reached a crescendo. Anticlimactically the batsman prodded the ball back along the ground from where it had come. The game was under way.

Unmesh fiddled with his glasses and carefully opened a small notebook on his bare knees. As each ball fired down towards my compatriots he noted the outcome in minute figures with a stub of pencil. The others chattered excitedly in between balls, pausing with each delivery to watch with all the intensity of the fervent fans that they were. Sahas and Prakash had borrowed a huge Indian flag from Old Saran, the slum shopkeeper in Tanjiwadi, who had lent it to them on the understanding that he would see them wave it on his fuzzy portable television. Dutifully, at appropriate moments, they stood as tall as they could and stretched it out between them. Sanjay joined us after a little while, having deposited the charabanc in a safe location. He seemed to be friendly with nearly everybody in the crowd and kept us supplied with any variety of refreshments.

By the time lunch arrived a number of the opposition had wandered despondently back to the dressing room, each departure providing very great pleasure for my friends. Strangely, however, they did not seem to connect me with the opposition and anyway were quite even-handed in their applause, cheering just as loudly for a well-hit four as they did a fine catch or the sudden collapse of the bails. We laid out the various pots and packages of food on the ground and crouched on the cement steps, the children tucking their left hands away, eating only with their right. Someone had thoughtfully included a spoon for me as, despite a great deal of practice, if I ate with my hand the general result was that I ended up covered in food along with anybody else in even reasonably close proximity.

As the sun swung over the stadium to grill the other half of the crowd, the public lost some of its initial enthusiasm and I found myself occasionally gently closing my eyes beneath the brim of my absurd but vital hat. It was not the easiest place to snooze because just as I found myself nodding off something exciting would happen on the field and there would be an almighty roar. There must have been a lull at some stage because I drifted off into a dream in which I was the star batsman for the morris dancers' team in a mighty battle against a combined team of *zamindars* and property developers. I was about to score yet another century when a huge shout rose from the ground and I woke with a jolt just in time to see another Englishman make his desultory way back indoors. I looked around at our group who were still rapt with attention at the proceedings on the pitch. Old habits dying hard, I did a quick head count. Despite the leaden feeling of weariness that held me as if tied to my seat, I quickly worked out that Unmesh was missing.

'Sahas, where has Unmesh gone?'

'Oh, he has gone talking with the scorer. He is thinking he has made a mistake so he is asking him to look in his book.' He smiled and shook his head as if incredulous that anybody would go to such lengths about something that he quite clearly considered to be of next to no importance. At the next roar of the crowd he stood and waved his country's flag with fervour.

'How long ago did he go? Anyway, where is the scorer's box? Is he on his own?' Ever since I had got lost in the bazaar, and realising the enormous concentration of the crowds, I was always deeply concerned about the whereabouts of the youngsters.

'Oh, about twenty minutes ago but I think he is being all right. That is the box over there.'

Twenty minutes! Christmas! I followed the direction of his arm to a stand diametrically opposite us across the ground. I looked out at the pointillist canvas of faces and realised that if the little boy got caught up in the waves of people pouring back out into the streets of Bombay, he might well be sufficiently disoriented for us never to see him again. Without fully thinking through what I was doing I made my way down to the boundary barrier and started to skirt around the pitch. This was almost certain to prove much longer than I had imagined as hundreds of children lined the picket fence, leaning over with their carefully curated autograph books, attempting to attract the attention of their heroes. Tripping and apologising, stumbling and slipping on the mounting rubbish and the odd limb, I slowly edged around. When eventually I arrived at the box that contained the scorers I found it heavily guarded by security men wearing hats that looked as if they had been bought as a second-hand job lot from an outlandish, ousted South American dictatorship. I enquired whether anybody had noticed a diminutive scorer attempting to gain entry and received the reply that 'only official are going inside'.

On their feet applauding another fine stroke, the crowd

waved squares of cardboard above their heads showing the number four to the field lest the umpires had failed to see the ball bobble over the rope. The pieces of card had been handed out at the gates by a very sweet soft-drink producer. The number four on the one side and six on the other, when the cards were not being waved in the air in celebration they were used to take a little of the hardness out of the concrete steps which everyone was sitting on.

As the supporters settled back down I began to realise the impossibility of ever being reunited with Unmesh. All that I could do was to hope that he would return under his own steam. He seemed quite a sensible little boy, and I could see our group sitting tightly together on the other side of the pitch, so he, too, would surely be able to spot them. Sighing, I carried on round the other half of the stadium, glancing at the scoreboard as I went. The last English batsman had just come out on to the field and the crowd were now baying if not for his blood then certainly for his wicket. They whooped and shrieked each time the Indian bowler ran in. I was much enjoying the atmosphere and felt strangely unpartisan about the outcome. As I wandered along I stopped to admire the next delivery from the bowler and clapped along with everyone else. Once again, I made small progress between balls but when I looked back at the pitch, strangely, the action seemed to have ceased. How odd, I thought. And peculiar too that all the players seemed to be staring at me – and so were the umpires and the now strangely silent crowd. Stopping again I waited for them to resume the game and leaned back on the large white panel behind me. Nothing happened. One of the umpires, a somewhat coarse-natured Australian, came striding towards me. He informed me in words of one syllable that I was standing in the wrong place – had I never heard of the bowler's arm?

No, yes, well, really. Sorry about that. Yes, carry on.

I hurried away among some good-natured giggling and rejoined the children. They were good enough to pretend that they had not noticed this last embarrassing episode.

A few minutes later Unmesh returned in high dudgeon.

Not only would they not let him into the scorer's box but they had not corrected their mistake – and a mistake it was. He had checked with various other people in the ground. Relieved that he was back, I suggested that I thought it probably didn't matter too much and received a stare as if I had implied that the moon was made of cheese.

Kundanika carefully removed the small earthenware cups from the wrappings of newspaper and uncorked the flasks of treacly sweet tea, whiffs of cardamom floating across the terraces. Sipping their drinks slowly, cupping the little pots protectively with their hands, the children thought that this was a great treat. Normally tea drinking was a luxury reserved only for the adults, the ingredients too expensive for everyone to consume. Some delicious samosas were handed out and we happily mopped up the last golden flakes of crisp pastry and soft, spiced potato. My digestive tract seemed to have coped admirably with its transition to Indian cuisine and I was now happily consuming curry twenty-one meals a week. This was a considerable advantage today as it meant that I did not have to visit the facilities available at the Wankhede Stadium, which would almost certainly have been beyond my powers of description. It also meant that I would not be tempted to cite, as so many other recorders of Indian experiences seem impelled to do, a litany of gastric close-misses.

Tea was finished for the players too and the English team, having performed reasonably well with the bat, now re-appeared on the field. Although the crowd had been vocal during the English innings they had clearly reserved the best part of their energies to support the incoming batsmen. Now they were almost silent as the first ball was delivered, waiting for the moment when it would flash away towards the boundary rope to unleash their vocal applause. A tall lanky Englishman with big ears pounded in from a long way out, dwarfing the umpire and the waiting batsman. The thirty thousand breaths held were released not in a shout of joy, but in a whooping sigh of disappointment as the batsman, confused, failed to attack or defend the ball and instead discovered that it had slipped between his pad and bat, crashing into the stumps and forcing the bails to reel into the air as if they had been pulled away on strings. Tucking his bat under his arm, he walked very slowly towards the stand from where he had appeared only a couple of minutes earlier. As he approached the picket fence another player trotted past him in the direction of the pitch, stretching and twisting at the waist and rolling his arms in big circles, as if he was trying to take off. Occupying the position of his defeated colleague, he made a great show of preparing himself, placing his bat in front of the wicket for the approval of the umpire and then, scratching a line with his foot, prodded the pitch in front of him to smooth out any imperfections. Sticking his bottom out he turned to face the bowler, thumping the ground with his bat. As if in action replay the bowler came bustling in. The batsman, disguised by his helmet, dithered just as his predecessor had done, missed the ball completely and again the stumps were broken, this time one of them flip-flapping backwards to be caught by the wicket keeper. The band went quiet, hooters and whistles fell silent too and, for the first time that day, the car horns that could be heard honking reminded me of the churning chaos that was swirling around outside the stadium. For a second time, the batsman made his way back to the dressing room, where, it seemed from his walk, he expected to find a hooded executioner awaiting him. This time it was a few seconds before the next batsman appeared but when he did it was extraordinary how palpably the spirits of the crowd were lifted for this was he: 'the Little Master' – the greatest player of his generation, the man on whose diminutive shoulders so much of India's cricketing aspirations rested.

When the next ball appeared, he clobbered it – if that is the correct cricketing expression – so hard along the ground that when it clattered into hoardings in front of us, it sprang straight up into the air, to be caught as if a gift from the gods by a jubilant little boy who jumped around in a circle showing it to his friends. With this cause for celebration, thousands of hands scrabbled around to pick up their cards, abandoned after the recent disappointments, and demonstrated with a display of their number fours their appreciation of this latest shot. As I watched, Unmesh reached down and picked up one of the orange squares, one amongst the dozens that lay scattered around on the ground. As he stretched to his tallest so that it might be seen by his hero, it was suddenly snatched out of his hands.

'Oi, yer fooking cheeky fooker! Yer a thieving fooker, yerar! Yer little fooking bastard. You trying to fooking rob me, innit!'

A man that I had not noticed before, his mouth snarling and his shoulders hunched in anger, had turned to shout at the little boy as he snatched the card out of his hand. Anybody in earshot froze, not because they had understood what he had said, but because his aggression and anger was so out of place in this good-natured crowd. Unmesh, who fortunately had not understood what had been said either – my teaching had not yet included this range of vocabulary – was clearly frightened by this response and took a step backwards and upwards to stand by me.

Angry that this man should have scared the boy so much, I stepped forward to say something and caught the man's eye. Although he was clearly of Indian origin his accent was pure Brummie. His dress, in stark contrast to the almost uniform beige shirt and trousers worn by nearly all the men in the crowd, was clearly Western: a shiny tracksuit, trainers and a cap, promoting some American baseball or football team, that was turned back to front on his head. Sunshine lit up a number of gold rings and chains that glinted as he turned away from us.

'Look, I don't think you should—' I didn't need to continue because as I started to remonstrate with him, I was interrupted by an elderly, respectable-looking Sikh in shirt and tie who spoke to the young man in front of us in a low serious tone.

'*Haanji, haanji*, sorry Uncle,' the man muttered, readjusting his cap.

'So, please, go on and present your apologies to this young boy,' pressed the older man in formal English.

Although obviously not acquainted, the younger man was immediately respectful of the older stranger.

'*Haanji*,' he turned to us. 'Look, I guess, I'm really sorry about that, you know. Sorry mate, right. No hard feelings, right?' He blushed and then hurriedly turned away towards the match. I sensed Sahas stiffen. Looking up at me, angered, he put his hand round Unmesh's shoulders to protect him. His natural sense of right and wrong had been wounded, even if he, too, had not fully understood what had been said. Indeed, if he had done, he might well have been considerably angrier. Confrontation was unlikely to resolve anything so I smiled at Sahas and taking his arm we all sat down again.

India fared better in the last session of the day and her favourite son put on a tremendous display of shots that rattled round the signboards to the delight of the crowd, and which finally won the game. When eventually play came to an end we made our way to the exit turnstiles, the children sighing happily, contented after a satisfying day. Out in the street, of course, motorbikes, cars, trucks and every other type of human conveyance blurred into a fantastical merry-go-round from the middle of which Sanjay eventually appeared at the wheel of his battered machine. As the children climbed aboard with our hampers, bottles, memento four and six cards and their personal scorebooks, I counted heads again and looked round to check that there was no small person who might have been over-looked.

Out of the corner of my eye I caught a glimpse of something metallic glinting and when I turned further, I found myself, to my great suprise, looking at the man who had sworn so vehemently at Unmesh. He appeared to be coming towards me. I raised my eyebrows unsure of his intention but he seemed more nervous than angry, looking at me sheepishly from under his drooping quiff of hair.

By now I could sense that the children had seen him too and were all staring intently at us through the window of the bus.

'Look, mate. Look, I'm really seriously sorry about earlier

on. I didn't mean no harm to the nipper or frighten him or anything, innit.'

'Oh well, never mind, no harm done,' I mumbled in return. There didn't seem much point in pursuing this conversation. We had a longish journey home and I didn't always enjoy having to travel through the city at night when everything seemed to take on an even more frenzied, chaotic atmosphere than usual.

'So where you from, mate?' he asked with a small smile.

'Oh nowhere really, London way.'

'Oh right. I'm from Dudley – you know, near Birmingham. You ever been there?'

I replied that I had not and was sorry but we had a long journey ahead of us and had to leave.

'Where you all from then, mate?'

His chubby face looked positively animated when I told him.

'Poona? You serious or you having a laugh with me or what? Is that where you're going? That's amazing. Cool, eh? That's where I'm going too. That's where my nan lives – she's Indian, innit?'

'Right, OK, I see. Well . . . perhaps see you there sometime then?'

The shadows were growing longer now and darkness had fallen across the young man's face.

'Err . . . look, well, I wonder you know like, can I ask you something, like?'

'Sure.' There didn't seem too much point in bearing a grudge against the guy.

'Well, I came with this group, right? And they had a bus too like, and they said they were going to meet here – at least I think it was here,' he was beginning to gabble, his voice a little shriller. Some of the macho chrome was beginning to wear off. 'And, now I don't know . . . but now I don't know where they are.' He paused, swallowing. 'And now, and now, I don't know . . .' his voice faltered, 'I don't know how I'm going to get home . . .' He broke off.

'Oh I see. That's bad news.'

'Well . . . yeah . . .'

'Well, you can come back with us.'

I could remember quite clearly the sense of impending doom when, in a strange place, plans go awry.

'Can I really mate? Ohh, ta ever so much.'

Sanjay seemed astonished as we climbed up the steps. Sahas looked horrified and angry as he saw me invite the enemy aboard the bus and turned round to consult with Prakash. Touched by their loyalty, I smiled at them and shrugged as the man sat down in the front bench seat. Sanjay steered us out into the tumult of the traffic, oblivious to the almost incessant near-misses.

Garish, or Gary as he preferred to be known in the UK ('All me mates said Garish was a poof's name. Well, I mean what would you do, you know, first day in your new school and that?'), took the opportunity of our three-hour journey to give a woeful account of his life until now. He had been born of parents who had migrated to England from Bombay in the 1970s. He had grown up in Dudley and for the last twenty-two years had never really been anywhere else apart from weekend trips to Birmingham and the school excursion to London, which apparently, along with a few other select moments in his life, had been 'wicked'.

His parents tried to return to India every two years but he had always resisted their efforts to convince him to go with them, preferring instead to stay with relatives and 'hang out with me mates' which seemed to be a particularly favourite, if not entirely productive pastime. This year, however, his mother had been desperate that he come out to meet the grandmother he had never seen – the old lady was eighty and it might soon be too late. Reluctant, he had only been induced to come with the promise of a car on his return.

'Might get an Astra, they're pretty good, don't you reckon? But if I don't get one of them then I'll probably get some kind of Ford. Depends on the prices but one of me mates is a mechanic so he can probably get me a good deal. Really want to get some alloys. I got some good magazines about them.'

He glanced at me, seeming to seek some approval.

Uncertain how forgiving to be, I looked back down the aisle and noticed that most of the children had fallen asleep apart from Prakash, who was scraping out the remainder of the now cold dhal from one of the metal tiffin boxes that had contained our lunch, and Sahas who was staring crossly out of the window. Unmesh was still flicking through the cricket scores in his flimsy notebook making notes all his own with his little stub of pencil. He adjusted his glasses and shook his head again, no doubt at the unpardonable incompetence of the official scorers.

'So how are you enjoying India? Must be very interesting to find out where your family came from?'

Might as well be friendly.

'Well, not really, you know. I find it quite difficult, you know.' He looked at me with honest embarrassment. 'You know, I really have been trying to like it but it's so hot, and it's sooo dirty and my grandma lives in a really horrible house – and it's so small. You know, I really love her and she's my gran and everything and yeah, like I said, I do really love her, you know. But another thing is she only cooks curry. I mean, I like curry, don't get me wrong, but not all the bloody time! I like other stuff too like burgers and stuff like that.'

Finally he fell silent and gazed out of the window as an elephant, keen to get home to a few bunches of bananas, plodded noddingly through the maelstrom of traffic.

'Have you been anywhere else in India then? Seen anything interesting at all?'

'Well, I been up to the Ganges, with me uncle and cousins and that. That weren't too bad.'

'Oh, right, sounds interesting. It's a very holy place isn't it?'

'Is it? What's all that about then?'

'Well . . .' But it was too late and I was too tired and I probably wasn't exactly an expert anyway.

'Anyway,' he mumbled, 'I'll be pleased to get back home.' In the lights of the oncoming traffic, I watched unhappily as a tear bubbled, burst and ran a silvery trail down one of his cheeks.

Gary, I imagined, was only one of thousands who had been dispossessed of their original heritage by the tides of human migration. India was for him almost as much a foreign country as it was for me. This was not a visit he would ever have made out of choice.

I changed the subject. 'So, err, what you do back home then? You know, what is your business back in UK?' Suddenly I noticed India's influence on my English.

'Well, I'm like a carpenter, sort of joiner, you know.'

'Oh, I see. You mean doing up people's houses?'

'No, I work in this factory where we design stuff for films and adverts and stuff like that . . . Sets and furniture, like.'

'What? Film sets? Like theatre sets? Do you really? That's interesting – really interesting.'

'Yeah. Well I suppose so . . . it's like all right, you know. Why you wanna know?'

15

Mental Riches

Out of place in time and space, St Olive's, the private
secondary school that had offered to host our show, had
been designed in the British neo-Gothic style of the late nine-
teenth century and bordered the Christian cemetery which
was full of wonky crosses and dismantled mausoleums: the
final resting places of numerous Doras and Freds, Felicitys
and Gordons, most of whom had been 'carried away' by some
kind of pestilence and most at an alarmingly young age. Built
for the comfortable, pleasant education of the male offspring
of the colonisers, now St Olive's was encroached upon on all
sides by shanty housing. Although the spacious grounds of
the school were relatively tidy, laid out to cricket pitches and
netball courts, the long wall that surrounded the playing fields
had already provided a useful solid start for prospective slum
housing inhabitants. Now some of their roofs were beginning
to rise into view of the ornate porch where I was now waiting,
having yanked with a happy jangle on the door knob bell pull.
Sanjay, who had 'businesses' to attend to, was steering his
rickshaw back out on to the road that ran along the northern
border, once a quiet lane of clonking bullocks and fanning
memsahibs but now a permanent and deafening corridor of
traffic.

Yet, I thought, as I followed a uniformed and suitably
stooping porter with a bad cold and a big handkerchief through
the parquet-floored, dark, main entrance hall, it had managed

to maintain much of its original atmosphere. Exclusive, smelling of floor polish and beeswax, and strangely cold, it seemed to have remained oblivious to the changes that had taken place outside its portals. It exuded elitism and a fundamental belief that the St Olive's way was 'Right'. Sniffling, the man led me through an archway above which hung an honours board inscribed in gilt letters with the names of the school's most illustrious alumni. Serenely unaware, it charted some momentous changes in history:

1947 J J Newman
1948 V St J Peregrine-Hawthorne
1949 M P Chatterjee
1950 R R Rajasingham

The headmistress, a very pleasant and efficient woman dressed in a business-like dark blue sari, led me down a corridor of hushed classrooms. Quiet, earnest dialogues murmured out through the panes of glass that reflected lamps which lit a series of oil paintings of former principals. Two double courtroom doors, which she pulled wide open with obvious pride, revealed a magnificent theatre. I whistled appreciatively. Faded gargoyles and dusty cherubs smiled cheerfully from the walls of the auditorium which seemed to have been designed on the model of a West End London theatre. Boxes, a dress circle and stalls were all lit by a slightly awry chandelier that hung from a worryingly cracked ceiling, decorated to look like a celestial sky.

Although it all seemed, as so much in India, to be a little tired and worn, grimy and unkempt, it was still a wonderful hall. With some concern, I counted the enormous number of red, velvet seats. How would we ever find enough people to fill this room? Walking down a threadbare, red carpet that led to the front of the stalls, we climbed up a flight of wooden steps on to the stage and I looked back into the empty seats – it was terrifying. Realising rather guiltily that I was not going to have to face an audience here, I wondered how the children would cope. Although friendly and relaxed with me, their openness had, of course, only developed over some considerable period of time. Sahas and Prakash would have no problem, perceiving their performances as a duty as much as anything else, and Tanushri and Dulabesh would probably enjoy the limelight. Even now I could imagine the little boy cartwheeling across the stage, but in my mind's eye I could also see the younger ones, despite their normal willingness to give anything a go, terrified, wincing and shying away from the glare of the lights, paralysed by this rare public attention. Oh dear. We would undoubtedly have to work on some confidence-building exercises, probably American: 'Hi, my name is diddley-dee and I come from . . .'

The headmistress showed me backstage pulling aside thick burgundy drapes. The surprisingly wide open space alone, complete with ropes and pulleys, canvas screens and an incongruous stuffed bear, would have served admirably but behind the backdrops there were some clean dressing rooms with professional-looking light bulbs spaced equally in an arch over the top of the big mirrors.

'We can provide you with some make-up if you are interested, Mr Randall. It is not very professional equipment – like you are probably used to – but we find it all OK for our performances.'

'Oh, I am sure it will be fine!' I replied nonchalantly and tried to remember what they had scrubbed on my face every ten minutes on the set of *The Ideal Wedding*.

'Yes and, of course, you will be bringing your own props and costumes which you could keep in this room if you like.' She opened a door marked 'Costume'. That reminded me.

Although I was a little taken aback by the scale of the venue I was also invigorated. Now that I had seen where we were to perform, I experienced a sudden surge of excitement about our plan – even a drop or two of confidence. After a tour of the lighting box which was equipped with an incredibly modern-looking sound desk with myriad buttons and mysterious dials – 'Perhaps you will like to be responsible for this?

It is very expensive and needs to be operated by an expert' – we wandered back down the corridor as a bell somewhere outside began to ring enthusiastically.

'Ahh, the end of another day,' sighed the headmistress, not without a degree of relief. The doors along the corridor opened and out filed hundreds of little boys dressed in shorts, blazers, sailor-boy caps in their hands and satchels over their shoulders, knee-high socks and fairly shiny black shoes – like so many extras from *Goodbye, Mr Chips*. Giggling, pushing and shoving, they made their way out of the arched front door. A still reasonably practised eye noticed one of the boys take a swipe at one of the smaller ones, twisting something, a sweet or coin, out of his hand. Something about the manner in which he then skulked away suddenly made me realise that it was Devashva, the rude and rotund son of Mr Dikshin Doegar, owner of the Aakash Garden Restaurant. He must have sensed that I was staring at him because as he disappeared out of the door he turned and looked at me, frowning with surprise when he recognised who I was, before cantering off out through the door into the spacious, shaded playground.

Thanking the headmistress and telling her, not entirely truthfully, how much I was looking forward to coming to the meeting, I followed the youngsters out into the sun where Sanjay was energetically cleaning his rickshaw by beating it with an old cloth. Careering out into the traffic we set off in the direction of his home.

Sanjay still lived in his childhood home on the fringes of the Tanjiwadi slum. For more than fifty years the small one-room shack had stood at the edge of the municipal waterway. Once, when Sanjay had been a small boy, clear water had run down this gully; now it was a stinking, stagnant, dark brown sludge.

Sanjay had married when he was sixteen and had brought his wife back to his parents where, along with assorted siblings, they had lived in greatly cramped conditions. The death of his parents and the marriage of his sisters meant that the house belonged to the two of them and their three children alone.

There was now about enough room for the whole family to sleep on the floor at the same time. There was, on the other hand, hardly the space for everyone to sit cross-legged in a circle and as I sat down in his home, we jostled and shoved until we found ourselves settled. Only then could I take in the effort that had been made to arrange this small gathering.

Sanjay had been inviting me for several weeks to come and 'take luncheon' with his family and I, to my embarrassment, had had to refuse on two occasions. This time, however, all had gone smoothly and he had come to pick me up on his scooter. We had woven through the lanes of the slum and by the time we arrived I was much relieved that he had offered to take me home again afterwards because I was sure that I would never be able to make my way back to the Bombay Road alone.

At the door, Sanjay's family was waiting patiently for my arrival. We performed our *namaste* and I was secretly rather pleased by how well executed mine had been. The journey had given me quite an appetite, so when we sat down on the colourful rush mats, I was delighted to see the array of steel and copper-bottomed pots be brought in and placed on the floor before us. The colours were almost as appetising as the smells: spinach of the richest, deepest green steamed alongside the orange creaminess of slow-stewed chicken; soft, brown chappatis were piled high and accompanied by slices of lime and purple-skinned onion; sticky balls of sweet coconut were sprinkled with small orange crystals. Only when we had finished off the last crumbs and washed our fingers with scented water from a large clay bowl did I guess from the contented, sated faces of the children that this was not everyday fare in the Sanjay household.

Indians love conversation. There is never any need to worry that you will not find something to talk about because just about everything is of interest. Sanjay, despite the fact that by his own admission he had little formal education, set about dealing with religion, politics, art, music, economics and the United Nations, all in the space of two cups of tea. When I feebly suggested that I did not really know enough about India and felt ill-qualified to comment, he told me that I did not need to worry. For, after all, 'Life is a mystery to be lived, not a problem to be solved.'

'Anyway, Mr Williams, you are good friend of the ashram and so we can be happy together everyone. Yes? Very wonderful children, you agree? Working very hard for your play.'

Yes. Yes, I agreed.

'We like to talk with you too, you see. You have informations about India and our ashram and we have some about your place. Very nice. Remember, Mr Williams: mental riches are very important.'

True, I thought, but before too long we were going to need some other kind of riches. Otherwise there would be no informations about the ashram to be had.

16

One Fellow from England

If I felt reasonably confident about the efforts of the children, I was considerably more uncertain about how to tackle the technical hurdles that presented themselves, but help came from a number of surprising sources. Gary, although still full of reservations about his grandmother's accommodation – which transpired to be only a short rickshaw ride from the ashram – seemed to be more able to cope with life in India than he had been before. It became clear that he saw me as his friend and so soon he invited me to call him Gaz, 'most of my mates do'. I was in no doubt that an honour had been bestowed.

On a number of occasions I invited him to the ashram and he eventually became comfortable in the company of some of the older children, who were only a few years younger than he. Amused by his Indian appearance but his Western attire, they found it difficult to understand why he could not speak any of the Indian languages. He surprised me, however, when despite his remonstrations that he couldn't speak 'a bloody word of 'Indi' he did make efforts to communicate with them in their own language. In fact, in many ways, he had more success communicating in Hindi than he did in English. Most of the children found his thick Black Country tones almost impossible to comprehend.

Probably in an attempt to forget about some of the less attractive aspects of his stay, he threw himself into our project with great enthusiasm. He was an extremely talented carpenter, no challenge to much for his imaginative mind, but he was also often daunted by the lack of materials and resources. Despite this, or perhaps because of it, he proved himself to be extraordinarily inventive. He soon became a popular figure amongst the street vendors and hawkers who pushed their two-wheeled carts up and down the narrow streets of the slum selling anything that they had managed to find in the huge amount of detritus that was thrown up by such an enormous population. Often they had nothing more to sell than dented tin cans and empty glass bottles, bicycle wheels, more than half the spokes of which were missing, the broken wing mirror of a car or an old burnt-out pot or pan. With a list of props that we required tucked into his tracksuit pants, he would inspect each item carefully, dreaming up designs for his creations. Occasionally, when he could not find what it was that he needed, he led a small group of children up to the municipal dump, where endless convoys of lorries bearing skips disgorged their stinking loads; to my great admiration, he would tie the handkerchief that he sometimes wore pirate-like on his head around his mouth and nose and join the hundreds of other scavengers, animal and human, who stayed alive by picking over other people's detritus. Gaz even developed a curious friendship with poor, mad Vikram, who, dressed only in a piece of sackcloth that was tied round his waist with a piece of plastic twine, lived in the stinking rubbish. Pulling an old carpet or rotting vegetable matter over his near-naked body at night, he fell asleep among the refuse and the rats would come out to play with his matted hair. Each morning Vikram would leap high over the mounds to proudly show his latest find to Gaz, who, filthy and smelly, would return to the ashram proudly waving a bit of old wire or plastic which, under the ecstatic gaze of Unmesh, he would transform into the horns of a deer, a monkey's tail or a star to dangle in the night sky.

In a country where an expression of dignity, courage or beauty was always clothed in the most sumptuous of garments, the costumes for our piece easily presented the most costly challenge of our project. For in the same way that the French might spend a high percentage of their wealth on what they ate and drank, or the British might invest heavily in their homes, so the Indians, even those who would struggle to find the money to ensure the general well-being of their families, would make certain at any important or ceremonial occasion that they and their family were as gorgeously attired as possible. It was unthinkable therefore that characters as elevated as Rama, Hanuman or the beautiful Sita should not appear dressed in the most lavish clothes we could produce. Both sides of Mahatma Gandhi Road (or 'MG, MG' as Sanjay would cry as he pulled out into the traffic with *absolutely* no effort to see if anything was coming – even his rearview mirror was redundant, angled as it was so that he might better admire his beard) were lined with shops offering 'Suitings and Shirtings', the walls lined with deep recesses which held countless numbers of rolls of material. The proprietors would slide them out and, holding the loose end, flick the roll away from them ostentatiously, allowing the cloth to spread like a carpet across the floor of the shop to then be admired by the potential clients seated in rows cross-legged either side of the room. If the sample was not quite what was required then the material was scooped up unceremoniously and thrown to an apprentice to roll up and replace, whilst another possible pattern was pulled out and the performance repeated.

Mrs Chaturashringi, who until now had expressed only a passing interest in the affairs of the ashram, became suddenly enthused with the prospect of the possibility of producing so many fabulous outfits. For her real love, above and beyond discovering exciting new recipes in the *Maharashtra Bugle* and running her finger down the paper's matrimonial lists, was taking the lid off her pedal-driven Singer sewing machine. Her mouth bristling with pins, occasionally snap-snipping with a huge pair of scissors, she delighted in producing stunning, sometimes rather alarmingly exotic *salwar kameez* for her daughter, Leelatai. Soon she might be rustling up twenty-five or more creations! With a worrying excess of emotion, she clasped her hands together, clutched them to one cheek, and immediately offered to take me shopping.

During what proved to be one of my longest days in India, we must have visited very nearly every clothing outlet in the city. Things had started badly. Sanjay had been in a terrible mood. The evening before a pigeon, no doubt half-suffocated and confused by the pollution, had crashed into the wind-screen of his rickshaw cracking it in several places. Resourceful as ever, Sanjay had decided that rather than replace the glass – at prohibitive cost – he would paint a picture, in this case a vase of flowers, over the cracks to disguise them. Unfortunately his artistic efforts, painting as he had had to by the half-light of the slum, had not been totally successful. The result, exacer-bated by the running of the paint, was a green splodge rem-iniscent of an unkempt Gorgon's tresses. Still sticky, the paint was taking an age to dry and this meant that we had to stop every few hundred yards for our driver to check it was not dripping on to the bodywork.

More positively, Sanjay had successfully fitted a gadget to his machine so that every time he put his gears into reverse, two large speakers screwed to the back of the rickshaw blasted out, most bizarrely, an electronic version of *'Eine kleine Nachtmusik'*. Although this would have the beneficial effect of avoiding any more nasty reversing accidents, it also meant that the proud driver, the novelty not having yet worn off, insisted on driving backwards for much of our trip.

About tea-time and several dozen shops later we were still empty-handed – Mrs Chaturashringi was as keen to drive hard bargains as had been Maria-Helena von Würfelwerfer. Unfortunately she was not quite so capable of making deci-sions. Eventually the exhausted owner of 'Backlaid Fashions – Exclusively for every man, woman and child' suggested that we should buy a bolt of plain calico, which could then be dyed to whichever colour was required. Mrs Chaturashringi seemed to be confident that this would not be unduly difficult and as I had absolutely no understanding of the practicalities of dress-making, I stepped aside to allow her better judgement full rein. Then of course came the question of how much we should pay. To my great surprise, the tailor seemed to be keen to offer us the material for free. But then, he asked, didn't I perhaps need some new outfits myself? Within a few minutes, lengths of materials came riffling out across the floor, a tape measure had been strapped around my chest and Mrs Chaturashringi and two women, friends of hers who happened to be passing by, were earnestly discussing which colours would best match my complexion. Two days later I was the proud new owner of a pair of smart business suits – if I am ever to find myself a proper career they will undoubtedly come in very useful.

One evening at the Aakash Garden Restaurant, shortly after the suit purchase, I was having a beer and trying to recover from a particularly hectic rehearsal. The scene in which the monkey warriors do battle with the Devil's apprentices had unfortunately, due to the burning desire of the actors for realism, turned into an unruly and in my case rather bloody brawl. Kamal, my enthusiastic but often confounded Hindi teacher, and the other waiters looked more than a little bemused when I explained to them what we had been doing. They were convinced I should be involved in greater things because, as far as they were concerned, I was that semi-deified creature, that superior being – a film actor.

Dabbing my nose and sipping from a glass of Kingfisher, I realised with a shock that only two weeks remained before the final performance. Quite a good deal had been achieved but there still seemed to be no shortage of problems to be solved. At least Ali Baba, who had just left, ever-confident, for his twice-weekly poker evening, had promised to lend me as much of his jewellery as I wanted.

'Ali, I couldn't. What would happen if we lost some of it or it got stolen or, you know . . . anything could happen!'

He smiled and gave a grandiose twist to his moustaches.

'Ha, ha!' He bellowed a melodramatic laugh and I half-expected to see a long curved sword tucked into the scarf tied round his waist. 'I don't think there is much in my shop that

I would care about too much. Ha, ha! You want . . . I give it
to you!'

And with that he left, taking, as he went, an absent-minded
swipe at young Devashva, who scurried away into the onion-
cutting shed.

Smiling at this recent memory, I looked up and to my
surprise I noticed a long-haired white man, dressed in familiar
maroon robes, standing near me, drinking beer. He was
watching the television which hung from the ceiling by the
bamboo wall that separated the quiet of the garden from the
turmoil of the early evening traffic. As there were rarely any
visitors to Osho who ventured as far from the calm tranquil-
lity of the surrounds of Koregaon Park, I smiled at him and
he smiled weakly in return.

'Perhaps he is one fellow from England?' whispered Kamal
as he put down a plate of mixed *pakora* in front of me.

'Maybe,' I mumbled as I dipped one of the deep-fried onions
into chilli sauce. Kamal soon wandered over to the stranger
and began talking to him most animatedly, pointing at me as
he did so. Within a couple of minutes he had taken the man's
glass from his surprised hand and was guiding him over to
my table.

'Mr Williams, this is Mr Mitchell,' my friend said as he
hurriedly laid another place and unfolded a napkin on the
man's surprised lap.

Embarrassed, the tall, gaunt man smiled and readjusted his
ponytail before lighting one of an almost non-stop succession
of American cigarettes.

'Mike, my name's Mike. I'm with that bloody lot over there.'
He pointed sadly over my shoulder. Turning, I realised that
at several tables, pushed together at the back of the restaurant, there sat a couple of dozen *sanyasins* from Osho poring
over their vegetarian menus. Mr Dikshin Doegar twitched and
fluttered around them like a dowdy and rather bald puffin.

Mike had decided to come to India with his girlfriend – she
had always wanted to visit India, and the trip had started
well. They had seen many of the sights in the north, in

Rajasthan, had been down south to the coast in Goa, and then had been heading back up to Bombay in order to fly south. Unfortunately, Marina had developed a fascination for the courses offered at Osho and, although Mike had tried out a few of them, he had soon become disgruntled with all 'the bloody sitting around and all that chatter – nuh-nuh-nuh – me-me-me' at the café nearby.

I laughed at the memory.

'We've just come from the Laughter Club. You've 'eard about that one, I'd reckon? Bloody 'ell. Unbelievable. It really was. Bloody unbelievable.'

In fact a few weeks earlier I had heard and seen this particular association in action in Koregaon Park. Popular, not just at Osho but throughout India, these clubs convened their members to . . . well, laugh. Yet this was no Comedy Club. No jokes were cracked, no amusing anecdotes recounted; you just arrived at the appointed hour and place, stood in front of your equally ribald partner, and laughed. Laughter, it was thought, would serve to lighten the soul, a chortle might clear the mind. In mirth was to be found an escape from the stresses of daily life. Had Mike found this, I wondered?

'Not bloody likely, mate. Just gave me a bloody 'eadache. It were unbelievably hot out there and by halfway through I were gagging for a beer.' He promptly ordered two more Kingfishers, a 'luvverly drop', which Kamal delivered at a smiling dash, delighted with his success at having instigated this new friendship.

'Cor, you know, I really got to make a move out of 'ere soon. You know? I been thinking about it but she won't bloody budge. Reckon I'll have to do a runner, you know!' He winked and drank appreciatively. 'Yep, on the road again.'

With a foamy moustache.

In fact Mike had already travelled widely because for a long time he had been the roadie for an internationally renowned rock band. He was consequently rather deaf. He was on the other hand profoundly knowledgeable about stage lighting.

Very interesting, I mentioned, and explained about the play.

'They've got this enormous lighting desk. Totally beyond me.'

'Well, let me have a look. Anything to get away from all these bloody loonies in dresses!' He looked down a little despondently at his own and lit another Winston.

When he heard of this new professional on our team, and not willing to be outdone, Sanjay, a keen amateur musician, had found a group to accompany the performance. He was sure Mike could deal with the 'Mixing, mixing' as well as the stage lights. Mike agreed he probably could. Enormously enthusiastic about the project, and friendly as he was with many of the locals in the area, Sanjay was soon to be seen driving around town, his rickshaw packed with musical equipment and fellow musicians, his radio blaring possible tunes. Soon they were all regularly appearing in the classroom to practise, which only served to confuse our rehearsals further than Dulabesh and his antics were already doing. Unfortunately, Sanjay informed me, this musical accompaniment would also necessitate some form of dance performance – and if I thought I might be able to make a reasonable go of directing the play, I was certain that my choreography skills, despite some rather overzealous late-night performances at school discos, were next to zero.

Assistance came from an unexpected source. I had assiduously been pursuing my yoga classes – which always seemed to end in my falling deeply and beatifically asleep. Although Fenella's disappearance back to England and Ken had removed some of the delicious anticipation of the lessons for me and, I suspected, Ivor Patel, I was still nevertheless enjoying them. Soon, I was confident, I would be reaping all the benefits of yoga rather than waking up the next morning feeling as if I had suffered at the hands of a meat-tenderising butcher.

When I announced to Mrs Bindra, after she had roused me from my mat with my customary cup of jasmine tea, that I was trying to put on a play with music, she declared that, once upon a time, she herself had been a classical Kanak dancer.

'One of the most greatest in India,' she added without, I thought, an excess of modesty. Indeed so enamoured had Mr Bindra been of her skills that he had pursued her and made her his wife on the basis of one performance.

Her approach to rehearsals was robust, her headband-bound energy seemingly inexhaustible: after our first session with her a number of the children, despite their gentle, agreeable dispositions, threatened to go on strike and I, who had practised the steps to show willing, had had to put my feet in a rice pot of cold water on my return to Ashoka Villas.

Well, progress was being made, I thought, with a mildly self-satisfied smile, as I sloshed around.

Everything was more or less in place and going according to plan.

17

Everything Became Very Quiet

So involved had I become in the whole process of putting on our play that I had almost forgotten the reasons that had initially set us on our path. Of this I was rudely reminded a few days after the arrival of Mrs Bindra for our first dance lesson. With the help of the security guard from the office block I was accompanying the smaller children back over the road to the ashram for lunch, leaving the older ones to play a few quick overs of cricket in the car park before they too came over to eat.

Just as we had negotiated a line of camels loaded with panniers of apples, which were being led along by a group of barefoot boys, and had arrived at the central reservation, two of those unremarkable, ubiquitous white Japanese cars (the vehicle of choice for those who had any) pulled up on to the stretch of rough ground that bordered the west side of the slum. Four men dressed in semi-comical, cheap, Italian-style suits and sunglasses jumped out and disappeared down one of the side lanes. Unmesh looked up at me quizzically and, I thought, a little uneasily. We all crossed the remaining two lanes and, as usual, the children broke away from me skidding down the lane towards the ashram. Slowly I followed, saying hello to a few people as I went. Everything seemed very quiet. This lane was normally a vibrant thoroughfare full of carts and animals and playing children. Mothers, their babies swathed in soft material and wrapped tight to their bosoms, were normally seated on almost every doorstep, but now each one was empty. Someone seemed to have turned off the normal multilayered noises that accompanied this scene. They had been replaced by quite a different soundtrack.

I was about to turn the corner by the sugar cane juice stall into the little square when I heard the noise of smashing and harsh voices. Peering uncertainly around the cart, I saw the four men pulling Old Saran, the kindly owner of the little shop opposite the gates of the ashram, through the front of his store and out on to the ground where they kicked him a few times. From the pantomime movements I guessed this was designed more to frighten than to harm. This was a warning rather than a punishment. Instead they contented themselves with ransacking the shop, breaking the earthenware pots against each other so that the contents merged irredeemably one with the other. Chickpea flour and rice, lentils and dried peas poured in multicoloured streams on to the floor, glass shattered and metal drums were dented, their oily contents surging out in great glugs on to the rough stones of the square before slowing like a weakening pulse; shelves were cleared with a crashing, smashing sweep of an arm. Old Saran scrabbled around in the dirt and filthy water around the standpipe trying to rescue any unspoilt stock that was now littered in a wide are across the little square.

Shocked, I was pushed aside and could only watch the four figures run back, pull open the doors of their cars and leap in. Suddenly I felt little Unmesh grasp my hand, as he hid half-behind me.

'What's happening, Unmesh? What are they doing? What are they saying?' I could make nothing of the words shouted in Marathi by the four men, but it was plain to see that this had not been a social visit.

'They say, "Leave, Old Saran, you must leave. Now go, go." Oh, we will have to leave as well. Where can we go, Billbhaiya?' The little boy looked up at me entreatingly and I would have laughed at the wildly wonky angle of his glasses had his face behind them not been so anxious.

These men were employed by the housing developers. Old Saran, I knew, had been lobbying the elegant lady and anyone else of influence so that the community might stay on this land, a place that for anyone under the age of twenty-five had always been home. Presumably these *goondas* had been sent by the developers to encourage everyone to move. But where were they to go?

Many of the locals followed the men confused and angry, and I tagged along. As I arrived back on the road, Unmesh still clutching my hand, the cars were squealing away as their owners presumably thought they ought to. The first car pulled straight out into the traffic but the second one, gathering speed and following, suddenly slid and lurched in a pool of oil that shone permanently outside the small wreckers' yard. Losing control, the driver, swinging the steering wheel left and right to no effect, watched as his vehicle bore down on a small boy, a child called Sachin, who had often played with the little children in the miniature garden of the ashram. Sachin had been busy trying to lift up a bundle of sticks on to his bony shoulder. Now he turned his head slowly, just in time to react open-mouthed to the impending impact. With a thud that could be heard above the noise of the traffic, the slight figure, still half-bent over, his small hand outstretched, fingers splayed in a pathetic attempt at self-protection, flew over the bonnet of the car, slid up the windscreen and, thrown through the air, landed in the path of an oncoming truck.

With the lightest of bumps, the lorry rolled up and over his body.

Still squealing, the car made no attempt to stop. After sliding this way and that it found its own equilibrium and disappeared into the traffic. Only when it was gone did everybody find themselves able to react. The little boy, his body perfectly still, was quickly surrounded by a group of friends and relations.

On the far side of the traffic, I could see a khaki posse of police, gripping their *lathi* sticks, sturdy bamboo canes, Indian truncheons, behind their backs. Mad with anger, I rushed over to them as they smoked and chatted and laughed. Just yards from them lay a boy, seriously injured – or worse. Weren't they going to do something? Come on, for God's sake. I grabbed one of them by the arm and dragged him into the traffic. In hindsight, perhaps they hadn't noticed what had happened but I was furious by the way they dawdled along.

Once there, they seemed to snap out of their insouciance, busying themselves directing the traffic and taking notes from passers-by.

Charuvat, who had just appeared, attracted by the crowd, sighed.

'Waste of time, waste of time. What will they do? Nothing.'

'Surely it's better that they investigate?'

Charuvat snorted with surprising vehemence.

'Even if they ever find them, their bosses will buy them out of prison. Waste of time. You have money, it's no problem. You come out of jail and everybody forgets what you did. If you are poor man you go to prison and everybody forgets you!' He headed back down the lane.

I was enraged, and felt, for the first time since I had first settled properly in Tanjiwadi, an outsider, a stranger. Sending Unmesh back to the ashram, I took refuge in the classroom across the road where I aimlessly rearranged the second-hand children's books.

Later, as I crossed the road again and wandered down the lane, I could hear coming from the small courtyard of one of the houses near the ashram the heartbreaking, pitiful wailing that is the expression of grief in India. In the centre of the enclosure lay the small dead boy, his crushed body hidden by a white sheet; only his head, kindly unblemished, was visible. His face had been washed and his hair neatly parted. All around the small form petals had been scattered and from his neck hung garlands of marigolds. On either side of him were brass joss-stick holders and several dozen plumes of blue smoke rose angrily, fast and straight, into the still air. Seated cross-legged on either side, the men to the left, the women to the right, the mourners, streaming tears, rocked backwards and forwards as they moaned their anguish. Now would begin the process of Hindu grieving.

Death is an escape. Shedding the human body, the soul becomes free for a period of time to wander the earth as a ghost before entering into a new phase of life. Death is liberation – *moksha;* it is peace – *shanti; paramapada* – the ultimate place. An auspicious time had been selected for the funeral. The rituals performed with great care guaranteed that Sachin's soul would make its safe passage to the land of the ancestors.

Death had polluted Sachin's family. Amongst these orthodox Hindus, the close family would not shave, comb their hair, wear shoes or ornaments or even cook food. On the fourth, the tenth and the fourteenth days special ceremonies would be performed. Only after this period comes *shubasvikaram*, an acceptance of what has happened and the return to the auspiciousness of life. A purification ceremony allows the mourners to re-enter the world. Life, in its economic reality, would not allow any further time for mourning.

Early the next day, the boy was borne at shoulder height on a rough canvas stretcher through the narrow lanes of the slum, down across the wasteland and a few hundred yards along the riverbank to a rough concrete pad at the water's edge. On it had been assembled a funeral pyre. Had Sachin come from a wealthier home his pyre might have been constructed from timber – even sweet-smelling sandalwood. As it was, it was built from piles of grey-brown cow-dung cakes. At a small altar, prayers were offered up to Agni, the god of fire, begging him to accept the sacrifice of the deceased. Looking down the hill to the river I could smell the stench of petrol wafting up towards me on the hot breeze. Slowly, chimes marking out the tempo, the hundred or so mourners made their way down and gathered around the pyre as the father of the boy, now purified by the Professor's rituals, took a burning firebrand from a relative and deliberately lit the tinder heaped on all sides at the bottom of the pile. Within a few seconds the boy's body had disappeared in a huge sheet of flame. It would take six hours for his body to be consumed.

Only when his skull had exploded from the heat or been smashed by his father would Sachin's soul be released.

Hazy, black heat and smoke swirled briefly round the mourners, fluttering the scarves drawn up over the women's heads, before lifting, escaping through the sky above me as I turned away and walked numbly across the dead earth.

18

Ganpati

So it seemed that the developers, rather than risk the adverse publicity which would be caused by the wholesale eviction of the inhabitants of the slum, had decided that applying intermittent pressure would eventually unsettle everyone sufficiently that they would finally move out of their own accord. After the death of Sachin, the *goondas* had chosen to stay away for a few days. Disconcerted, we attempted to concentrate on our rehearsals. One afternoon, inevitably, the men returned.

Gary, Unmesh, Prakash, Sahas and I had been experimenting to see how best we might give the impression of Ravana's heads resprouting after they had been swiped off by Lord Rama's sword. Unmesh had devised an exhausting system which involved releasing the air from a balloon each time a blow was struck and then hurriedly blowing it back up again. In spite of some clever valves he had made from clothes pegs, allowing him to regulate the amount of air that was released, after four demonstrations the little boy was exhausted, panting and glowing. His glasses had misted up inside the sweaty headdress so he could often not find the correct nozzle. On one occasion he attempted to blow up an already inflated balloon, which very nearly resulted in him blowing a gasket, and one of the demon-king's heads exploding in a most alarming way.

'Back to the drawing board, innit, Garybhaiya?' asked

Unmesh, employing a newly learnt, not much approved of, but now much overused phrase.

'Yeah, that's right, mate! Back to the drawing board,' laughed Gaz as he hitched the boy further up his back and we made our way down the lane towards the ashram. Gaz and I were going to eat in the Garden Restaurant. He had wondered if they served burgers and I had been sorry to have to disappoint him. Sanjay was going to drop us off on his way to his 'cousin brother's' wedding.

As we rounded the corner, I was horrified to discover, lying in the dirt, part covered by a fine dust, a bloodied and mangled corpse. We stopped aghast. Just as we were about to approach it for a closer inspection another one, also covered in a shiny coating of gore, joined it. The two dead lambs had been torn down from the hooks in the butcher's shop and thrown outside by two of the thugs that had visited the slum before. When they appeared from the doorway, they blinked in some surprise when they saw me but pushed past us and started to make their way back to the road.

Sahas was outraged by this violation and, before we could stop him, threw himself at one of the men, his fists clenched. He swung hard at his chest but his hand was gripped by the powerful man. Pushing him against the wall with an audible thump, the man murmured something in his ear. Then, before any of us could react, he calmly lifted a military-style boot and stamped down on one of the boy's bare feet. Quite absorbed in the act, he then took hold of the middle finger of Sahas's right hand and very slowly, or so it seemed, twisted it round and back.

There was an audible crack that drained the colour from the boy's proud face. Everything stopped. The man let go. Sahas slid down the wall gripping his smashed and bleeding foot with his good hand. Without so much as looking down, the man and his colleague ran quickly up the alleyway. Torn between pursuing them and looking after Sahas, I hesitated and then, yelling at Gaz – who, poleaxed, still carried Unmesh on his back – to look after the boy, I ran after them, shouting, shouting what

I do not know, just an explosion of fury at the horrible injustice of the situation. As I slithered round a corner jumping over some startled chickens, I was reminded of the elegant lady's remark: 'They are just trying to feed their families.'

But what a way to do it! There was no excuse for their treatment of Sahas. It was inhuman but then in this growling slum was that so surprising? What would I do if I ever caught up with them? – a question that I was never to answer, as I slipped in something wet and stinking and fell, hands outstretched, on to the rough cobbles.

Panting, I returned to Sahas who was now breathing heavily and shivering, his head resting on Gaz's tracksuited arm. His dark lashes were beginning to wet with tears, which he wiped away hurriedly in case I should see them. Never at my best in a crisis, I looked closer at the boy's injuries. He was bleeding quite badly from beneath his toenails. His finger pointed at a right angle to the others. Tying the handkerchief that I normally used to mop my brow round his foot as tightly as I thought was sensible, I called out for Sanjay.

Some of the other children now gathered around and Harvada, who had appeared on her way back from the market, carrying a large box of vegetables, knelt down gently beside us. Suddenly Sanjay was with us as well and after a brief inspection of the scene he turned and hurried back to his rickshaw. Pumping the starter handle as if he was trying to bilge pump the *Titanic*, he eventually managed to kick it into life. Like a curious dodgem car, the rickshaw steered its way around the standpipe towards us.

The sun had disappeared behind the dusty, shabby roofs of the slum. The night-time shadows, the guttering fires burning smokily in oil drums, the racing, honking car headlights, all caused the city to take on an infernal character. From every corner of every side street, as we lurched, jerkily, painfully through the traffic, I expected devils, demons, horrible goblins, *goondas* to surround us.

Hospital services suffered, as did so much of the country, from the enormous number of people with which they had to deal. I was not looking forward to our visit. Even so, the scene that I found at the archaic government hospital horrified me. The single-storey building was dilapidated and dirty. Many of the windows were broken so that they were either permanently closed or open; the furniture was old and often in a terminal state of collapse; the beds were either bare or covered with well-worn, grimy sheets. And everywhere there were people. Two women to a bed; children, their eyes closed by sickness, slept fitfully on benches in the corridor; and outside on the narrow veranda beds had been pushed together to maximise the number of men, old and young, that could be squeezed on to them.

Inside, the consulting room milled with people suffering from every possible and unsightly ailment. Well, there was no doubt, I thought; if I ever got badly ill I was going to go straight home. Yes, get out; go straight home!

But then, of course, I could.

When Sahas limped into the room, supported between Sanjay and me, he desperately needed to sit down but the best we could do was to slide him down the wall to the floor, his rapidly swelling foot stretched out in front of him. His toes appeared to have stopped bleeding but he was clearly in a great deal of pain. I felt sorry for him, knowing these surroundings were not doing much to make him feel better. Above all, I fervently hoped he would get better in time for the play. I knew how much it meant to him – to us all.

Sanjay and I looked at each other grimly, realising how long we might have to wait, when suddenly out of the melee appeared Christian, the irritating, hearty student doctor that I had run into in the queue for train tickets in Bombay. It took me a couple of seconds to recognise him as he was much changed. He was thinner certainly and bearded now, but what struck me most was how much older he looked. So much more grown-up.

'Hello again,' he said pleasantly. 'There's a surprise. So what's the matter with you?'

'With me?'

'Yes, you look very pale.'

'No, no,' I'd touched my face to see if it was true. 'No, no, it is my friend Sahas. He has been in an accident.'

When I described to him what had happened, he knelt down and, with surprising kindness, inspected the boy's foot. He nodded and shook his head.

'I'm afraid we haven't got an x-ray here, or at least we have but someone's nicked all the bloody film – again. But I'm fairly confident that there is nothing broken. Luckily his finger is just dislocated.' He squeezed the joint gently which caused the boy to wince. Moving him to a table that had recently been vacated by a child who seemed to be convulsed by some sort of fit, he felt over his head to see if there were any signs of bumps or contusions. While he expertly wrapped the boy's foot in a bandage he told me about his Indian experiences.

'It's just the *scale* of the whole thing. It's not just the over-crowding, which is of course a massive problem, but it's also the fact that we have so little resources.'

He had been holding the boy's hand in his and quickly, without warning, he jerked the finger out and round. So sudden was the action that Sahas hardly realised what had happened. Checking that the boy was not in too much discomfort, Christian packed it round with ice and bound it up in a cloth.

'That'll be sore for a few days but it should be fine. He'll lose a couple of toenails though. But you'll be OK, won't you?' Sahas nodded. 'Anyway, yeah, so what was I saying? Yeah, not only do we not have any equipment, but there are not even enough medicines to help cure even the most straight-forward of infections. Whatever comes in gets nicked and sold to other hospitals so we end up having to buy stuff that's been nicked from some other hospital! But probably the most diffi-cult thing to cope with is the suffering that these people have got to put up with and it's totally unnecessary.'

He shook his head as he patted Sahas on the back and gave him a cheerful grin which the boy, despite his pain, returned gratefully.

'Well, what's the solution?' I shrugged my shoulders.

'God, I don't know . . . A huge international effort to create some form of greater equality, some crap like that. Not that it will happen.' He shook his head again fatalistically. 'I do know one thing though – I'm going to finish off my exams when I get back home and then I'm coming straight back here. You know the most heartening thing? Despite the pathetically small amount that we can do, all these people are polite, patient and grateful. Not like the nightshift in Hackney. More likely to throw up on you and then try and put you in a ward yourself.'

He laughed unhappily.

'So anyway, I'm afraid I didn't ask you when we first met – I wouldn't have done – but what exactly is it that you are doing in India?'

I explained about the ashram. Smiling, he looked most interested and asked if he could come and visit us. Sahas nodded enthusiastically, as he had developed a sudden admiration for this young doctor. We agreed a date and Christian managed to find a pair of crutches from somewhere.

Relieved to be out of the claustrophobic, unpleasant atmosphere of the hospital, I still could not help thinking that what Christian had been saying was, however simplistic, true. International effort needed to be massive and concerted. Governments' reliance on the therapeutic effects of charity on those that gave, and the efficacy of envelopes bearing the picture of a crying, African child falling on to doormats in Esher or Croydon, was not, in any way, enough. It was surely the grossest form of criminal negligence to allow people, millions across the world, to suffer to the point of premature death, when the world's resources were rich enough to prevent it. All I hoped to do was to offer the little help I could. How very much I wished that Sahas and all the other children might have the opportunities that I had had – I was confident that they would make a great deal better use of them.

Sahas had to spend some time seated with his leg elevated

and therefore, for a while, our rehearsals were a little static. Meanwhile, however, others in the background, our technical crew, were working with enormous enthusiasm and soon we were ready for our dress rehearsal.

With the agreement of the principal of the school we were allowed to go in late one afternoon after school, and from various corners of the town the now numerous participants in our show arrived.

Earlier that day, the Professor had assembled the children in the garden of the ashram and solemnly we had paraded to the shrine of Ganesh, that most popular of gods, to request *darshan*, an audience, and also to offer him homage, in the hope that he, the god of new endeavour, the remover of obstacles, would bless our undertaking.

The small room of the temple was filled almost completely with his statue: an enormous pink, shining effigy of the god with the head of an elephant and the body of a man. In one hand he held one of his broken tusks, poised to write, for he was also the god of scribes and authors. All around, in an exotic haze, burned cones of incense, rose, myrrh and expensive sandalwood, the smoke swirling around his outstretched arms as he welcomed us. From the doorway, which, partially through deference, partly through confusion and the fear of doing the wrong thing, was as far as I chose to venture, I could sense why, with his fantastic but cheerful visage and impressive size, 'Ganpati' as he was affectionately known was held in such high regard – a cheerful, positive, kindly influence in a world that was often sorely in need of such qualities.

Sahas, ever the leader, rang a brass bell that hung from the roof in order to make the deity aware of our presence and the children filed in, each bearing a gift, a piece of fruit, coconut or melon, or flowers that they laid reverently at his feet. Finally there was a sizeable meal laid out before him, such as would rarely have been served up in the ashram, and the children joined the Professor in kneeling and bowing in a complicated series of rituals before their favourite deity.

Strange, I thought, as I turned away, suddenly aware,

perhaps wrongly, of intruding, but then not as frightening or worrying as the Western adoration of Mammon. In fact, I thought, as I watched a small boy sleep peacefully face down on the seat of a motorbike, considerably less odd.

When the ceremony came to an end, the Professor announced that all should be well and the bell chimed again as we set off for St Olive's. Ganesh was going to be a busy man – or elephant.

When the costumes appeared at the porter's lodge in a yellow and black taxi it was almost impossible to see if Mrs Chaturashringi and Leelatai had accompanied them, but finally they burst their way out of a great confusion of taffeta and ribbon; Gary arrived with his grandmother, who was clutching baskets of chapattis and samosas, and he proudly produced the remaining props: swords, daggers, crowns, stars and the numerous heads of Lord Ravana all crafted from his discoveries on the rubbish dumps of the town. Mike lowered himself from the roof of the theatre, attached to some sort of harness better suited to caving; a miner's lamp was strapped to his forehead – he never left home without it.

Sanjay unpacked an enormous amount of musical equipment from the boot of our bus and shortly his fellow musicians appeared on bicycles, buses, six-seaters and on foot. With good humour they set up their instruments.

We were ready.

'OK. Action!' My voice echoed in the empty theatre.

Suffice it to say that the rehearsal was, on all fronts, a disaster, although thankfully the children did not seem to realise quite how badly things had gone. When finally they had all left in the bus with Sanjay and Charuvat, the rest of us sat gloomily in the half-light of the auditorium and commiserated.

'Not to worry,' muttered Mike. 'The sound check for Motorhead gigs was always a disaster too.'

19

The PBB

'Smash, splash! Sploosh!'
Noises of cascading glass and metal glancing on metal came from behind the peeling, grimy, pale blue door of the small house some thirty or forty yards down the lane from the ashram. Loud men's voices and even louder women's commands echoed off the poster-plastered wall of the small shop. Momentarily the hustle of the slum paused, heads turning curiously in the direction of the commotion.

Silence.

Suddenly the door was blown open as if by some explosive blast and four middle-aged men ran out, their gait high-legged as if they were pursued by a swarm of wasps. Oblivious to the surprise that they had aroused in the neighbourhood, they bounded down the alleyway, four fearful ostriches in search of some sand.

'Down with this drinking! Very bad for all you people!' From the same house appeared a dozen smartly dressed women, flicking the scarves of their *salwar kameez* back round their shoulders from where they had slipped down on to forearms. A number of the older women were clearly exhausted by their exertions, having to pat their brows with delicate wisps of handkerchief, whilst the others triumphantly slid large, new-looking axes and surprisingly dangerous-looking knives back into their shopping bags. The Poona Booze Busters (the PBB, as I had now named them in my mind) had eventually decided on direct action.

'Quickly, Billbhaiya. Quickly, let's go and have a look!' Dulabesh and I had been practising his lines, which were by a long way less than perfect but seemed to be causing me considerably more concern than him. Sitting on the steps of the ashram and distracted by the loud voices and sounds of destruction, we had witnessed this strange scene. Now, the nimble boy bounced to his feet and cartwheeled his way to the gate, before peering out and then beckoning me to follow him. Slipping the rather smudged sheets of the play script under the corner of a mat inside the door, I followed. What exactly had the PBB decided to do this time? Slightly daunted by the gang of prohibitionists who were now marching back three abreast towards their chauffeur-driven cars, we hung back from the road until they had disappeared out of sight, still handing out fluttering leaflets as they went.

With two or three hundred other people we tiptoed to the door that, weakened by the violence of the incident, now hung, melancholic, from its bottom hinge. Dulabesh wriggled his way through the forest of inquisitive legs and I craned forward. From my considerable height advantage, I could see that the ladies' furore had caused some significant damage. Although the room was small, as they all were here, our debut-ant distillers had obviously given some significant thought to its design. The walls were shelved from floor to ceiling and on them stood innumerable small corked bottles and half-empty paper bags containing a variety of different herbs and spices, roots and berries, flavourings to be mixed carefully for the secret brew. Sacks of rice, presumably the stock ingredient, were heaped up behind the door, the top one sliced open from corner to corner. Small white grains were still sprinkling and bouncing on the smooth, earthen floor.

It was the strange contraption in the middle of the room that had been the real object of the PBB's ire. Hollow balls of glass broken from a larger structure had rolled to the furthest reaches of the room and a triangular metal stand, although still upright, now bent low on one leg as if in apology.

Spluttering, a small spirit lamp was all but extinguished; it seemed that the distilling process was at an early stage, not yet possessing the inflammatory qualities that the PBB so feared. Even so the air stank of something corrosive and, more worryingly, the atmosphere was heavy with protest.

Initially I thought that this had only been a symbolic success for the PBB, as Sanjay told me (and his smile suggested where his sympathies lay) that they had only found the factory.

'They are never finding the storeroom for it is kept in a most secret place.' Clearly, somewhere in the vicinity a significant cellar had been laid down.

When the men finally returned, somewhat shamefacedly, to see the results of the raid, they were aghast. Nobody realised how long it had taken them to construct the still. However, plenty of supplies remained, it just meant that precious profits would have to be spent re-equipping, and how was Old Saran going to be able to afford his third daughter's wedding? All those plans for new clothes for the children and some nice baubles for the wife would have to be shelved for quite a long while now. It made you sick. Nobody realised quite how important this micro industry was to the slum. It wasn't only so that the producers could have a drink now and again. Mind you, that was going to have been a particularly nice batch. After all, the man from the medicine tent up the road had given them the recipe this time. What a waste!

Poking around at the blackened, broken remains of their industry, the men's dismay quickly turned to anger. Who did they think they were, these women? (And it seemed to be made very much worse by the fact that they were women.) Life was hard enough without their intrusion and, anyway, what was wrong with having a drink now and again? All right, so some of the young lads could get a bit overexcited and Shyam had lost his hand when he fell while crossing the train tracks. Even that could have been worse.

Nobody chose to mention the several occasions in the past when somebody had slightly misjudged which alcohol was the right one to drink and dozens of women had been left widowed or, almost worse, having to deal with their blind, half-batty husbands.

What made them angrier than anything, though, was how condescending these people were. After all, they lived in nice comfortable flats; they didn't have to worry about where the next meal was coming from. Why did they think that they knew so much better than anybody else? Just because they had more money didn't mean that they could tell everyone what to do all the time. Oh, they made you sick. Look at the clothes they wore, the cars they drove. And, Mr Williams, they send all their childrens to private schools where they have everything that is the best. Why is that being fair?

I wobbled my head from side to side in the most non-committal, not-really-sure way that I could manage.

'Hang on, Mr Williams,' asked one of the men as he was scooping up the spilt rice from the floor with a metal scoop. 'Where were you planning to put on your play for the children?'

'It's in one of those schools, isn't it? That's what you told us, isn't it?'

'Well . . . it's not really . . .' It was true that I had gone on about St Olive's quite a bit after I had looked round the first time.

'Surely you shouldn't let any of the children from the ashram go along, should you, Charuvat? Not when they coming messing around with us all the time,' an indignant voice demanded. The mild man stroked his beard and looked at me attentively. Secretly, I suspected, he did not really approve of the distillery but it was important for him, for the children too, that they should be well thought of in the community. They relied, after all, on the generosity of their fellow slum-dwellers. He would have to have a think about it, he supposed. He did see their point, probably, but it seemed like a shame at this stage. What did I think?

My opinion on the matter was probably fairly academic and in many ways I was happy to sidestep any part of the decision-making. The centuries of caste and class differences were infinitely complicated and I thought it unlikely that I would or indeed will ever make any rational sense of them. My generally speaking optimistic personality, of course, hoped that in time tempers would settle and the slum-dwellers would be happy for us to proceed. My second visit to St Olive's was unfortunately to give this positive outlook what Gary might have described as a 'good shoeing'. The elegant lady had reminded me about the parents' and teachers' meeting which I was to address in order to explain our project and summon up some support. Remembering with dread my last experiences of such an evening, of Neeta et al., I had attempted a number of ploys to avoid attending, but I was no match for her determination and had only in addition to suffer the embarrassment of Drupad's graphically describing a prostectomy, all fingers in holes, when she came to collect me at the gates of Ashoka Villas.

An oak-panelled hall had been laid out with rows of straight-backed chairs in which we sat for not too long before I was called upon to explain our proposal. The audience comprised mainly mothers and a smaller number of fathers who gazed unblinkingly at the ceiling as they probably had done throughout their careers as parents of school-age children. They listened patiently and applauded politely before it was time for everyone to socialise over cups of tea and small snacks provided by schoolgirls in uniform.

Smiling, Mr Dikshin Doegar, the owner of the Aakash Garden Restaurant, came over to me, his hand outstretched as if he were to show me to my table.

'Mr Rambo. How *nice*. Thank you.'

Ushering me along, he introduced me to a Mrs Gupta. She seemed vaguely familiar.

'So, we both *very* much are enjoying your speech,' said Mr Dikshin Doegar clasping his hands and bowing slightly at the middle. 'How *interesting*. You know, of course, that my boy, Devashva, is attending St Olive's. He's a most promising student. *All* the teachers say so. I am *very* proud of him of course. I imagine he will be growing up to be a suitable young man to take over from his father. Would you agree?'

Somehow, I managed to refrain from replying.

'So, I am right in thinking that these children you speak of come from the Tanjiwadi area of our town?' To my surprise I found myself being addressed by Mrs Gupta, one eyebrow archly raised.

'Err . . . yes, that's right. Why, do you know it?'

'I most certainly do,' she replied in tones that were definitely louder than strictly necessary for the purposes of our chat. 'That is where they are making the liquor. Fortunately my friends and I have taken measures to stamp it out.'

She looked about her triumphantly, conveniently ignoring the fact that in Mr Dikshin Doegar's own establishment far more alcohol was consumed each night than possibly ever had been in the history of the Tanjiwadi Distillers.

Mr Dikshin Doegar stopped bobbing backwards and forwards abruptly, swiping his scrapeover hair back into place aghast. Supplicant-like, I raised my hands in an effort to get his friend to exercise some restraint. I failed.

The room seemed to have suddenly become deeply frozen.

'Oh yes, we all know Tanjiwadi very well, I think, ladies?' Only then did I notice the faces of numerous prominent members of the PBB amongst the crowd. 'We all know what kind of people they are. Not the sort of people we are looking for at St Olive's. Anyway, what is the point of offering those children such hopes? They will never be able to make anything of themselves.'

Immovable, Mrs Gupta was a sari-clad Lady Bracknell. I do not care to remember the semi-public address that she gave concerning the risks attached to allowing 'these people' on to the premises, the lice, the disease, the wanton drunkenness of the men; the list continued for some time, a terrible litany of failings interrupted only by the occasional, shrill interjections of 'Can you believe that, Mr Rambo?'

Soon, I found myself surrounded by a gang of militant women, all strongly supportive of the triumphant Mrs Gupta. Unfortunately, my two supporters, the elegant lady and the headmistress, had withdrawn for a meeting in camera and Mr Dikshin Doegar had retreated to bob back and forth with the ceiling gazers, leaving this particular Daniel in the lionesses' den.

So that, it seemed, was that. None of the children from Tanjiwadi would be allowed to go to see the play, let alone perform in it. Whereas I felt sick with fury, disappointed beyond measure, the children, the actors who were to have been acting in our production, met the news, which clearly came as a big disappointment, with astonishing stoicism. Life, they knew, was not in the habit of doling out chances; life was full of setbacks and disappointments and they, the powerless, had no choice but to battle on. But still it hurt and angered me. Sahas, in particular, I knew had been looking forward to the event as an opportunity to prove himself. It was to have been a watershed moment for him that might, after all his unhappinesses, give him the chance to prove his bravery. Somehow I wanted to commiserate with him.

'Look, there will probably be another . . .' I attempted to make things better with adult promises for the future, which never come near to making up for a child's loss in the present. He managed a smile and a light, small laugh.

'Well, now you will not have to be getting nervous about Tanushri making all her mistakes! Or maybe Unmesh falling down?'

He turned away and cocked his foot up on the low wall, as was his wont when he wanted to dream himself away from the here and now.

He coughed as if to clear his throat. 'Thank you, Billbhaiya.'

I left him alone with his thoughts and walked away through the swirling dust, down to the bridge over the thick brown sludge of the river.

20

Come on you Ashram!

Imperceptibly the yellow stick of light that ran along the bottom of the closed curtains faded away as Mike dimmed the auditorium from his position in the lighting box high above the ranked seating. Glimpsing through a chink in the proscenium arch, I could see the audience expectant in its finery – *tout* Poona was there.

On the stage, bathed in a nocturnal blue, the younger children were arranged, costumed in branches and plastic-bag leaves, ready for the appearance of the adventurous Rama and his dear wife Sita in the enchanted Ashoka Grove. Sahas nodded seriously at me from the wings on the far side, smoothed down his *kurta* and wiped a small spot of sweat from his forehead. Tanushri wriggled as she fiddled with the gold chain, lent to her by Ali Baba, that ran from her nose stud to her intricate earring, and waved at Mrs Chaturashringi who was trying to stitch a small monkey into his costume. Smiling confidently, I hoped, I nodded back at Sahas and lowered my arm. At the signal, Drupad, having removed his front of house shirt and tie and rolled up his white Long John sleeves in the heat, took firm grasp of the rope and began to pull it down, the white feather in his beret bobbing with the effort. Sanjay began to beat out a quiet, mysterious rhythm on his tabla as the mildewed, heavy drapes drew back with only the quietest squeak.

Perhaps I should have remembered what it was that Pawan

had said to me the morning of the turban debacle at the Sikh Gurudwara: 'Remember, William, anything is possible in India.' And so it seemed to be. Just when I had given up all hope of being able to perform our play, all the obstacles that I had seen erected so quickly seemed to disappear with equal rapidity. It appeared that Sanjay, who had been looking forward to his part in the performance perhaps more than anybody else, and was not going to take any hindrance lightly, was a good friend of the Tanjiwadi Distillers. Over a few teacups of one of their better brews, served up surreptitiously from behind the rickety wooden bar at the entrance to the slum, he had succeeded in calming their irritations. Fortunately, too, a glass blower in the bazaar had managed to repair their condenser and they had managed to get back into business much more quickly than they had hoped. As the afternoon wore on, they softened and relented. They had even supplied him with a small bottle of viscous, sickly yellow liquid which he had hidden in his dhoti and would be used, he told me with a confident smile, as we wove a little more erratically than usual through the early evening rush hour, to celebrate the success of our venture.

As she seemed to exert an almost mystical power over the parents at St Olive's, the elegant lady's opinion and general snob value seemed to hold a great deal more sway than that of the virago Mrs Gupta. A few gentle words in social circles, accompanied by some kindly gestures and graceful *namaskars*, had meant that a few days after the meeting she had come to the ashram to tell us, in tones as close to triumph as she would ever have allowed herself, that 'The Committee' had agreed that our performance could certainly go ahead. What was more, the faint atmosphere of embarrassment engendered by Mrs Gupta's uncharitable remarks had meant that the parents would redouble their efforts to ensure a capacity crowd.

Despite the two or three days that had been wasted when a general pall of depression had mixed with the smog that hung over the ashram, I was delighted by the resurgence of excitement among the children and the helpers. Slipping out of the morose mood that had descended upon us, we all returned to the normal rush of the world around us.

Backstage roles were finalised: I would be stage manager, Charuvat my assistant, Gary was to be in charge of props, Mike, the lights. Sanjay took control of transport and music with his normal ingenuity and Harshada and Kundanika would organise the children, ensuring they were correctly attired by the fastidious Mrs Chaturashringi. Drupad was to greet the guests and tear the tickets – with as little extraneous medical information as possible, he promised. He also volunteered to organise the smooth drawing of the curtains. He had had plenty of experience, he told me cheerfully. At the hospital, every time a patient died on the operating table it was he that would pull the curtain round the corpse.

Cast members seemed to be well acquainted with their roles and even Dulabesh, sensing perhaps, despite his happy-go-lucky approach, that we had been granted a fortunate last reprieve, learnt his lines in a couple of hours sitting cross-legged on top of the water tank. It was uncertain who was the more delighted, he or I, when he proved that he knew them. At any rate, we spent a long time shaking hands and thanking each other.

Tanushri was a great deal more cause for concern. Far from knowing where she should be and what she should say at any given moment, she seemed hardly to realise that the performance was almost upon us. For as long as she was surrounded by the beautiful costumes that Mrs Chaturashringi occasionally brought to the ashram for fittings, she was happy. She did, it was true, help our wardrobe mistress greatly, stitching embroidery on dresses and tying ribbons in little girls' hair, but this left little time for line-learning or remembering any of the stage directions. Finally Harshada took her aside and, kneeling down with her on the floor, made her come to realise how important it was that she should concentrate. With luminous, honest eyes she came to me to promise to do her best.

'Sorry, Billbhaiya. I am sorry if I am not being a good girl.

But now I try, really trying so it will make you happy with me. You still nice man, Billbhaiya,' she whispered before bringing her hands together and bowing slightly, then running inside with small quick steps to join the other girls. Blinking, I looked away and smiled at a passing cow.

Everything else was more or less falling into place. Soon the cupboard in our classroom was filled with assortments of costumes, props and equipment. Occasionally, to my delight, as I wandered round the periphery of the ashram, I would come across groups of children acting out small scenes from the play, although a number of our neighbours must have wondered what sort of effect I was having as they watched a dozen or so seven-year-olds come 'Uh-uh-uh'ing their way down the alleyway pretending to be monkey soldiers.

Our arrival at St Olive's in the late afternoon of the day of the performance had not gone entirely without incident. Sanjay had managed to summon up from somewhere a vehicle that was beyond the realms of antiquity and on this occasion, of all occasions, it proved not to be up to the task. Once the bus had been loaded with all thirty-odd children, half a dozen adults (the musicians arriving separately), umpteen costumes and one goat, we set off across the bridge in the direction of the school. Sanjay negotiated with skill the racetrack of rick-shaws that zoomed in perpetuity round the railway station and bumped with what proved to be excess zeal over the sleeping policemen on Boat Club Road. Squealing with delight, the children on the back seat loved it – the engine sadly did not.

Nearing the turning into the road that ran north along the perimeter of St Olive's, our driver steering like a slalom skier, we heard a muffled detonation that seemed to emanate from the lower intestines of the bus. The subsequent explosion from the exhaust pipe seemed to propel us forward at double speed for a few yards and then we stopped.

'Bloody bastard is broken,' was Sanjay's considered dia-gnosis of the mechanical failure of the bus. On the other side of the Christian cemetery I could see the crenellated towers of St Olive's. There was nothing for it.

Beckham leading the way, tugging Tanushri over fallen gravestones by his rope leash, we stumbled along in the darkening light, clutching heaps of clothes and the enormous number of different props that Gary had created.

'Don't bloody drop any. We'll all be in terrible shite,' he muttered from behind a pile of cheerful goat-hair and cardboard monkey masks.

'Yeah, bloody 'ell!' agreed Tanushri, as she disappeared, with a great jerk, behind a mausoleum.

'What is this place then please, Billbhaiya?' asked the normally equable Kundanika.

'Well, it's where people from the Christian religion,' we had discussed the different religions in our lessons, 'where they are buried in the ground – you know, after they are dead. Careful, Unmesh, maybe you shouldn't be writing in your book right now. Ooh, are you OK?'

'You mean there are dead people here?' She looked up at me with what I thought was curiosity but turned out to be dread. She turned in reply to a question from one of the little girls and, once what I had explained had been translated, the general pace quickened. It was true that in this gloom it did all seem a little spooky.

'Yes, but there's nothing to worry about – they're all err . . . dead . . . Oh, Christmas, what's that?'

Leering over the crux of a fallen monument was a truly hideous visage, a devil, with stumpy gnarled horns. We stopped walking and, in a couple of cases, breathing, gasps released only when the fiend reached up slowly and tore off its face.

At least Dulabesh thought it was funny as he returned the papier-mâché Devil's mask with its ice cream cone horns to Mrs Chaturashringi and scampered about the girls with horrid shrieks and impish pinches.

By the time that we had arrived at the porter's lodge there were some very anxious faces. A number of the smaller children had grasped the hands of anyone taller and were standing tight alongside them, only some of them daring to glance back at the graveyard.

Not a good start.

'Right, are we all here?' I asked as breezily as I could. Thankfully it appeared that we all were – even if some of our knees were knocking. Fortunately, the headmistress was standing at the threshold. Her warm smile and unflappable nature went some way to soothing the more jittery, and, even though we had been to the theatre before, many of the youngsters were suitably distracted by the grandiose buildings.

After-school clubs, the pride of St Olive's, were just finishing and the corridors were milling with sailor-suited boys struggling to put their satchels on to their backs and pulling absurd pom-pommed caps on to their heads. They stopped still when they saw our strange, straggly party of troubadours making its way towards the theatre. As we passed, I was struck not only by the difference in the standard of dress but also in their physical size. Just as we reached a crossroads in the passageway a portly figure leaned out of the crowd and muttered something to our group as it passed.

Abruptly, Sahas lifted his head and looked furiously at the fat boy. It was Devashva Dikshin Doegar who now wrinkled his fluffy little moustache and held his nose with his two pinched fingers, glancing slyly sideways at his fellows, seeking out their encouragement. A strangely simian-looking creature beside him sniggered but most of the others looked hotly embarrassed and busied themselves with their belongings.

Sahas flared; tensing his muscles he looked as if he might take a step towards Devashva. Prakash, dumping his pile of costumes on to Dulabesh who all but disappeared, was immediately at his friend's side. But then, with a glance towards the theatre, Sahas straightened and relaxed. He sighed deeply.

'Go home, little boy, go home to your mother,' he said levelly in clear English and made to turn away.

Clearly surprised by Sahas's excellent English, Devashva still expected to have the last word.

'At least I have a mother to whom I may go home . . .'
Furtively he grinned at his friend again.

Pause.

Pandemonium.

Sahas threw himself forward at the odious schoolboy,
Prakash hard behind him. With a surprising fleetness of foot,
considering his bulk, Devashva made off down the side
corridor with his crony in tow. The boys followed and
Dulabesh, dumping his huge pile of costumes on to an even
smaller child, who completely disappeared, pursued them
determinedly, pausing only to grab a surprised St Olivian by
the cheeks and pat him cheerfully on the head before pinching
his cap.

'Go ferrit, Sahas, mate, go ferrit. Go on, mash him mate!
Come on you . . . err . . . Come on you Ashram.'

Gary stopped skipping around like an East End boxer, legs
swinging from side to side, and readjusted his pile of masks
self-consciously when I glared my disapproval at him.

'Yeah well, he bloody deserved it! Look at him, the little . . .'

The headmistress and I set off after them, but our progress
was considerably hampered by a crowd keen to see the
outcome of this altercation. By the time we had waded
through the sea of blue and white uniforms and reached the
double doors, we had time only to see Sahas and Prakash
seize the wriggling Devashva who was squealing in the most
unseemly manner. Grabbing him by his shoulders and the
seat of his voluminous shorts, they lifted him easily from the
ground. Suddenly Devashva seemed to go limp as he recognised his fate. With a surprisingly graceful 'One, two, three',
Sahas and Prakash launched him headfirst into an enormous
and thankfully half-full metal wheelie bin. He landed with
a dull 'boom' that was followed very shortly afterwards with
an agonised wail. As the two boys walked back towards us,
half-triumphant, half-embarrassed, the rubbish bin began to
wobble violently.

It was only when I turned to the headmistress that I realised
I had one arm raised, punching the air. I lowered it hurriedly.

'Look, I'm terribly sorry. What a disastrous start!' I fully expected that we would be promptly asked to leave.

'Oh, no, don't worry,' she replied and laughed. 'Boys will be boys! Come along; let's go and get you set up.'

And then as we walked back along the parquet floor I could have sworn that I heard her mutter, 'Serves him right!'

21

Curtain Up

'I can never be tired walking after you. The dust thrown up by the winds to cover me will seem, dear husband, rich sandalwood powder.' I mouthed the words as the young girl spoke them beautifully, clearly. 'With you it is heaven, away from you hell. So it is. Be certain of it, oh Rama, and be perfectly happy with me.'

Tanushri was clearly hoping to win some sort of award. It was all going very well. Her bare feet skipped across the stage as she threw herself into the arms of her heroic, but mildly embarrassed husband.

Cue Beckham – much against my will, the children had insisted that he take part.

As the goat had little or no acting experience it had been decided that his appearance would be kept short. Dressed up in the costume of an enchanted deer, complete with coat hanger and brown paper antlers and a smelly old bit of carpet (but which was in no way as malodorous as the performer that wore it), he could hardly be expected to follow any complicated stage directions. An incarnation of the devilish Ravana, the deer's only role was to lure Rama away from his beautiful Sita.

So it was decided, based of course on a design from Unmesh's little notebook, that before the performance a rope would be laid the width of the stage. When the moment came for Beckham's entrance, one end of the rope would be attached to his collar and the other end pulled until he had crossed the scene. Sahas would follow and, hey presto!, he would be lured away. In order to encourage the goat to make his way from one side to the other, I would, out of sight of the audience, wave a number of attractive vegetables in his direction. They had been selected for their succulence and their high colour-quotient. No ruminant in his right mind would do anything but scamper in their direction.

Animals in India, I should have realised after my experiences on the set of *An Ideal Wedding*, were not to be trusted as compliant. 'Never work with animals or children' was a theatrical adage I remembered much, much too late. Abhishekh gingerly attached the rope to Beckham's collar as he threw his head up and down and his antlers wavered worryingly. Stepping smartly back the assistant stage manager raised his thumb. Charuvat yanked hopefully on the rope. No interest was expressed in the carrot that I waved as enticingly as possible, or indeed the banana, the orange or the small melon. Princess Sita was still hanging uncomfortably round Lord Rama's neck as the Ashoka Grove shifted slightly as if in a light breeze.

Desperate measures were called for. Abandoning my fruit and veg, a pomegranate rolling precariously towards the stage, I joined Charuvat in this impromptu tug-of-war. Beckham entered into the contest with gusto. Slowly, his hooves slipping on the wooden floor, creating, I tried not to notice, two deep grooves, he slid into view to the surprised applause of the audience. Not one to give up without a fight, the goat, his legs stuck straight out in front of him, shook his head up and down and twisted one way and the other. One of his antlers swung sideways like a broken branch. Succeeding in wrapping the rope round one of the backstage pillars, between us we managed to winch the uncooperative beast over to our side. Finally he gave up, deposited, in a last gesture of defiance, a scattering of brown oval droppings on the smooth boards, and trotted smartly into the wings, scooped up the carrot and disappeared off into the dressing rooms, dragging

Charuvat behind him. Mrs Chaturashringi squeaked audibly when she was suddenly nuzzled as she sat on the floor carrying out some last-minute repairs.

Calm was restored, perhaps a little too successfully, as the princess settled down to rest in the quiet woods, lulled to sleep by some rather authentic bird noises that came from the tree-tops. So soothing was this noise that even the arrival of the fearsome Ravana, come to abduct her, was not enough to stir the sleeping figure. A long wooden stick inserted between the flaps of the backcloth, and jammed into the small of Tanushri's back by a gleeful Dulabesh, finally roused her. Yawning authentically, she was dragged away to captivity amongst the Devil's other women in the kingdom of Lanka.

A wayward arrow tipped with a charm given to Rama by Lord Brahma landed somewhere in the first few rows of the stalls, but the rest of the performance passed off without any serious disaster. Apart, of course, from a very alarming moment when Unmesh, excelling in his role as Ravana's head, made the mistake of covering up Prakash's eyes as he hurled down a few paper poison darts. Prakash, momentarily losing his direction, disappeared off stage and became entangled in the complicated set of ropes used to operate the stage scenery. By great good fortune he trod heavily on the toe of the slumbering Drupad, who woke quickly enough to redirect the demon-king, with a firm push, back towards his mighty combat.

When the last note of the sitar faded away across the auditorium and Sanjay stroked his drums for the last time, Sita finally rested her head on her valiant husband's shoulder. Surrounded by adoring monkey warriors and the now softly sagging trees of the forest, the actors became still as the lights began to fade. A palpable pause of emotion descended over the theatre.

Then suddenly, like a wave that crashed and burst over the front of the stage, the applause of the audience almost frightened the performers. The ovation was fulsome, and the happiness on the faces of the public quickly transferred itself to those of the children. Dulabesh somersaulted his way to the front of the stage to join the glowing Sahas and Tanushri who delighted in a lengthy and elegant curtsy. Little Unmesh slid from the shoulders of the steady Prakash and joined the others, now surrounded by the younger children, in several final bows.

As I looked across at the tableau I was suddenly reminded of the old lady who had accosted me with *pooja* in the street in Bombay as I made my way back to the Salvation Army Hostel: '. . . many people who will bring you great riches. See a sparkle in the sand, pick it up, for maybe it is a diamond.' The sparkle that had been my meeting with Abhishekh certainly turned out to have been a gem. And each of these children was a facet that had shone for me; each one of them, and I knew this to be real despite the mist of sentimentality that now settled down over me and through which I now found myself looking at them. Every one of them had certainly brought me great riches. More by far than any career in the City might have done, more than any amount of conversations over herbal teas and cakes that were good for you at Osho could have provided, these children had offered me something intangibly, inexplicably pure; something, too, that was about to reduce me to tears if I didn't stand now with the rest of the audience and applaud loudly. However small my input had been, I was content, proud even, to have added my small drop of assistance to the ocean.

'Bravo!'

Eventually Drupad remembered to draw the curtains closed but still the applause continued and so, with a broad grin, he opened them again one final time.

Charuvat beamed as the children knelt down one by one to touch our feet before they climbed back aboard a St Olive's charabanc, lent to us for the trip home. Many yawned despite the excitements as Harshada snatched back the last bits of costume from tired heads.

Sanjay, beside himself with the anticipation of trying out

this wonderful machine, eased up the clutch and, with a grunt and a creak, the bus rumbled forward.

Waving through the smoky back window, the children headed back to the slums.

Epilogue

India flickers through my mind like speeded film.
But it is not the commotion of the traffic, the endless liquid
movement running up and down every street, road or
alleyway, nor the concentration of humanity and the indus-
trious bustle that arrest my attention as I replay my experiences. For all this becomes the norm, the patina of the surface
of India; it is now as much a part of the country as the moun-
tains, hills and rivers. Humanity has rubbed a slightly grimy
finger over the map and doubtless this mark will spread all
the wider as the population continues to increase at such a
dizzying rate.

No, it is not these most immediately arresting aspects of
everyday life that I think of most, for they are simply the background against which life is played out. Nor, interestingly, is
it the numerous images of sadness or poverty, illness and
disease, or the more seldom but still regular and contrasting
displays of the rich and the exotic, the historic and the brazenly
new. Nor is it the profoundly opulent and complex combinations of smells, nauseating and arousing to the senses in equal
measure, without which the whole would only be observed
in vacuumed sterility. It is none of this that will take the fore-
ground when I am reminded of India.

Rather, and this is strange to me, considering the clamouring
competition of the surrounding world, it is the quiet moments;
snapshots, when the film stops and I can see the event clearly:

Tanushri taking my face in her hands, Drupad at the gate, Sanjay at the wheel, Sahas, leg raised on the low wall, gazing across the sprawl of the slum to a distant more agreeable future, the little boy lying motionless in the road, the still tableau on the stage at the end of our play, the pride on faces.

The soundtrack to these images is softer than the roar of traffic and voices, both human and animal; it is instead a murmured word, a compliment, an intimated thank you and the gentle agreeable laughter of the children in the ashram.

And always finally washing into the edge of this sound-scape is the strange white noise of applause, the applause of recognition, of recognition that within the swirling world that surrounded these children, often obscuring them in dust and noise, each of them existed; each of them was real, an individual, able to live with some greater degree of self-determination than they had before.

Happily it was true too that not only had we presented a theatrical masterpiece – or so I certainly thought and insisted on telling anyone and everyone for several months to come – but financially, too, it had been very rewarding. Cheques from the Banks of Baroda and Maharashtra, carefully made out in black fountain pen, were slipped discreetly into the elegant lady's hand as the guests departed or were delivered by chauffeur the following morning to the smoked-glass office across the road from the slum. Funds had been raised and were enough, immediately, to purchase the plot of land on which the ashram stood. In the longer term, too, the children's future was assured, for the play had aroused the interest of a large charitable organisation from Bombay with sufficient capital to help ensure a better education and a greater future for the children of the ashram. A lawyer in our audience took it upon himself to put a number of weighty legal sticks in the spokes of the developers' bulldozers, thereby guaranteeing the future of the Tanjiwadi slum for some considerable time to come.

On the afternoon before I returned the keys of Ashoka Villas to Mr Rentaparti and made my way back to Mumbai, the children of the ashram had arranged a farewell for me. Flowers decorated the gateway and around the walls Tanushri and Kundanika had used coloured rice to trace intricate patterns in white, pink and blue. Plastic-bag flags designed by Unmesh fluttered from the roofs. Everyone had dressed in their best clothes, Charuvat looking particularly fine in a borrowed silk *kurta*. Even Beckham had a bow around his neck and pretty unhappy he looked about it too, I was delighted to see.

The Professor, who was presiding, read a little from one of his pamphlets and thanked me for being 'jolly fine', hoping at the same time I would be happy and fulfilled.

'Remember,' he said, 'what you fellows say in your Bible: "What shall it avail a man if he gain the whole world but lose his soul?"'

Smiling, I thanked him. To think that I might have become a stockbroker – and not a very good one at that.

Sahas and Prakash wished me well on behalf of everybody and hoped that I would be back soon. Yes, yes, I promised. Then, on the boys' instruction, all the children followed me across the wasteland to the bridge where Sanjay was waiting. As I climbed aboard, Dulabesh leapt on to Sahas's shoulders so as to wave me a better goodbye.

Mrs Chaturashringi never quite got round to popping the question; the elegant lady continues to visit the children at the ashram and help Charuvat and Harshada to care for them, hoping all the while, as I do, that a greater international resolution will provide a longer-term solution to the poverty of India. Gary has surely returned to Dudley and taken proud possession of his Astra – he deserves it. Mike abandoned his girlfriend to the tender mercies of Osho and returned to his roots in rock 'n' roll. One day soon, Christian will certainly return to his patients in Poona General. Sanjay is doubtless somewhere, finding something, selling something or tinkering with the engine of his autorickshaw. Beckham still services the nanny goats of Tanjiwadi, and Drupad, I very much hope, still bellows 'Appendectomy!' at residents as they return home in the evenings to Ashoka Villas.